PRAISE FOR

The Angelical Language

"*The Angelical Language* is the single most comprehensive text ever written on the subject of the Enochian magical system and language of Elizabethan luminary Dr. John Dee. This two-volume magnum opus demonstrates Aaron Leitch's familiarity with practical magic as well as his skill as a meticulous researcher. A must-have book."—Chic and Tabatha Cicero, Chief Adepts of the Hermetic Order of the Golden Dawn

"A profound step in the evolution of magickal understanding…Aaron Leitch has taken it upon himself to deeply explore the ins and outs of the Angelical language, examining its linguistics and origins with accuracy and an eye for detail. For serious practitioners interested in an approach to Enochia that is both scholarly and mystical, I can't suggest this book highly enough."—Raven Digitalis, author of *Shadow Magick Compendium*

"In this hardbound book, ideal for researchers, the curious, and serious magicians, Leitch gives the most comprehensive history and overview of the system and language ever published…This book and its companion deserve a place on the bookshelf of every serious magician. They truly bring Enochian magick into the twenty-first century."—Donald Michael Kraig, author of *Modern Magick*

"*The Angelical Language* is an exhaustive examination of the underlying springs of Enochian magic…Anyone seeking to get at the very roots of Dee's Enochian language and at the meaning of Enochian angel magic will find this work of great utility…The most in-depth analysis of the Enochian alphabet and the Enochian language that has appeared to date."—Donald Tyson, author of *Enochian Magic for Beginners*

"In *The Angelical Language*, Aaron Leitch is to be congratulated on producing what is surely by far the most lucid, thorough, practical, and coherent study of the apparently diverse workings of Dr. John Dee and Edward Kelley to date."—David Rankine and Sorita d'Este, authors of *Practical Elementary Magick*

The *Essential Enochian* Grimoire

About the Author

Aaron Leitch has been a scholar and a spiritual seeker for nearly three decades. He is a member of the Hermetic Order of the Golden Dawn, the Gentlemen of Jupiter, and the academic Societas Magica. His writings cover such varied fields as ancient Middle Eastern religion and mythology, Solomonic mysticism, shamanism, Neoplatonism, Hermeticism and alchemy, traditional Wicca and Neopaganism, the Hermetic Order of the Golden Dawn, Thelema, angelology, Qabalah, Enochiana, African Diaspora religions, hexcraft and hoodoo folk traditions, psychology and consciousness expansion, cyberspace and virtual reality, and modern social commentary. He is the author of *Secrets of the Magickal Grimoires* and *The Angelical Language, Volumes I* and *II*. Visit his website at kheph777.tripod.com or his blog at aaronleitch.wordpress.com.

The Essential Enochian Grimoire

An Introduction to Angel Magick from Dr. John Dee to the Golden Dawn

AARON LEITCH

Llewellyn Publications
WOODBURY, MINNESOTA

First Edition
Ninth Printing, 2024

Aquisitions editor: Elysia Gallo
Art director: Lynne Menturweck
Book design: Donna Burch and Rebecca Zins
Cover design: Ellen Lawson
Cover illustration: © SuperStock/995-3626/Albrecht Durer
Interior illustrations: James R. Clark
Production editor: Rebecca Zins

Library of Congress Cataloging-in-Publication Data
Leitch, Aaron, author.
The essential Enochian grimoire : an introduction to angel magick from Dr. John Dee to the Golden Dawn / Aaron Leitch.—First edition.
pages cm
Includes bibliographical references.
ISBN 978-0-7387-3700-3
1. Enochian magic. I. Title.
BF1623.E55L46 2014
133.4'3—dc23

2013038931

Llewellyn Publications
A Division of Llewellyn Worldwide Ltd.
2143 Wooddale Drive
Woodbury, MN 55125-2989
www.llewellyn.com
Printed in the United States of America

Other Books by Aaron Leitch

The Angelical Language, Volume I

The Angelical Language, Volume II

Secrets of the Magickal Grimoires

As a Contributing Author:

Both Sides of Heaven

Diabolical

Commentaries on the Golden Dawn Flying Rolls

At the Crossroads

The Holy Guardian Angel

Contents

An Enochian Grimoire

Chapter Twelve: Neo-Enochiana 207

Introduction

The Enochian system of magickal evocation is considered one of the most advanced in the Western world. The angels whose attentions it gains are among the most powerful and dangerous—mighty spiritual beings who are concerned with the motions of the stars and the rise and fall of earthly governments. Respected magickal orders such as the Hermetic Order of the Golden Dawn reserve Enochian magick for their highest Adept grades. Academics and researchers have spent generations attempting to decipher and understand the journals of the men who first recorded the material. Even beyond those original journals, the Enochian system has had a profound effect on Western occultism over the last several hundred years, much of which has been little understood until fairly recently.

Therefore, I must admit that it was difficult to imagine writing an Enochian magick book written for "beginners." Imagine, for example, attempting to write *An Introduction to Atom Smashing* or *Brain Surgery for Beginners*. What information could such books contain that would be understandable and useful for someone just beginning on his or her path? For a while I was stumped and even unsure whether I should take on the project.

Thankfully, some close friends quickly pointed out an error in my thinking. Whether the subject is nuclear physics, neural surgery, or Enochian magick, you have to start somewhere. Writing a beginner's book on a complex subject does not mean creating a watered-down version of the system and presenting it as "safe" for the courageous neophyte. Instead, it should serve as an introduction to the more complex material. It should include some basic history and define the terms and lingo the student will encounter later. Most importantly, it must present a simplified overview of the entire system, thereby allowing the student to see the whole proverbial elephant *before* focusing upon the trunk, ears, legs, or other elephantine components in detail.

Thinking about the project in this way also brought another fact into focus: in its original form, Enochian magick was never restricted to magickal masters alone. In fact, the Enochian journals record a system that was very much for beginners at the start and proceeded into more advanced practices as the system unfolded over months and years.[1] Therefore, a modern Enochian beginner's book can follow the same pattern, introducing the student to the very basics and preparing him or her for the more advanced material encountered in later study and practice.

Once I had considered all of the above, I realized I had been given the opportunity to create an Enochian grimoire, presenting the practice of the magick without dwelling upon every detail of the system (such as endless magickal squares made from other magickal squares, complex methods of name decryption, long-winded quotes from Dee's journals, etc.). All these aspects of the system are certainly important—they are the underlying foundation of the magick—but they are not necessary in an introduction to the system. An Enochian grimoire should be light enough to carry around a magickal circle or temple and include the information you need to create the tools and perform the ceremonies. (All of the underlying details of Enochiana will be covered in depth in a later work, to which this book can be considered a primer.)

Of course, John Dee himself created the world's first Enochian grimoire. It still exists today, cataloged in the British Library as Sloane MS 3191 and also published in Geoffrey James's *Enochian Magick of Dr. John Dee* (a book I highly recommend you obtain). However, Dee apparently did not intend his grimoire as a primer. It includes very little instruction for the creation of the tools and presents even less information about how to use them. Instead, Dee's grimoire is a collection of working notes intended for his own use and therefore assuming the reader is already well-versed in the system. A modern Enochian primer needs to present the tools along with what they represent and, most importantly, how to properly use them.

The book you are now reading is intended to fill this gap in Enochian literature. Here I will briefly cover some of the history behind the system, so the beginner will know something about the men who first recorded the material—Dr. John Dee and Sir Edward Kelley—and what they were attempting to accomplish with their work. Then I will present an overview of each phase of Dee's magick as it progressed through his journals—from the Heptarchia (planetary magick), Gebofal and the *Book of Loagaeth* (including the famous forty-eight Angelical Callings), to the Parts of the Earth and the Great Table of the Earth (which concern world-changing magick). I will then trace the thread of Enochian history from John Dee through the Golden Dawn and beyond to illustrate how a set of journals that Dee never shared with the public became some of the most influential magickal documents in Western history.

Next, I will present my Enochian grimoire. It will present the Heptarchia, Gebofal (the use of the *Book of Loagaeth*), the Parts of the Earth, and the Great Table of the Earth (Watchtowers) systems of magick. It will outline Enochian cosmology and the magickal tools, furnishings, angels, and spirits of the system. Then it will provide step-by-step instructions for Enochian magickal ceremonies. This grimoire will focus upon Dee-purist Enochiana, meaning it will not borrow material from any of the sources that came after the man himself passed away.

After the Dee-purist material, I will present an overview of the neo-Enochian current that is rooted primarily in the Golden Dawn tradition. This material focuses upon a modified (or "reformed") version of the Great Table of the Earth and a curious method of applying the forty-eight Angelical Callings to the Great Table itself. (Traditionally, there is nothing concerning the Heptarchia, Gebofal, or the Parts of the Earth in the neo-Enochian material; however, this has been changing recently as more students are discovering Dee's original material.) This may be the first book in history to present the Dee-purist and neo-Enochian systems side by side in an easy-to-understand format.

A Note on the Basics of Magick

Due to space restrictions, it is impossible for me to include detailed instructions for the basics of Renaissance angel magick or the lodge-style rituals of the Golden Dawn. However, there are many points in this book where I will instruct the aspirant to perform basic purifications, write invocations, and perform Golden Dawn rituals like the Lesser or Greater Rituals of the Pentagram.

Most students who are interested in Enochian magick will likely have previous experience with either Renaissance (Solomonic) or Golden Dawn styles of magick and will not need step-by-step instructions for these things. However, if you do need or desire further information or teaching for either system, here is a list of great books to get you started. Each of these can be considered perfect primers for the magick you will learn in this text.

For Dee-Purist Enochiana:

My own *Secrets of the Magickal Grimoires* is, to my knowledge, the only existing primer for Renaissance / Solomonic magick on the market. There I cover magickal timing, ritual purifications, consecrations, writing invocations and conjurations, talismans, magickal tools, summoning angels, and more. Plus, I wrote *Secrets* with this current book in mind, so it includes a lot of examples from Dee's journals, angels that you'll find in this book, and more. It is a perfect companion to *The Essential Enochian Grimoire*.

For Golden Dawn Neo-Enochiana:

If you're looking for a great introduction to Golden Dawn–style magick, you won't find a better source than Donald Michael Kraig's *Modern Magick: Twelve Lessons in the High Magickal Arts*. He covers everything from basic pentagram and hexagram rituals to Golden Dawn grade signs, the Opening by Watchtower, creation of talismans, angelic evocation, and much more. Plus, if you feel particularly drawn to the Golden Dawn path itself, you would gain much by working through Chic and Tabatha Cicero's *Self-Initiation into the Golden Dawn Tradition*. If you work through the courses outlined in those two books, there will be nothing in the neo-Enochian magick presented in this book that will be beyond your grasp.

Finally, if you want a great resource for creating Golden Dawn robes, altars, and magickal tools, see *Creating Magical Tools*, also by Chic and Tabatha Cicero.

Zorge,

Aaron Leitch

Chapter One

Who Was Enoch?

Enoch is perhaps one of the most mysterious figures in the Old Testament. Legend tells us that he was taken by angels into the heavens and, while there, recorded hundreds of books of wisdom. When he returned to earth, he wrote his story and passed his wisdom down to later generations. The same legends claim that Enoch's books and wisdom were lost in the great flood of Noah's time. All that survived was his autobiography, called the *Book of Enoch*.

It is quite curious that so much to-do should be made over a person who is hardly mentioned in the Bible at all. The New Testament book of Jude quotes briefly from the *Book of Enoch*, though it makes no reference to the legends about Enoch himself. In the entire Old Testament Enoch is mentioned only once, and even then in a seemingly off-handed manner. His name appears in the book of Genesis as part of a longer list of forefathers. In chapter 5, verses 18–24, we learn that Enoch was the father of Methuselah and the great-grandfather of Noah, each of whom have their own important places in biblical literature and legend. There are only three details that might explain why so many have found Enoch so fascinating:

First, he is the seventh generation from Adam, and seven is a sacred number throughout biblical traditions. Second, he is said to have lived 365 years, which is the number of days in a solar year and therefore also a sacred number. Finally, and most importantly, he is the only forefather in the list with no recorded time of death. The passage simply reads "And Enoch walked with God: and he was not; for God took him" (Genesis 5:24), and no more is said of the man. These small details were very interesting to Jewish (and later Christian) mystics. Eventually the legends about the life and deeds of Enoch arose to "flesh out" the skeletal description given by Genesis.

The famed (or infamous, depending on your view) *Book of Enoch* is the oldest known recorded version of the Enochian legend. It was not likely written by Enoch in the mythical time before the great flood. Instead, it appears to have been written during the very real Hebrew captivity in Babylon (about 600 BCE). This legend describes a Babylonian-influenced cosmology and mythos wherein Enoch is taken bodily into the heavens several times and given grand tours of its seven regions. He holds familiar conversations with both angels and fallen angels, beholds the throne of God, and is allowed to read from the celestial Book of Life (a divine record of the destinies of every created thing in the world—past, present, and future). In the end, Enoch is taken (without dying) to live permanently in Paradise, well before God destroys the world with the great flood (Genesis 6).

The *Book of Enoch* became foundational not only to Jewish religion, but also to the early Christian faith. Many early churches included the scripture in their bibles before it was rejected by Catholic authorities and excluded from the canon. Eventually the *Book of Enoch* faded into obscurity. By the medieval and Renaissance eras, no living person known to the Western world had ever seen it, and the Enochian legend existed only in oral form.

Of course, Eastern Orthodox churches did not recognize the authority of Catholic councils. Thanks to this fact, the book was rediscovered in the eighteenth century as part of the Ethiopian Orthodox Bible—where it had been preserved all along. Thus, we tend to refer to the original *Book of Enoch* as the *Ethiopic Book of Enoch* or simply as *1 Enoch*.[2]

John Dee and the Enochian Legend

John Dee was an English scholar and mystic who lived and worked during the reign of Queen Elizabeth I. He was one of the most influential men in England at the time—an expert in navigation, mathematics, astronomy, astrology, chemistry, languages, encryption, and even occultism (to name only a few of his specialties). During his lifetime, very little of import was done in England—even by the queen—without first seeking his advice or direct involvement. Dee's home was England's first unofficial library and scientific lab, which attracted a long list of famous scholars, artists, mystics, and early scientists.

When Dee began to summon angels in 1581 CE, he stated that he merely wished to follow in the footsteps of Enoch and other biblical prophets who conversed with angels and were thus granted direct access to the secrets of heaven. Before long, Dee found himself—with the help of a medium named Edward Kelley—holding daily conversations with archangels such as Michael, Gabriel, Raphael, and Uriel. These entities introduced the men to an entire host of previously unknown angels who would eventually reveal a new system of angel magick.

As Dee recorded the angels' early lessons regarding the tools and furniture needed for the magick, he decided to ask them about the *Book of Enoch*. Like most Christian or Jewish mystics of his day, he desperately wanted to get his hands on the long-lost record of Enoch's life. Since finding and obtaining lost books is listed among the powers of angels, he asked them if they might be able to bring him a copy of the book. I imagine his heart must have raced when they agreed to grant his request—but the angels had a surprise in store for Dee and Kelley.

The spiritual entities certainly upheld their promise: they did bring a Book of Enoch to Dee. However, it wasn't the *Ethiopic Book of Enoch* or some other record of the life and deeds of the biblical prophet; it was a far greater and much more valuable treasure. The angels revealed nothing less than the mysterious "book" Enoch had read and copied from in heaven—the Book of Life itself, the ultimate record of all things in the universe. Dee's angels would eventually call this the *Holy Book of Loagaeth* ("speech from God"). It contained the words God had used to create the world, entrances into forty-eight gates of heaven, and it recorded the destinies of all things in creation—past, present, and future.

The *Book of Loagaeth* became the heart and soul of Dee's entire corpus of magick. From it was derived the language of the angels, along with several systems of magick intended to influence the physical world. Its primary purpose, however, was to open the gates of heaven and either call out angels or spiritually enter the gates—as Enoch had done—to visit the celestial realms directly. The angels explained that Enoch had been the first to undertake this process, and they also outlined exactly how he had accomplished it. This was apparently intended as instruction for how Dee himself was expected to perform the same work.

That is why Dee's system of magick is called "Enochian" today. By linking the magick directly to the legend of Enoch, Dee's angels had established the new material as part of the historical Enochian saga. The angel magick of Dr. John Dee is "Enochian" in the exact same way the Keys of Solomon are "Solomonic" or the books of the Torah are "Mosaic"—because they each purport to be directly descended from (or written by) the biblical hero whose mythos they adopted.

Further Reading

The Books of Enoch: A Complete Volume Containing 1 Enoch (The Ethiopic Book of Enoch), 2 Enoch (The Slavonic Secrets of Enoch), 3 Enoch (The Hebrew Book of Enoch) by Joseph B. Lumpkin

Jewish Meditation by Aryeh Kaplan

Origins of the Kabbalah by Gershom Scholem

Major Trends in Jewish Mysticism by Gershom Scholem

Chapter Two

What Enochian Magick Is

Technically, the term "Enochian magick" can indicate any system of occultism that draws upon the writings or mythos of Enoch. By far the world's most famous system of Enochian occultism is that recorded by John Dee and Edward Kelley.

John Dee was introduced to Edward Kelley in late 1582. Dee had already employed a skryer (Barnabas Saul) to speak with angels but was unsatisfied with the man's results. Kelley, it turned out, was an excellent medium—not to mention a fellow student of alchemy—and the two men quickly became partners in their spiritual pursuits. Over the next six or seven years, Kelley would spend hours each day gazing into a crystal ball while Dee recited prayers and invocations to call down angelic entities. Once Kelley reported seeing visions in the stone, Dee would question the angels and record what they revealed.

What the angels revealed is what we usually call Enochian magick today. This new system was given to Dee and Kelley in three phases: the Heptarchia, Gebofal, and the Parts of the Earth and the Great Table of the Earth (Watchtowers).

1: The Heptarchia ("Sevenfold Rulership")

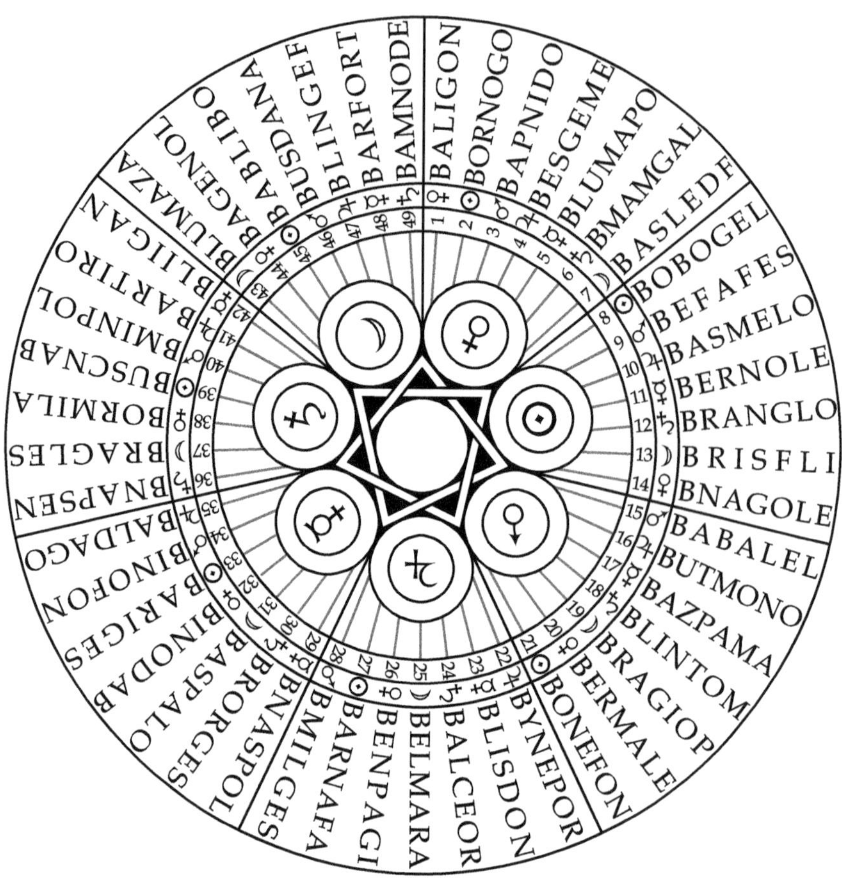

Figure 1: *The Round Table of the Forty-Nine Heptarchic Royal Angels*

The Heptarchia is a system of planetary magick that calls upon the angels of the seven biblical days of Creation. There are forty-nine of these angels—seven for each of the days of the week (or the seven classical planets). There is no reference to Enoch in this phase of the system, and it largely resembles other systems of Renaissance angel magick (such as found in the *Arbatel of Magic*, the *Heptameron*, the *Pauline Arts*, the *Almadel of Solomon*, etc.).

Most importantly, this phase is where the tools and furniture necessary for all three phases of Dee's magickal system are revealed. They include a skrying table with wax seals and purified tin talismans, a magickal lamen, and a golden ring of Solomon to be worn by the conjurer.

2: *Gebofal (The* Book of Loagaeth *and the Forty-Eight Angelical Callings)*

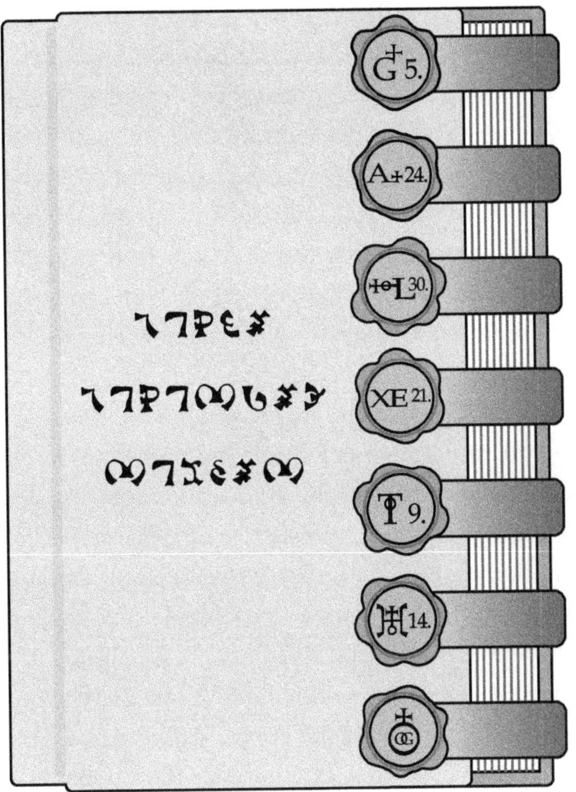

Figure 2: *The Book of Life with Enochian Seals*

The *Book of Loagaeth* ("speech from God") is supposed to be one and the same with the Book of Life described in the legends of Enoch, the Old Testament, the book of Jubilees, and elsewhere. As such, it should also be one and the same with the famous Book of Seven Seals described in the Revelation of St. John:

> And I saw in the right hand of him that sat on the throne a book written within and on the backside, sealed with seven seals. And I saw a strong angel proclaiming with a loud voice, Who is worthy to open the book, and to loose the seals thereof? And no man in heaven, nor in earth, neither under the earth, was able to open the book, neither to look thereon (Revelation 5:1–4).

As the angels explained to Dee, the *Book of Loagaeth* embodies the seven days (or we might say the seven ages) of creation outlined in chapter one of Genesis. This includes our modern age, which is mystically interpreted as the seventh age (day) of the universe, during which God rests from the Creation. Taken all together, the holy book represents the entire span of history from creation to destruction. It includes all wisdom and knowledge from the past, of the present, and into the future. In short, it is the ultimate tome of universal knowledge.

However, the text of *Loagaeth* is written in a mysterious language with which God is supposed to have spoken the universe into existence. (Consider the many instances of "And God said..." in the first chapter of Genesis.) The angels never offered a translation of the text, and it continues to elude attempts to translate or decipher it to this very day.[3]

The holy book appeared to Kelley in the skrying stone as a collection of forty-nine leaves[4]—each with a 49 × 49 table that has a front and a back side (thus taking up both sides of each leaf), filled with the letters of the mysterious Language of Creation.[5] Each leaf's table represents a mystical gateway into one of the twelve kingdoms of heaven, which likely indicates the twelve zodiacal houses or their signs (Aries, Taurus, etc.). These gates swing both ways, allowing the aspirant either to call angelic teachers through them or to enter and (like Enoch) explore the celestial cities beyond them.

In order to access the wisdom of the holy book or gain entrance to the gates of heaven, the aspirant must invoke the aid of the angels who guard each gate. The system given for achieving this was called Gebofal by Dee's angels, though they never offered a translation of the name.

Gebofal is a lengthy forty-nine-day ritual that uses a series of forty-eight invocations designed to attract the attention of the necessary angels. The invocations are described as "callings" as well as "keys" (because they are the keys to the gates of heaven), and they are written entirely in the Angelical language.

The Angelical Language

Graph	*Un*	*Or*	*Gal*	*Ged*	*Veh*	*Pa*
E	A	F	D	G/J	C/Ch/K	B

Drux	*Ger*	*Mals*	*Ur*	*Na*	*Gon*	*Tal*
					/	
N	Q/Qu	P/Ph	L	H	I/Y	M

Gisg	*Fam*	*Van*	*Ceph*	*Don*	*Med*	*Pal*
T	S	U/V	Z	R	O	X

Figure 3: *Letters of the Angelical Alphabet*

The forty-eight Angelical Callings are written in another version (or dialect) of the *Loagaeth* tongue, which modern students and practitioners often refer to as Enochian. Dee himself referred to it variously as "Angelical," the "celestial speech," the "first language of God-Christ," or "Adamical." That last name—Adamical—was used by Dee (briefly) after the angels told him that Adam had spoken the language fluently in Eden and had even used it to apply "true names" to all things in creation. (In my own work, I have chosen to stick with "Angelical.")

According to the legend revealed by the angels, Adam lost the language when he fell from paradise (Genesis 3); he then attempted to reconstruct it from memory. This reconstruction was the first primordial version of Hebrew, though it's not a Hebrew we would recognize today. Some time later, the confusion of tongues took place at the Tower of

Babel (Genesis 11), and the primordial Hebrew was similarly lost. After that, biblical Hebrew—the language of the Old Testament—came into existence, and the rest is linguistic history.

After Adam's fall, only one human was deemed worthy to read the original tongue of Eden, and that was Enoch. It is possible to interpret the Enochian legend as a failed attempt to reseed the language into humanity. It failed, of course, due to the events that led up to the great flood (Genesis 6–8), during which all of Enoch's wisdom was lost.

Fortunately, the Angelical Calls revealed to Dee were given loose translations, and there have been several efforts over the years to create workable dictionaries of the words. I have made my own contribution, which I published as *The Angelical Language, Volume I: The Complete History and Mythos of the Tongue of Angels* and *The Angelical Language, Volume II: An Encyclopedic Lexicon of the Tongue of Angels*. Those projects were fairly massive, taking ten years and over nine hundred pages to complete. Because I cover the subject in such exhaustive detail there, I will save space here and refer the reader to those books to learn more about the tongue of the angels.

As I stated previously, *Loagaeth* is the central linchpin of Dee's entire system of magick. The angels of the Heptarchia are associated directly with the book—they are mentioned in the text and were also involved in transmitting it to Dee and Kelley. Also, the practice of Gebofal requires the same skrying tools and furniture used in the Heptarchic system.

Finally, *Loagaeth* appears to be the primary source of the third phase of the Enochian system, the Parts of the Earth and the Great Table of the Earth (Watchtowers).

3: The Parts of the Earth and the Great Table of the Earth (Watchtowers)

r	Z	i	l	a	f	A	u	t	l	p	a	e	b	O	a	Z	a	R	o	p	h	a	R	a
a	r	d	Z	a	i	d	p	a	L	a	m		u	N	n	a	x	o	p	S	o	n	d	n
c	z	o	n	s	a	r	o	Y	a	u	b	x	a	i	g	r	a	n	o	o	m	a	g	g
T	o	i	T	t	x	o	P	a	c	o	C	a	o	r	p	m	n	i	n	g	b	e	a	l
S	i	g	a	s	o	m	r	b	z	n	h	r	r	s	o	n	i	z	i	r	l	e	m	u
f	m	o	n	d	a	T	d	i	a	r	i	p	i	z	i	n	r	C	z	i	a	M	h	l
o	r	o	i	b	A	h	a	o	z	p	i		M	o	r	d	i	a	l	h	C	t	G	a
c	N	a	b	r	V	i	x	g	a	z	d	h	Я	O	c	a	n	c	h	i	a	s	o	m
O	i	i	i	t	T	p	a	l	o	a	i		A	r	b	i	z	m	i	i	l	p	i	z
A	b	a	m	o	o	o	a	C	u	c	a	C	O	p	a	n	a	B	a	m	S	m	a	l
N	a	o	c	o	T	t	n	p	r	a	T	o	d	O	l	o	p	i	n	i	a	n	b	a
o	c	a	n	m	a	g	o	t	r	o	i	m	r	x	p	a	o	c	s	i	z	i	x	p
s	h	i	a	l	r	a	p	m	z	o	x	a	a	x	t	i	r	V	a	s	t	r	i	m
m	o	t	i	b			a	T	n	a	n		n	a	n	T	a			b	i	t	o	m
d	o	n	p	a	T	d	a	n	V	a	a	a	T	a	O	A	d	u	p	t	D	n	i	m
o	l	o	a	G	e	o	o	b	a	u	a		o	a	l	c	o	o	r	o	m	e	b	b
O	P	a	m	n	o	O	G	m	d	n	m	m	T	a	g	c	o	n	x	m	a	l	G	m
a	p	l	s	T	e	d	e	c	a	o	p	o	n	h	o	d	D	i	a	l	e	a	o	c
s	c	m	i	o	o	n	A	m	l	o	x	C	p	a	t	A	x	i	o	V	s	P	s	И
V	a	r	s	G	d	L	b	r	i	a	p	h	S	a	a	i	z	a	a	r	V	r	o	i
o	i	P	t	e	a	a	p	D	o	c	e		m	p	h	a	r	s	l	g	a	i	o	l
p	s	u	a	c	n	r	Z	i	r	Z	a	p	M	a	m	g	l	o	i	n	L	i	r	x
S	i	o	d	a	o	i	n	r	z	f	m		o	l	a	a	D	a	g	a	T	a	p	a
d	a	l	t	T	d	n	a	d	i	r	e	r	p	a	l	c	o	i	d	x	P	a	c	n
d	i	x	o	m	o	n	s	i	o	s	p	a	n	d	a	z	N	z	i	V	a	a	s	a
O	o	D	p	z	i	A	p	a	n	l	i	x	i	i	d	P	o	n	s	d	A	s	p	i
r	g	o	a	n	n	ꟼ	A	C	r	a	r	e	x	r	i	n	h	t	a	r	n	d	i	⅃

Figure 4: *The Original Great Table*

The Parts of the Earth

The final phase of the magick came in two pieces. The first is called the Parts of the Earth, wherein the world is divided into ninety-two regions of geopolitical influence (kingdoms, nations, and even cultures) governed by the signs—and the ruling angels—of the zodiac.[6] These zodiacal kings govern their areas (or "parts") of the world with the help of large numbers of servient angels. All of these entities have direct influence over their own Part of the Earth, and thus apparently over the nation(s) that reside there. By summoning these angels, Dee likely hoped to exert his own influence over foreign nations, or at the very least spy upon them via remote viewing.

The Parts and the Thirty Aethyrs

There are ninety-two Parts of the Earth listed in Dee's journals, though one of them is hidden; therefore, Dee often referred to them as the "ninety-one Parts of the Earth."[7] Those ninety-one parts are divided amongst the final thirty tables of *Loagaeth*, which represent the thirty circles of heaven called the *Aethyrs* (or Ethers or Aires). During Dee's lifetime (and, in fact, until fairly recently in scientific history), the word aethyr/ether meant "the upper regions of space, the clear sky, the heavens."[8] Thus, the thirty Aethyrs of the Enochian system are actually thirty heavens that extend from the earth all the way to God's throne.

Each of these Aethyrs (along with their Parts of the Earth) can be accessed by reciting the Angelical Call for the appropriate *Loagaeth* table. The mage then has the choice of viewing that nation through the crystal stone or even spiritually visiting the nation directly via a form of etheric (or aethyric) projection.

Though these aethyric heavens are described as stacked one atop the other, this is only for illustration. The ninety-one (or ninety-two) parts are better envisioned as stretched out horizontally across the earth. The thirty Aethyrs represent the visible firmament (sky) where the stars (angels) dwell, while the parts represent the areas of the world governed by those stars.

The Great Table of the Earth (Watchtowers)

Once Dee had received the Parts of the Earth, he was given the second piece of phase three: the Great Table of the Earth. This is a large magickal table (or word-square) formed by taking all of the names of the ninety-two parts and arranging them upon a massive 25×27 grid. The resulting table can then be broken down into four separate 12×13 tablets bound together by a large central cross containing a few letters and several blank squares. Dee would refer to this central cross as the "Black Cross" (likely an alchemical reference) and the "Cross of Union." The four surrounding tablets are called "Watchtowers," based upon biblical imagery such as the following:

> I have set watchmen upon thy walls, O Jerusalem, which shall never hold their peace day nor night (Isaiah 62:6).

Compare that to the following statement about the Great Table made by one of Dee's angels, Ave:

> The four houses are the Four Angels of the Earth, which are the Four Overseers, and Watchtowers, that...God...hath placed against the... Great Enemy, the Devil.

These four angelic overseers are likely the four kherubic archangels (lion, eagle, man, and ox) found in the vision of Ezekiel (Ezekiel 1) and in St. John's apocalypse (Revelation 4). They would also have close relations to the four archangels—Michael, Gabriel, Raphael, and Uriel—who were the primary angelic contacts for Dee and Kelley throughout their work. However, Dee never explored this aspect of the Great Table in his journals, so I will reserve my findings on them for another publication.[9]

According to Dee's journals, the four Watchtower tablets are supposed to represent the quarters of the earth. Note that this does not necessarily mean they represent the four philosophical elements (Fire, Water, Air, and Earth). Today, it is traditional in many Western systems of occultism to assign the elements to the four points of the compass, and this has led many to assume the four Watchtowers at those compass points should also represent the four elements. However, this is not how Dee recorded the system. In his journals, the primary focus was upon the direction associated with each Watchtower, and they were never described as "elemental" tablets at all.[10]

Whereas the Parts of the Earth system grants one influence over individual nations, the Great Table covers entire quarters of the world at once. When Dee asked exactly how the four quarters of the map were to be divided amongst the Watchtowers, the angels gave the cryptic and unhelpful answer, "In respect of your poles." That's all well and good for north and south, but where exactly are the eastern and western "poles" of the earth? We have the prime meridian today; however, that is an arbitrary point that has changed many times throughout history. (Our modern prime meridian was set in 1884, long after Dee's lifetime.) There is no indication in Dee's journals where the eastern and western quarters of the earth should be divided.

I feel the quarters covered by the Watchtowers are intended to be geopolitical rather than geographical—that is, much like the Parts of the Earth, they don't represent specific tracts of land as much as they represent communities of people. Whereas the parts focus upon individual nations, the quarters represent the four "civilizations" of the world. You hear about these more often than you might think, in terms like "Western nations" or "Eastern culture." Below is a list of the four world civilizations and a few examples of countries or regions that traditionally fall into each category:[11]

Western Civilization: Western Europe and North America. Britain, USA, Canada, Spain, France, Germany, Italy, etc.

Eastern Civilization: Eastern Europe and Asia. Russia, India, Mongolia, China, Japan, Korea, Thailand, etc. (Also including the Middle Eastern nations such as Egypt, Israel, Palestine, Iran, Iraq, etc.)

Northern Civilization: Northern Europe. Norway, Sweden, Greenland, Iceland, the Inuit and Siberian peoples, etc.

Southern Civilization: Nations south of the equator: southern Africa, South America, Australia, countless inhabited islands, etc.

These four classifications likely developed in ancient times—perhaps when Rome ruled the Western world, or maybe even Greece before it. Therefore, the area of Greece and Italy became the center point of the known world for geographers and mapmakers. Dee likely felt that his beloved England should be the center of the world—and the four classifications would later be preserved once England indeed became the ruling world empire. These are the same classifications we use to this very day.

The letters of each Watchtower—taken from the Parts of the Earth but rearranged into the form of the Great Table—create the names of dozens (maybe hundreds) of angels and spirits who govern their particular quarter of the earth. There are angels of medicine and alchemy, transportation, transformation, and the revelation of secrets (to name just a few) associated with each civilization. Thus, if one desires to influence the Western nations, one would call the angels of the Western Watchtower; if one desires to influence the nations of Asia, then one would call upon the angels of the Eastern Watchtower. As Dee's angels instructed, "But when thou wilt work in the East, thou must take such as bear rule there; so must thou do of the rest."[12]

The Reformed Great Table of Raphael

You might be surprised to learn that there were two versions of the Great Table of the Earth recorded in Dee's journals: the original and one called the Reformed Great Table of Raphael. The reformed version is largely the same as the original except the four Watchtower tablets have been rearranged and some of the lettering has been changed.

I suspect that nothing in the Enochian system has caused more controversy than the debate over which version of the Great Table is the "proper" version. In fact, this single conflict is at the center of a major split within the Enochian tradition—where two entirely different magickal systems (called "Dee purist" and "neo-Enochian") have developed around the opposing tables.

Even Dee himself seems to have been unsure on the matter. He received the original Great Table at the same time as the rest of the Enochian material. At first, he placed the Watchtowers in the wrong order within the Great Table,[13] but the angels quickly corrected him. Nothing further was said about the arrangement of the Watchtowers until years later, long after the Enochian transmissions had run their course.

When the Reformed Table was later revealed by the archangel Raphael, it was presented not as a major correction to the system of angel magick but merely as a method of decrypting a mysterious message for Dee, Kelley, and their wives. Nonetheless, Dee felt it was important enough to record the Reformed Great Table in his personal grimoire alongside the original, though the rest of the magick in his grimoire is based strictly upon the original version. It would appear that he never made up his mind or that he felt either version had its uses.

In order to give you the complete picture, I will briefly explain the origin of the Reformed Great Table. Later we will explore the two schools of Enochian magick that have developed over the centuries and how the two Great Tables are at the heart of the schism:

r	Z	i	l	a	f	A	y	t	l	p	a	e	T	a	O	A	d	u	p	t	D	n	i	m
a	r	d	Z	a	i	d	p	a	L	a	m		a	a	b	c	o	o	r	o	m	e	b	b
c	z	o	n	s	a	r	o	Y	a	u	b	x	T	o	g	c	o	n	x	m	a	l	G	m
T	o	i	T	t	z	o	P	a	c	o	C	a	n	h	o	d	D	i	a	l	e	a	o	c
S	i	g	a	s	o	m	r	b	z	n	h	r	p	a	t	A	x	i	o	V	s	P	s	N
f	m	o	n	d	a	T	d	i	a	r	i	p	S	a	a	i	x	a	a	r	V	r	o	i
o	r	o	i	b	A	h	a	o	z	p	i		m	p	h	a	r	s	l	g	a	i	o	l
t	N	a	b	r	V	i	x	g	a	s	d	h	M	a	m	g	l	o	i	n	L	i	r	x
O	i	i	i	t	T	p	a	l	O	a	i		o	l	a	a	D	n	g	a	T	a	p	a
A	b	a	m	o	o	o	a	C	u	c	a	C	p	a	l	c	o	i	d	x	P	a	c	n
N	a	o	c	o	T	t	n	p	r	n	T	o	n	d	a	z	N	z	i	V	a	a	s	a
o	c	a	n	m	a	g	o	t	r	o	i	m	i	i	d	P	o	n	s	d	A	s	p	i
s	h	i	a	l	r	a	p	m	z	o	x	a	x	r	i	n	h	t	a	r	n	d	i	L
m	o	t	i	b			a	T	n	a	n		n	a	n	T	a			b	i	t	o	m
b	o	a	Z	a	R	o	p	h	a	R	a	a	d	o	n	p	a	T	d	a	n	V	a	a
u	N	n	a	x	o	P	S	o	n	d	n		o	l	o	a	G	e	o	o	b	a	u	a
a	i	g	r	a	n	o	o	m	a	g	g	m	O	P	a	m	n	o	V	G	m	d	n	m
o	r	p	m	n	i	n	g	b	e	a	l	o	a	p	l	s	T	e	d	e	c	a	o	p
r	s	o	n	i	Z	i	r	l	e	m	u	C	s	c	m	i	o	o	n	A	m	l	o	x
i	z	i	n	r	C	z	i	a	M	h	l	h	V	a	r	s	G	d	L	b	r	i	a	p
M	o	r	d	i	a	l	h	C	t	G	a		o	i	P	t	e	a	a	p	D	o	c	e
o	c	a	n	c	h	i	a	s	o	m	t	p	p	s	u	a	c	N	r	Z	i	r	Z	a
A	r	b	i	z	m	i	i	l	p	i	z		S	i	o	d	a	o	i	n	r	z	f	m
O	p	a	n	a	l	a	m	S	m	a	P	r	d	a	l	t	T	d	n	a	d	i	r	e
d	O	l	o	P	i	n	i	a	n	b	a	a	d	i	x	o	m	o	n	s	i	o	s	p
r	x	p	a	o	c	s	i	z	i	x	p	x	O	o	D	p	z	i	A	p	a	n	l	i
a	x	t	i	r	V	a	s	t	r	i	m	e	r	g	o	a	n	n	P	A	C	r	a	r

Figure 5: *The Reformed Great Table of Raphael*

Dee and Kelley received the original Great Table from the angels in mid-1584.[14] This remained the one and only Great Table throughout the transmission of the Enochian magickal system(s). The events that led to the Reformed Great Table took place in April of 1587[15]—when we learn that Kelley has asked the angels to relieve him of his skrying duties.

The angels appear angry at Kelley's request but agree to grant it if, after fourteen days, he still wishes to quit. Dee spent those two weeks attempting to train his son Arthur to skry in Kelley's place, but he did not have great success. On the day before the deadline, Kelley returned with every intention of ending his employment with Dee. The angels appeared in the stone but were dressed in the most filthy and disordered manner—quite the opposite of the splendid royal clothing they normally wore. It was then the angels gave Dee and Kelley their most infamous commandment: to bond together as one by sharing all things in common between them. Kelley understood at once that the angels meant even their wives must be shared.

At first, Dee did not accept Kelley's interpretation. He instead took the commandment to mean a kind of Christian brotherhood and communal living. However, Kelley would later tell Dee that he had received a vision of Raphael, who confirmed the sharing of wives and gave Kelley a message from God to prove it. The message was encrypted—nothing more than a collection of numbers. The angels explained the key to decrypting the message was to number all the squares of the Great Table of the Earth from 1 to 624, then replace the numbers from the message with the letters found in each numbered square.

Sadly, when Dee wrote out the resulting message, it was nothing but gibberish. So the men set to summoning the angels once more and demanded to know the correct method of decrypting the secret message from God. The answer, they were told, was to rearrange the Watchtowers within the Great Table, then number the squares as previously instructed. Dee did this, decrypted the message, and this time obtained a letter written in Latin. It contained a statement of divine permission for Dee and Kelley to share their wives in common.

That was the one and only time the Reformed Great Table of Raphael was used in Dee's journals. Dee wrote out this new table in his entry for April 18, 1587. Above it, he included a note explaining that he had originally been unsure about the correct placement of the Watchtowers. Beneath it, he explained how Kelley had received this new version of the Great Table from the archangel Raphael and that it made him "greatly rejoice in spirit." This makes it appear that Dee rejoiced at getting a correction to his ordering of the Watchtowers, and it has led many to believe the Reformed Great Table should overrule the original version. However, Dee had long since received the correction to his ordering of the Watchtowers. His great rejoicing was because this new Reformed Great Table allowed him to decrypt the message from God.

Yet, as I said before, it would appear that Dee did suspect the Reformed Great Table had practical uses. At least, he felt there was some reason worth including it alongside the original Great Table in his personal Enochian grimoire.

Those who oppose the use of the Reformed Great Table point out that Kelley received it alone in his bedchamber, while the rest of the Enochian material was received strictly when both men were present. A more cynical segment of Dee and Kelley scholars insist that the commandment to share wives in and of itself is proof that either they were no longer talking to angels (if, indeed, they had ever been speaking with true angels) or that Kelley was merely lying to get into bed with Jane Dee.

Personally, I can't accept either of these simplistic conclusions. First, I find it odd that people generally accept angels who dictate such things as war and famine but become suspicious if angels suggest that humans should share love. In my opinion, a suggestion of polyamory (multiple loves) would have been quite ahead of its time in Dee's day, but it's hardly proof that the entities were demonic.

Second, it is entirely possible that Dee and Kelley were influenced by certain social experiments that were, indeed, centuries ahead of their time. One of these social experiments was called the "Family of Love"—which practiced communal living and group marriage. Dee and Kelley seem to have known several members of that group and thus could have been introduced to their philosophies. While that subject is a bit beyond this book, the above should be enough to illustrate that the polyamorous episode between the Dees and the Kelleys should not be written off with short-sighted moral judgments (against either the angels or the humans involved) nor without further historical study into the matter. In any case, it does not automatically invalidate the Reformed Great Table of Raphael.

Of course, there is nothing that ultimately proves its validity either, so the issue remains unresolved. In a later chapter we will discuss the historical development of the Enochian tradition, and we will see what role the Reformed Great Table has come to play in its own right.

Further Reading

Dee's Occult Sourcebooks:

Steganographia by Trithemius

De Septum Secundeis by Trithemius

Three Books of Occult Philosophy by Henry Cornelius Agrippa

Liber Juratus

Arbatel of Magic

The Heptameron

The Pauline Arts and *The Almadel of Solomon* (both found in *The Lemegeton*)

Dee's Angelic Journals:

John Dee's Five Books of Mystery edited by Joseph Peterson

A True and Faithful Relation of What Passed for Many Years Between Dr. John Dee…and Some Spirits by Méric Casaubon

The Heptarchia Mystica by John Dee

Digital Scans of the Enochian Manuscripts (i.e., all of Dee's original journals)

The Enochian Magick of Dr. John Dee by Geoffrey James

Books About Dee's Original System:

Enochian Magick for Beginners: The Original System of Angel Magick by Donald Tyson

The Angelical Language, Volume I: The Complete History and Mythos of the Tongue of Angels by Aaron Leitch

The Angelical Language, Volume II: An Encyclopedic Lexicon of the Tongue of Angels by Aaron Leitch

The Complete Enochian Dictionary: A Dictionary of the Angelic Language as Revealed to Dr. John Dee and Edward Kelley by Donald Laycock (especially see the introduction)

Enochian Magic in Theory by Dean F. Wilson

Chapter Three

An Enochian Cast of Characters

Dee and Kelley spent their years together traveling across Europe, meeting powerful people, and attempting to establish themselves as occult leaders. Dee hoped to be recognized as a prophet due to his angelic contacts, while Kelley hoped to become an accomplished alchemist. Only Kelley would achieve his goal during his lifetime, while Dee, sadly, would not become a world-famous angel worker until many years after his passing.

As you expand your Enochian studies beyond this primer, especially if you read Dee's journals or biographies, you will quickly find yourself lost in a labyrinth of obscure names. Some of them will be familiar (such as Queen Elizabeth I), while most of them will be entirely new. There will be names of humans who aided or persecuted Dee during his travels, and there will be names of angels who have never appeared outside of Dee's writings.

Therefore, I feel it would be useful to provide a program of sorts so you can keep track of all the players. The following list is not in alphabetical order but is instead arranged so that each entry will provide another piece of Dee's story in (roughly) chronological order. Once you have read through this section, you will have a basic understanding of the greater Enochian saga.

The People

Queen Elizabeth I (1533–1603): This famous monarch guided England through one of its most exciting and frightening periods. Her father, King Henry the VIII, had broken away from the Catholic Church and proclaimed himself the leader of a new Church of England. This new faith was basically similar to Catholicism (in its rites and liturgy) but did not recognize the authority of the pope. After Henry's passing, his son Edward reigned for a short time and continued what his father had started. This was not destined to last, however, as Edward soon died and the throne was seized by his very Catholic sister Mary. Mary began a reign of terror across England to uproot and destroy the new Protestant faith. For this campaign, Mary is known to this day as "Bloody Mary."[16]

Meanwhile, Princess Elizabeth had been raised and educated in the Protestant faith. As Mary's popularity as Queen diminished, the people began to view Elizabeth (and the Protestant faith) as a probable alternative. The princess was therefore arrested, spending some time in prison and then confined to her home. According to Dee, he made visits to her while she was imprisoned and worked "under cover" for her in support of the Protestant cause.

Mary passed away after a reign of only five years. She had failed to produce an heir, so Elizabeth finally ascended the throne. She quickly began to rebuild the shattered Church of England and even took it beyond its "just like Catholicism but without the pope" origins. It was Elizabeth, not her father or brother, who truly created the Church of England that we know today.

Emperor Rudolph II (1552–1612): The Holy Roman Empire has a long and not well-defined history. Its origins are often attributed to the crowning of Charlemagne as "Emperor of the Romans" by the pope in 800 CE. A bit over one hundred years later (962 CE), Otto the Great was the first to officially take the title Holy Roman Emperor. In 1576 (Dee's lifetime), the Austrian Rudolph II inherited the position from his father, Maximillian II.

Rudolph was the black sheep of the Catholic Hapsburg family. He was largely uninterested in politics or the affairs of the empire, and gave his attention instead to the arts, alchemy, astrology, and occultism. His court in Prague became a center for artists, philosophers, and alchemists from around the world who knew they could study and practice their arts there without fear of persecution. Rudolph even employed teams of alchemists in the hopes they would discover the secret of turning base metals into gold. (This was actually not uncommon in royal courts across Europe. At the time, alchemy was considered a serious mainstream science.)

John Dee (1527–1609): During the Renaissance, England was not yet the grand empire it would become. In fact, Dee was among the first to insist that England should build its defenses and act quickly to secure the northern seas and parts of (the newly discovered) North America. Dee was also the only man in England with the necessary knowledge of navigational equipment to launch such expeditions. England's earliest trips to America, as well as its first meeting with Russia, were undertaken only after consulting with Dee.

Dee even coined the term "British Empire"—though that empire would not arise until after he passed away. During his lifetime, England was still a backwater burg—a hick town on the outskirts of the world that was just beginning to take its place in the larger European community. Of course, its turbulent shift from Catholicism to Protestantism only intensified its isolation from the Holy Roman Empire. In this state, England did not have the finances to afford royal status symbols such as "court philosophers," but that didn't stop England from filling that role unofficially.

This is where John Dee came into the picture. His European education was more extensive and current than that of anyone in England. He was already famous as a mathematician, scientist, physician, astronomer, and navigator, and he soon found himself serving the queen as her adviser, court magician ("philosopher"), and even undercover spy. He spent his life in the hopes that he would one day be compensated for his service to the crown, but those hopes mostly would be dashed. The queen usually did her best to look after her old friend, but politics and finances often came between them.

Not long after Dee began his angelic evocations with Edward Kelley, the two men decided to seek their fortunes in Europe. They first traveled to Poland in the company of their friend and benefactor Albert Lasky, the Polish prince (see later in this chapter). Their time with Lasky was rather short, and Dee and Kelley soon moved on to the court of Rudolph II in Prague. Dee hoped that his angelic journals would prove his status as a prophet, and he attempted to transmit "messages from God" directly to Rudolph. Sadly, as is most often the case for prophets, Dee's messages were not welcomed (or truly believed), and Dee quickly found himself out of favor and beating a retreat back to England. Kelley would not return with him, nor would Dee ever see him again.

Edmund Bonner (1500–1569): After King Henry VIII founded the Anglican Church, England struggled to establish itself as a Protestant country. Bonner had been instrumental in the schism from Rome and was appointed bishop of London. However, he generally disliked the reformations proposed by the new church and was eventually removed from his position and imprisoned.

After Mary ascended the throne, her primary goal was to bring the kingdom back under Catholic control—and that meant the arrest and persecution of anyone associated with Protestant politics. Bonner was freed from prison, restored to his former position, and became, to put it simply, England's grand inquisitor. Mary sent Protestants and sympathizers to him for interrogation (and likely torture), and many of the accused were never seen alive again. Thanks to this role, Bonner is known to this very day as "Bloody Bonner" (clearly an association with the name "Bloody Mary").

Dee was one of the Protestant sympathizers arrested and sent to Bonner. He had drawn up horoscopes for both Mary and Princess Elizabeth that indicated Elizabeth was more fit to rule. This seems like a rather stupid thing to do under the circumstances, unless Dee was trying to get arrested. The records of Dee's arrest and interrogation are slim. All we know for certain is that Dee went to see Bonner under accusation of treason. Then, the next time we see Dee, he is working *with* Bonner in the interrogation room, helping to prosecute Protestants! Dee lived in Bonner's household for some time and possibly earned a doctorate of divinity while he was there. (This may be the origin of his "Dr." title.)

It appeared to many people at the time that Dee was a coward who merely wished to "side with the winner" when his own life was on the line. This did some damage to Dee's reputation and likely contributed to the social struggles he faced most of his adult life. In his later years he would claim that he never sided with the Catholics but had, in fact, been working undercover for Princess Elizabeth (who had been in prison at the time). This claim is difficult to dismiss in light of the fact that the young Queen Elizabeth—once she finally took the throne—accepted Dee into her inner circle as one of her primary advisers with open arms and no questions asked.

Sir Edward Kelley (Talbot): Dee began his magickal work with another skryer by the name of Barnabus Saul (see next page). However, things did not work out with Saul, and Dee was soon introduced (by a Mr. Clerkson) to a man named Edward Talbot. Dee wasted no time in putting Edward's skrying skills to the test, and that test was passed with more than flying colors. Kelley easily established contact with the most powerful of archangels, and Dee seemed to know he had found his working partner.

Later, Edward Talbot would turn out to be Edward Kelley. (It is unclear, but the revelation of his true identity may have caused a row with Dee's wife.) It is uncertain whether Talbot or Kelley is his real name; it is possible that Kelley was traveling undercover at the time he met Dee[17] or that he gave a false last name in case Dee turned out to be hostile. In any case, we know little to nothing about Kelley's life before he appears in Dee's journals. It is certain, however, that he lived his life as Edward Kelley from the time he revealed his name to Dee until his death.

Kelley may have been a top-notch skryer, but his real interest was in alchemy. It is possible that he desired to meet and work with Dee in order to learn what alchemical knowledge Dee possessed. He also spent some of his free time away from Dee in the pursuit of alchemical mysteries and buried treasures. When the two men traveled to Prague to meet with Emperor Rudolph, Kelley found his true calling among the court alchemists he met there.

During their stay in the Empire's capital city, Dee ceased to be the leader of the pair and began to take a back seat to Kelley and his alchemical exploits. When Dee finally decided to leave Prague and journey back toward England, Kelley remained as one of Rudolph's primary court alchemists. He was given several estates—including silver mines, castles, and even an astronomy tower—by a William of Rosenburg (see later in this chapter), and Rudolph even made him a "baron of the kingdom." This title was equivalent to knighthood back in England, and it is the reason he is called "Sir" even though he was not technically knighted by the queen.

Legend has it that Kelley was successful in transmuting base metals to gold, and English authorities spent many years vainly attempting to convince Kelley to bring his knowledge back to England. Kelley refused and lived the rest of his life as a successful alchemist.

In the end, Kelley was arrested and imprisoned on two separate occasions. This may have been due to his own volatile temper, or it may have been done for political reasons. Some even suspect he was locked up for failing to produce the amounts of gold he promised. Dee's journals indicate Kelley was killed during an escape attempt from prison in 1597; however, new Czech documents are currently coming to light (untranslated as of yet) that may prove Kelley lived on and had a very influential life in Prague.

Barnabas Saul: Before Dee met Kelley, he attempted his work with another medium named Barnabas Saul. Saul appears as the skryer for only one session in the magickal journals (the very first one), after which he claimed that his mediumistic abilities had left him. He leaves the story in the company of a Mr. Clerkson and does not appear again.

Soon afterward, the same Mr. Clerkson introduced Dee to Mr. "Talbot" (Kelley), who warned the good doctor that Saul was secretly slandering him. Dee had already recorded his own doubts about Saul's honesty, so there is reason to believe Dee took Kelley's warnings at face value. Later, Kelley would report that the angels agreed and had declared both Saul and the information he had skryed corrupt. On one hand, all of this could easily be Kelley selling himself as a skryer over Saul. On the other hand, if Kelley's accusations were true, it could explain why Saul suddenly gave up skrying and departed the scene just before Kelley arrived.

Very little is known about Barnabas Saul. Dee's records suggest he was a cleric or preacher of some type. I suspect his name is not real, because Barnabas and Saul are the names of two early church fathers who worked together for a time (see Acts 11–15 in the Bible). They eventually began to work with a third (Barnabas's nephew John Mark) and had a falling out over his involvement. It resulted in Barnabas and Saul going their separate ways, with John Mark going with Barnabas. The whole story seems a bit similar to the incidents between Dee, Saul, and Kelley.

Mr. Clerkson: We know nothing at all about Mr. Clerkson. He first appears in Dee's journal as a friend or associate of Barnabas Saul. When Saul quit skrying and left Dee's household, he left in the company of Mr. Clerkson. Then, a mere two days later, Mr. Clerkson arrives once more to introduce Dee to Edward "Talbot" (Kelley).

It would seem, then, that Mr. Clerkson had an important role in finding skryers for Dee to hire. This would not have been unusual. At the time, skryers sold their services much as astrologers and psychics do today. What we do not know is what interest Mr. Clerkson had in Dee's work, or what (if any) compensation he received for introducing skryers to potential employers.

Arthur Dee (1579–1651): For a very brief time, Edward Kelley refused to continue Dee's skrying work; thus, Dee attempted to employ his eldest son, Arthur, instead. The attempt was a failure, and soon Dee convinced Kelley to come back to work.

As an adult, Arthur would claim that he witnessed his father and Kelley transmuting base metals into gold in Prague, and even used to play with gold and silver ingots that littered the house like toys. He would go on to follow in his father's footsteps as a physician and alchemist, and he would serve powerful men in this capacity. James I (king of England after Elizabeth) recommended his appointment as physician to the czar of Russia, and during his years there he would compile his own famous alchemical text: *Fasciculus Chemicus*. Later, he would return to England and become physician to King Charles I.

Thomas Kelley: Thomas, supposedly Edward Kelley's brother, is another shadowy figure in Dee's journals. He appears quite suddenly in the story, bringing news that Edward is about to be arrested for alleged crimes committed elsewhere. Edward vanishes from Dee's household before authorities arrive and returns later claiming to have been fishing.

Thomas Kelley would appear several times throughout Dee's journals, almost always in the role of a courier taking messages between England and Prague. He would also marry into the von Pisnitz family, a noble Bohemian family with connections in Rudolph's court. This is interesting because Kelley would himself become a Bohemian noble while working for Rudolph.

Dee never recorded the name of the family into which Thomas Kelley had married. He also did not record when Thomas and his family moved to England, nor did he ever mention them again. Scholars who view Dee's journal as a complex spy thriller (and it certainly is!) have suggested that Thomas Kelley may be a false name.

Albert Lasky (b. 1527): In 1583, this Polish prince made an elaborate royal appearance in Queen Elizabeth's court. It is not entirely clear why Lasky made this visit; however, it is strongly suspected that Lasky was hoping to claim the Polish throne. The flamboyant noble was popular with the people of Poland and was perhaps attempting to gain the blessings and support of certain foreign monarchs such as Elizabeth and Rudolph. Of course, this put him very much at odds with Poland's king Stefan Batory.

Lasky was also interested in alchemy and wished to meet with Dee as much as he wished to see the queen herself. Thus, after his visit to the royal court, he took another elaborate royal procession to Dee's front door and quickly became part of the Enochian saga. He was allowed to sit in on the skrying sessions and was even allowed to ask questions of the angels.

Dee hoped he had found his benefactor and soon packed up his household (including Kelley and his family) and headed off for Poland in Lasky's company. Unfortunately, Lasky quickly ran out of money and finally parted ways with Dee. It is unclear, but he may even have run afoul of King Batory, as his royal aspirations were never achieved.

William Cecil (Lord Burghley) (1521–1598): William Cecil served as Queen Elizabeth's chief adviser for most of her reign, first as secretary of state and then as Lord High Treasurer. He and John Dee knew one another personally, and it was Cecil whom Dee often appealed to for compensation for his services to England. Sadly, it was also Cecil who denied many of Dee's requests.

Once Kelley became a famous alchemist in Prague, Cecil seemed to largely forget about Dee and focused instead upon Kelley. Through an intermediary agent named Edward Dyer (see next page), Cecil made valiant efforts to convince, cajole, and lightly threaten Kelley to return to England with his alchemical knowledge. Kelley, of course, refused to return.

Francis Walsingham (1532–1590): Walsingham was Elizabeth's secretary of state after William Cecil moved into the position of Lord High Treasurer. During most of the period that concerns us, Walsingham was responsible for establishing government policies both foreign and domestic. He is even more famous as the queen's spymaster, who single-handedly built England's famous network of "intelligencers" (spies) throughout England and Europe.

Dee and Walsingham knew one another, and their roles in English history brought them together on several occasions. When Walsingham took over as spymaster, he found it necessary to consult with the only man in England who understood encryption ciphers and who (legend has it) had long since served as the queen's spy: John Dee. Sure enough, Walsingham would go on to establish the world's most famous spy network, made famous for its dependence upon encryption and secret messages.

Of course, spies trust no one, and Walsingham would later develop suspicions against Dee, Kelley, and their occult work. In response, Dee took to hiding his journals in a secret compartment inside his chimney. When Dee and Kelley left with Prince Lasky for Poland, they did so in the dead of night to escape the eyes of Walsingham's agents. Later, Dee and Kelley made a rather large show of burning the journals in their entirety—very likely so Walsingham's spies would report that the records were destroyed. (Later, the journals would reappear, which Dee would claim as a miracle.)

Count William of Rosenberg (Vilem Rozmberk; d. 1592): The Rosenberg family was the most influential clan in Bohemia and were often called the "real lords of the kingdom." William, in particular, made his hometown a center of Bohemian politics and culture. He was also a friend of Dee and Kelley, acting as their patron and benefactor after they left Rudolph's court. The two mystics slept in a house owned by Rosenberg in Trebon and even worked in an alchemical lab he provided for them. Czech sources (only now coming to light) have indicated that Sir Kelley's later knighthood may have been compensation for finding silver in one of Rosenberg's mines.

Sir Edward Dyer (1543–1607): Dyer is perhaps the ultimate example of an Elizabethan poet-intelligencer. England made much use of poets and writers as agents because they were prone to travel and could influence public opinion. Dyer was called an ornament of the queen's court—outwardly for his poetry and secretly for the missions he ran on Elizabeth's behalf. For his efforts he was knighted and given land.

Dyer was also a personal friend of John Dee, even becoming godfather to Dee's son Arthur. As a secret agent he worked directly for William Cecil, and he, in turn, directed the Garland brothers (see next entry). As Dee and Kelley traveled across Europe, Dyer and the Garlands kept track of the two mystics and their doings. Apparently at the direction of Cecil, Dyer became an alchemical student of Kelley's for several months in Prague—until the two had a violent falling-out and ended up in jail together. England never got its hands on Kelley's alchemical knowledge.

Garland brothers: In his journals, Dee mentions four men by the name of Garland: Francis, Edward, Robert, and Henry. However, Dee's journal is the only place these men can be found. They appear in no English or European records, nor in the personal journals of others who encountered them, such as Arthur Dee.

Yet two of the so-called Garland brothers were present at a public demonstration where Kelley transmuted mercury into gold. At least one of them—Francis—appears several times, carrying messages to and from England. They appear to be most active during the period in which William Cecil attempted to lure Kelley back to England for his alchemical knowledge. Francis Garland specifically seems to work for Edward Dyer. All of this suggests quite strongly that the Garland brothers of Dee's journals are English secret agents; they were not likely brothers and "Garland" was a false name.

Sir Walter Raleigh (1552–1618): A friend and neighbor of John Dee, their children used to play together. Sir Raleigh is most famous for his involvement in the founding of Virginia in the New World. He established the town of Roanoke, Virginia, which is famous for the later disappearance of its entire population. (It is assumed the colonists decided they had been abandoned by England and thus went to live with the Native Americans.) Sir Raleigh is also famous for his attempt to find El Dorado—a mythical city of gold—in South America. It is nearly certain that this famous explorer consulted with Dee on the subjects of navigation and English claims to North America.

Gerardus Mercator (1512–1594): Mercator was a world-famous cartographer who lived in the French county of Flanders in the Low Countries (directly south of England on the continent). In his youth, Dee studied with Mercator in France and there gained expertise in the latest navigational techniques and equipment. Upon returning to England, Dee was the only person in the country with this knowledge, and that is why he was consulted by the captains of every major English maritime expedition during his lifetime.

Sir Robert Bruce Cotton (1570–1631): Sir Cotton is best known for the collection of the Cotton library, which still exists in the British Museum today. About a decade after Dee's passing, Cotton obtained rights to the land around Dee's house and began to search the grounds for valuable books or artifacts. This resulted in the discovery of the second half of Dee's angelic journals, which Cotton claimed had been buried in the ground. (We have never learned why Dee divided his journals in half and hid them in two radically different places.)

Later, during the mid-1600s, a scholar by the name of Méric Casaubon (see next entry) would obtain these journals from Cotton's son and publish them, thereby bringing Dee's magick back into the light half a century after Dee hid it away. Unfortunately, the first half of Dee's records (which included much vital information about his system) would not be found until some time later. (See the entry for Elias Ashmole.)

Méric Casaubon (1599–1671): Casaubon was a French-English classical scholar with a focus upon religious and esoteric subjects. He is known for his literal belief in such spiritual things as angels and demons, and he supported the inquisitorial definition of "witchcraft." As a conservative Protestant—much like King James I, whom he served—he disagreed with such things as divine inspiration or, indeed, any individual's claims of personal spiritual revelation.

To "prove" himself correct, he obtained several of Dee's journals from Robert Cotton's son, wrote a disparaging introduction to them, and published them in 1659 as *A True and Faithful Relation of What Passed for Many Years Between Dr. John Dee...and Some Spirits.* In the introduction, Casaubon asserts that Dee was truly in contact with spiritual beings, but that they were, in fact, demons who were deluding an old fool with the help of a young con artist (Kelley). Even though *A True and Faithful Relation* would eventually become foundational to the Western Esoteric Tradition (certainly not what Casaubon intended!), the introduction also cast Dee in a negative light that has only been overturned in the last few decades.

Elias Ashmole (1617–1692): Ashmole was an antiquarian, esoteric student, and early Freemason. He was also deeply involved in the collection and cataloging of priceless manuscripts, so it is no surprise that this man was acutely interested in the magickal journals of Dr. John Dee.

About ten years after Casaubon published *A True and Faithful Relation*, Ashmole was contacted by a man who claimed to possess several papers written in Dee's hand. The story the man gave was nothing short of fantastical: His wife owned a cedar chest that she had acquired during her first marriage. She kept the chest after her husband passed away, and even rescued it from the Great Fire of London in 1666. (She could not say why she had chosen to carry a large wooden chest with her during such an evacuation.) She later remarried, and the chest remained in her household for many years. One day, they were moving the chest and heard a faint rattle in its bottom. Sure enough, the chest had a false bottom, and when it was pried open, a large stack of papers was found, along with a small rosary.

These papers turned out to be the missing first half of Dee's magickal journals, along with a small grimoire Dee had compiled from information in the journals. Sadly, the couple failed to secure the documents, and their illiterate maid found and destroyed several pages of the material. (She infamously used them to drain pies.) Once this mistake was discovered, the couple gathered the remaining pages and took them to Ashmole. The year was 1672, though these journals would not have a significant impact on the Enochian tradition for several centuries.

"Dr. Rudd": Thomas Rudd (1583–1656) was born just as Dee and Kelley began their angelic séances. He would become a military engineer and mathematician, and thus may have had a natural interest in the life and work of John Dee. A manuscript by a "Dr. Rudd" entitled *A Treatise on Angel Magic* (which included Enochian material) would be published in the late 1600s, but it is unlikely the actual Thomas Rudd had anything to do with it.

A long-standing legend has it that Dr. Rudd knew Dee personally, and that Rudd continued Dee's angelic experiments after the older man passed away. As you will discover later, this is not likely the case. However, the name "Dr. Rudd" still has an important place in the Enochian saga.

The Angels

Annael ("Grace of God"): More commonly spelled *Anael*, he is the archangel of Venus as found in *The Heptameron*. He appears only once: in the very first session recorded in Dee's journals and the only session featuring Barnabas Saul as skryer. During this appearance, Annael claimed to be the successive ruler of the entire universe. There are six others who take their turn in the supreme position (all of whom are also found in *The Heptameron*): Cassiel, Sachiel, Samael, Michael, Raphael, and Gabriel.[18] These are the seven spirits who stand before the face of God (Revelation 4:5).

Annael also explained that the archangel Michael was attached to the skrying stone. (Later, Dee would learn that Gabriel, Raphael, and Uriel were also attached to it, but that Michael was chief among them.) Annael further offered instruction for how to proceed in the work, and then he left for good. The implication is that Annael brokered the meeting between the two men and the four archangels who would oversee the transmission of the entire corpus of Dee's magickal system.

Michael ("Who Is Like God," Fortitudo Dei): Chief of the four archangels, high priest of heaven, and general of the angelic hosts. In *The Heptameron* he is the archangel of Sol. Other sources list him as an archangel of Mercury and a psychopomp who directs souls to paradise, or Gehenna. In Dee's journals, he also goes by the name of Fortitudo Dei ("Fortitude of God").[19] Legend tells us that Michael was the patron of Solomon and gave the king the famous Ring of Solomon by which he worked miracles. Michael would also reveal a special Ring of Solomon to Dee and Kelley, as well as the other magickal tools and furnishings necessary for Enochian magick.

Gabriel ("Strength of God"): Best known as the angel of the Annunciation (who told Mary she would give birth to the son of God) as well as the angel who revealed the Koran to Muhammed. In *The Heptameron* he is the archangel of Luna.

In Dee's journals, Gabriel was in charge of the transmission of the forty-eight Angelical Callings and the thirty Aethyrs. He did not reveal them personally but directed two angels under his charge—Nalvage and Illemese (see later entries)—to transmit the information. He did step in to answer questions about the material, such as when he spoke to Dee about the relationship between the words of the calls and certain numbers that Nalvage had attached to them.

Raphael ("Healing of God," Medicina Dei): The physician of heaven, he is often called Medicina Dei ("Medicine of God") in Dee's journals and sometimes by the shorthand "Me." This should not be confused with an angel named Me that appears elsewhere in Dee's magickal system but with whom Dee never spoke directly.[20]

Raphael, meanwhile, revealed the *Book of Loagaeth* and the "Language of God-Christ" with which it is written. He referred to this as a divine elixir that would heal all of the world's afflictions. He began transmitting the text of *Loagaeth* in a letter-by-letter fashion that quickly overwhelmed Dee and Kelley. When they requested an easier way of doing the work, the archangel agreed but swore he would not appear to the men again. From that point onward, "a voice" revealed the remaining text of the holy book.

Uriel ("Light of God"): The divine avenger and an angel of death, Uriel is the divine light shining within the darkness. This archangel appeared to Kelley during his very first skrying session with Dee, and he remained the archangel in charge of the transmission of the entire Enochian corpus. When the men had questions or made a mistake, it was Uriel who would appear to elaborate points or chastise the men for their shortcomings.

Galvah ("The End," Wisdom, I AM): Galvah's name means "the end"—most likely in the sense of "Omega" from the biblical phrase "I am the Alpha and the Omega, the Beginning and the End." Galvah is the Mother of Angels and is once called "Wisdom" (Greek: Sophia) by one of Dee's angels. She introduced herself to the men with the name I AM—the same name given to Moses at the burning bush (Exodus 3:14).

Without a doubt, Galvah is one and the same with the Gnostic mother goddess Sophia, which also links her to such figures as Inanna, Ishtar, Isis, the Shekinah (or Aima Elohim of the Qabalists), Mother Mary, and the Hermetic "Soul of the World." In short, she is the wife of God and represents the presence of the Divine in the physical world.

Galvah's main role in Dee's journals was the revelation of the forty-ninth table of *Loagaeth*, the very last in the book. It would appear that she is linked directly to the powers represented in that table.

Madimi: An angel of the Heptarchia, a Daughter of the Daughters of Light. Madimi appeared as a young girl and was one of Dee's primary (and favorite) angel contacts. When he later fathered a daughter, Dee would name her Madimia. The angel Madimi appeared throughout Dee's journals, usually in an unofficial capacity. Dee would ask her questions, and if she could not answer them she would point Dee toward the right angel(s).

During the final weeks of Dee's work with Kelley, Madimi appeared as a fully grown woman and instigated the infamous wife-sharing incident.

Nalvage: Also called *Fuge Terrestrium* ("Flee the Earth"). He is one of the rare angels in Dee's records whose name is *not* found upon one of the many cipher-tables that make up the Enochian system. (That is, he is not in the Heptarchia, nor upon the Great Table of the Earth, etc.) He appeared to be under the direct authority of Gabriel. Nalvage revealed the Corpus Omnium Table (otherwise called the Round Table of Nalvage)[21] and the first eighteen Angelical Callings. (Illemese would reveal the Calls of the Aethyrs—see next entry.)

Illemese: An angel of the Heptarchia and a Son of the Sons of Light. Dee sometimes abbreviated Illemese's name to "Il," but that should not be confused with the Heptarchic angel named El (or L), who never spoke directly with Dee.

Illemese, like Nalvage, seemed to be under the authority of Gabriel. (Also see Mapsama.) When Nalvage's time as teacher had expired, Gabriel assigned Illemese to complete the lessons. It was thus Illemese who revealed the names of the thirty Aethyrs and the Angelical Call(s)[22] that open them. He was also the angel who introduced Dee and Kelley to Mother Galvah (who went by the name Wisdom at the time).

Ave: An angel of the Heptarchia, a Son of the Sons of Light. This angel had more to do with the "Enochian" aspect of Dee's magick than any other. It was Ave who revealed the system of Gebofal (the forty-nine-day ceremony for opening the tables of *Loagaeth*). Most of the instruction was contained within a "Prayer of Enoch," which outlined exactly how Enoch had gone about opening the holy book and how Dee was to do it as well. (Further instruction would be given by the angel Mapsama.) Ave was also the angel who revealed the Great Table of the Earth and its system.

Semiel ("Name of God"): This angel appears in only one place in Dee's journals, and his name does not appear elsewhere in the Enochian system. He was called by Michael to reveal the outer circumference of the Seal of the True God,[23] which contains a forty-lettered name of God. Michael told Dee that Semiel alone knew the mysteries that were about to be revealed. It was Semiel, then, who called in forty childlike angels who revealed the forty characters in the circumference of the seal.

Mapsama: Mapsama's name means *Dic Illis* ("Say Unto Them"). He is one of the rare angels who appears in Dee's journals but does not appear elsewhere in the Enochian system. (Also see Nalvage.) Mapsama was active during the transmission of the forty-eight Angelical Calls and gave Dee and Kelley further instruction on the nature of the calls and how to use them for Gebofal. He is under the authority of Gabriel, the archangel in charge during the transmission of the calls and seems to work directly with Nalvage. (Also see Illemese, who later took over Nalvage's role in the journals.)

Levanael (Luna of God): An angel of the moon and one of the angels of the Heptarchia. Levenael is the angel who first referred to the practice of the *Holy Book of Loagaeth* as Gebofal.

Murifri: An angel of the Heptarchia, though his name does not appear on any of the magickal tools or furnishings. Instead, his name is found upon one of seven cipher-tables used to generate the names of the forty-nine angels of the Heptarchic royalty. Although Dee wrote much about the forty-nine royal angels, he recorded very little about the other names that could be found in the seven tables. Murifri was the only one from that group to appear to Dee.[24] He appeared later in the journals to give instructions on the creation of a Heptarchic talisman for a client of Dee's.

Aath: An angel of the Heptarchia, a Daughter of the Daughters of Light. She appeared once to explain the proper use of the *Book of Loagaeth* to Dee and Kelley, and to assure them they would not be able to use it to find buried treasure.

Salamian: An angel of the sun who first appears in *The Heptameron*. In Dee's records, he comes to warn the men that the demon Mammon threatens them and is trying to hinder their work.

The Dee Journals (and Where to Find Them)

***Mysteriorum Libri Quinti (Five Books of the Mysteries)*:** Acquired by Elias Ashmole in 1672 and now cataloged in the British Museum as Sloane MS 3188. Currently published as *John Dee's Five Books of Mystery*, edited by Joseph Peterson. Includes records from 1581 until 1583 concerning the Enochian magickal tools, Heptarchic angels, and the first parts of the *Book of Loagaeth*.

Liber Mysteriorum Sextus et Sanctus **(Sixth and Sacred Book of the Mysteries):** This is a copy of the tables of *Loagaeth* in Kelley's handwriting that were not included at the end of the *Five Books.* Also acquired by Elias Ashmole in 1672 and now cataloged in the British Museum as Sloane MS 3189. The forty-nine tables of *Loagaeth* are currently available only online or on the Esoteric Archives CD available from Joseph Peterson's Esoteric Archives website.

Dee's Personal Grimoire: Also acquired by Elias Ashmole in 1672 and now cataloged in the British Museum as Sloane MS 3191. Currently published as *The Enochian Magick of Dr. John Dee* by Geoffrey James. Includes choice parts of Dee's entire system of magick.

***De Heptarchia Mystica*:** In 1983, Robert Turner published excerpts from Dee's personal grimoire concerning the Heptarchic system of magick. This is now readily available online, and I recommend Joseph Peterson's Esoteric Archives website.

The *True and Faithful Relation...* journals: The final thirteen books of Dee's records. Acquired by Robert Bruce Cotton in about 1620 and now cataloged in the British Museum as Cotton Appendix XLVI, Parts 1 and 2. Currently published as *A True and Faithful Relation of What Passed for Many Years Between Dr. John Dee...and Some Spirits* by Méric Casaubon. Covers the period from 1583 to the end of the work in 1585. Contains some instruction on the Heptarchia and *Loagaeth* / Gebofal (though there is little context for them), the forty-eight Angelical Calls, and the entirety of the Great Table of the Earth and Parts of the Earth systems. This book was the sole source for all post-Dee Enochian practices for nearly four hundred years.

Further Reading

The Queen's Conjuror: The Science and Magic of Dr. John Dee, Advisor to Queen Elizabeth I by Benjamin Woolley

John Dee (1527–1608) by Charlotte Fell-Smith

John Dee: The World of the Elizabethan Magus by Peter J. French

The Private Diary of Dr. John Dee: And the Catalog of His Library of Manuscripts by John Dee

Writings of Dr. John Dee (1527–1608) at the Esoteric Archives website

A Golden Storm: Attempting to Re-Create the Context of John Dee and Edward Kelley's Angelic Material by Teresa Burns

Francis Garland, William Shakespeare, and John Dee's Green Language by Teresa Burns

Chapter Four

The History of Dee's Enochian Tradition

So far, I have given you the very basics of the Enochian tradition, John Dee, and the magick he recorded in his journals. You should now be generally familiar with certain terms—such as Heptarchia, Gebofal, Great Table, Watchtower, and Part of the Earth—that were once mysterious. In this chapter, we will explore a general historical overview of Dee's Enochian tradition.

I will begin with some thoughts about Dee's own intentions and motivations behind recording the Enochian material. The discussion will briefly touch upon subjects such as Jewish and Christian mysticism. Next, I will explore the development of the Enochian tradition after Dee's passing, starting with a brief summary of how the journals escaped from Dee's hiding places into the hands of later occultists. Then I will trace the Enochian influence through the scholar-philosophers of the Royal Society of England, the Adepts of the Golden Dawn, and on into the occultism of the twentieth century. This will illustrate how drastically Dee's material was altered by those who followed him—occultists who rarely had access to all of Dee's journals and largely misunderstood what they could find. This resulted in an entirely new Enochian tradition, which I have called "neo Enochian" in previous writings.

The Enochian Magick of Dr. John Dee (or "Dee Purism")

It is important to consider the work of Dee and Kelley within the context of the Renaissance world in which they lived—where Protestantism was diluting the previously unchallenged authority of the Catholic Church, where the Church of England was still young and endangered, where Britain was on the verge of empire and the New World was newly discovered. Dee's magick appears very different through this lens than it would look much later, after passing through the Age of Enlightenment and magickal groups like the Hermetic Order of the Golden Dawn. This study of the original version of Dee's magick—as recorded by the man himself—is today called "Dee purism."

All too often, Dee purism is mistaken to mean that only Dee's own writings are important to the study of Enochian magick. Nothing could be further from the truth! Dee himself studied several mystical traditions, such as the Hebrew Qabalah and Merkavah mysticism, the Christian Qabalah, Gnosticism, and even the Solomonic grimoires. (We will explore these further below.) All of these show their mark upon Dee's personal system of angel magick and are therefore an important part of the Dee-purist study of Enochiana.

When we compare Dee's magick to his source material, we begin to get an idea of his unspoken intentions. The first phase of his system—the Heptarchia—appears to be his own version of the magick found in the Solomonic grimoires. Precursors to the Heptarchia (and other phases of the Enochian system) can be found in texts such as Agrippa's *Three Books of Occult Philosophy*, *Arbatel of Magic*, *Liber Juratis*, *The Heptameron*, *Lemegeton* (especially the *Pauline Arts* and the *Almadel of Solomon*), and many more. Like many of these texts, Dee's Heptarchia is a system of planetary angel magick intended to gain the attentions of the seven entities who constructed and currently maintain the universe.

One of the grimoires in particular contains an essential occult primer for anyone who wishes to attempt a Heptarchic working: the forty-nine magical aphorisms found in the *Arbatel of Magic*. These aphorisms outline both an occult philosophy and a cosmology that seem to provide the foundation upon which the Heptarchic magick is built.

The second phase of Dee's system—including Gebofal and the *Book of Loagaeth*—appears to be greatly influenced by Jewish mystical practices such as "Counting the Omer" and Merkavah mysticism. Counting the Omer is an observance that spans the fifty days between Passover and Shavuot. During this time, the Jewish mystic could engage in the practice of "Entering the Fifty Gates of Understanding (or Binah)." This involved daily meditations upon different aspects of God as recorded in the Torah. Each meditation leads the aspirant closer to the Divine and should ultimately open a channel of direct communication from God to human.[25] This would appear to be the inspiration behind the forty-nine-day practice of Gebofal, during which a different table from the *Book of Loagaeth* is meditated upon each day until it culminates upon the final day in direct divine revelation.

The *Ma'aseh Merkavah* ("work of the Chariot") was an early form of Jewish shamanism that existed alongside the *Ma'aseh Berashith* ("work of Creation"). In the study of Berashith, the mystic would pray and contemplate the manner in which God created the universe and how the soul became incarnate in flesh. In the study of Merkavah, the aspirant would perform techniques to generate visions of the throne of God (called the Merkavah, or divine chariot) and the seven circles of heaven. This carried over into early Christianity as well, as we can see especially in chapter four of the Revelation of St. John.

Later, in about the thirteenth century, both Ma'aseh Berashith and Ma'aseh Merkavah would become vital foundations for the Jewish Qabalah (as well as the rest of the Western Mystery Tradition). Aspects of Merkavah mysticism run throughout Dee's system of angel magick, especially in the *Loagaeth* system, which promises that one can enter the forty-eight gates of heaven and explore the realms beyond.

The third phase of Dee's magick is broken into two aspects: the Parts of the Earth and the Great Table of the Earth. The parts system appears to be drawn from Agrippa's work[26] (with some reference to Merkavah mysticism), while the Great Table of the Earth appears to be a diagram of the Merkavah (throne of God) itself and has a largely alchemical focus.[27]

Even Dee's Angelical language did not arise in a complete vacuum. Long before he penned his journals, scholars and mystics had been searching for the "primordial tongue"—that is, the first human language, supposedly spoken in Eden. Other famous mages (such as Trithemius and Agrippa) had already attempted to create some form of this language. However, they usually produced a version of Hebrew written with obscure "Hebrewesque" characters. Dee was one of the first (perhaps the very first) mystics to record a truly unique celestial language with its own grammar, syntax, alphabet, and so on.[28]

Finally, there is a heavy Gnostic influence underlying most of Dee's system. Gnosticism is a mystical religion that arose around the dawn of the Common Era in the area of Egypt. It drew much from the ancient Egyptian and Greek philosophies that were common to that area at the time. It arose independently of Christianity, but after a couple of centuries it had become closely associated with early mystical Christian sects. (A Gnostic text even became one of the four biblical Gospels: the book of John.) This perhaps reached its peak when a man named Valentinus (100–160 CE) formed a Gnostic sect within the Catholic Church.

This and other Gnostic sects had been all but abolished by the time Dee came along. However, their mysteries—especially those of the Valentinian sect—had long since become foundational to the Western Esoteric Tradition. Traces of Gnostic doctrine can be found within the Hebrew Qabalah, alchemy, Hermeticism, the Solomonic grimoires, etc. In Dee's system, the Gnostic influence is most obvious in the poetical imagery of the forty-eight Angelical Callings.[29]

Taken all together, it would appear Dee wished to formulate his own Christianized versions of the most powerful occult systems he had encountered. This makes perfect sense when we consider that the Christian Qabalah was newly born and gathering steam during Dee's era. The Christian Qabalah (often spelled Kabbalah or Cabala as well as other variations) is a mixture of Christian, Jewish, and Hermetic mysticism.

One of the first Christian Qabalists, Pica Della Mirandola, had lived in Italy in the late 1400s, about one hundred years before Dee's journals were written. Another famous Christian Qabalist, Johann Reuchlin, lived in Germany during the late 1400s and early 1500s, passing away just a few years before Dee's birth in 1527. Therefore, Dee stood in a good position to add his name to the list of great Western Christian Qabalists. Had the kings and emperors who glimpsed Dee's journals understood the significance of what they saw, he would have achieved his goal, and his name would now be spoken alongside Mirandola's, Reuchlin's, and those who followed them.

However, that dream was never fulfilled. Too many powerful people were suspicious of Dee's angelic revelations. Remember, this was a time when anything that smacked of occultism or that attempted to contradict religious authority could get you arrested and tortured to death. Besides which, kings and rulers do not generally take kindly to would-be prophets who insist on issuing commandments from God. Thus, instead of being hailed as an accomplished philosopher, Dee found himself hastily leaving several towns in the dead of night. Kelley (whose aggressive personality made him few friends) would escape with Dee on several occasions until he finally found a home with Emperor Rudolph and left Dee's employ.

Dee would eventually return to England in 1589, where he would spend his remaining years seeking fair compensation for all he had offered his queen and country, including his skills as a navigator, cartographer, mathemetician, physician, astrologer, philosopher, cryptographer, and perhaps even intelligencer. In this quest he would meet with some successes and quite a few defeats. Complicating matters was Dee's growing infamy as a "sorcerer" and consorter with "devils," which caused him to spend a portion of his spare time defending his reputation.

In the end, Dee hid his magickal journals away. His personal grimoire (compiled from information recorded in the journals) and the first five journals (containing the Heptarchia and a portion of *Loagaeth*) were secreted in the false bottom of a cedar chest. They would remain hidden there for over fifty years, and it would be nearly four hundred years before the magickal systems recorded in them would be seriously studied by Western occultists.

The remaining journals appear to have remained hidden on Dee's property. About ten years after Dee's passing, the land was purchased by Robert Cotton, who claimed he found the journals buried there. Later, Cotton's son would give these journals to Méric Casaubon, who published them in 1659 as *A True and Faithful Relation of What Passed for Many Years between Dr. John Dee (A Mathematician of Great Fame in Q. Eliz. and King James their Reignes) and Some Spirits*. This publication, especially Casaubon's introduction to the material, was quite sensational for the time. Casaubon described Dee as a naive fool who was duped by devils posing as angels—a characterization that would haunt Dee's memory until the latter parts of the twentieth century.

Today there is a marked increase in both scholarship about Dee and Kelley and in the practical application of the magickal systems they recorded. This new movement has led to the Dee-purist practice of Enochian magick, seen for the first time in over four centuries.

Of course, if Dee's magickal system was largely unknown and unused until the past couple of decades, then how did Enochian magick become foundational to the Western Mystery Tradition in the meantime? Let us continue the saga in the next section:

The Neo-Enochian Tradition

As discussed in the previous section, Dee did not become famous as a co-founder of the Christian Qabalistic tradition. After his passing, few people knew of the existence of the journals, and absolutely no one attempted to carry on his work. Much of the material important to working the system was hidden in the cedar chest, and Casaubon would not publish *A True and Faithful Relation* for nearly half a century.

Dee had, however, died with the reputation of a conjurer, and this would provide the perfect audience for Casaubon's later publication. The world wanted to know what Dee and Kelley had been up to behind the closed doors of their study. Like tabloid readers today, they wanted dirt and drama—and Casaubon was more than happy to provide them with both. In his introduction, he described Dee as a poor zealot who was fooled by a bunch of "devils" and a con artist (Kelley). Casaubon's take on the story became accepted as fact, and no scholar would challenge that view for nearly four hundred years.

Thankfully, some people were nonetheless interested in Dee's actual magickal work. The Age of Enlightenment was just getting underway, and Western culture was shifting its focus from religion to science. Several members of the Royal Society (a late seventeenth-century English organization of Enlightenment scholars, scientists, and philosophers) took Dee's journals seriously and began to experiment with his material.

Of course, since most of Dee's system was still hidden away, what these scholars found in Casaubon's book was a very intriguing yet incomplete system. It led to the (mistaken) idea that Dee had only recorded a skeletal outline of a system, and that it needed "fleshing out" with outside material to make it workable. Thus, occultists began to incorporate Dee's material (such as the Watchtowers, the Holy Table, and the forty-eight Angelical Callings) into their own established magickal traditions. This resulted in something entirely new and different from what Dee had intended—and I call it "neo-Enochiana."

This was the era of men like Elias Ashmole—a founding member of the Royal Society—who is rumored to be among the philosophers who experimented with summoning Dee's angels. (This is by no means confirmed.) It was also the period during which the mysterious "Dr. Rudd" comes into the picture (see below). Other major contributors to the neo-Enochian current would come along later, such as the Hermetic Order of the Golden Dawn and Aleister Crowley.

Rudd Enochiana

Legend has it that Dr. Rudd knew Dee personally and directly inherited his system of angel magick. This would mean that Rudd's Enochian material—published in *A Treatise on Angel Magic*—should represent the final form of Dee's system as the man himself would have used it. It would reflect what Dee and Rudd worked on together, and it is said that Rudd led his own English mystery school, continuing a secret tradition of Enochian magick descended directly from Dee.

Sadly, this legend does not stand up to the facts. First of all, the Enochian material found in Rudd's treatise shows no familiarity with Dee's entire system. It includes only the portions published by Méric Casaubon, which only includes about a third of the system. Many of the mysteries associated with the Enochian material were recorded in the journals Casaubon did not have, and Rudd's treatise makes no reference to them whatsoever.

All of this means the *Treatise on Angel Magic* was most likely written after Casaubon published his book in 1659. And since the Thomas Rudd of historical record passed away three years earlier (1656), it is quite unlikely that he wrote the treatise. Plus, there is no proof that Thomas Rudd knew John Dee. It would appear the treatise was written by someone long after Dee passed away, and Dr. Rudd's name was simply used to give the manuscript occult authority.

For these reasons, I consider "Rudd's" material to be the first example of neo-Enochiana. Rudd did what hundreds of neo-Enochian practitioners after him would do: he picked and chose interesting bits of information from *A True and Faithful Relation* and incorporated them into the magickal system he was already using. Rudd stands out in this regard because he published before the existence of the Hermetic Order of the Golden Dawn, so you won't find any GD elements in his neo-Enochian material.

Rudd focuses primarily upon the construction and use of the skrying table, which Casaubon had illustrated near the front of *A True and Faithful Relation*. Ironically, this was perhaps closer to Dee's original intent than later neo-Enochian systems would come. Rudd did not seem interested in the Watchtowers, Parts of the Earth, the thirty Aethyrs, or (oddly enough) the forty-eight Angelical Callings, likely because he was already well-versed in his own systems of angel summoning (as outlined in the rest of the treatise). He might have been more interested in the Heptarchic system if that material been included in *A True and Faithful Relation*. I would find it hard to believe Rudd could have known about the Heptarchia and not mentioned it in his own analysis of the Holy Table and Seven Ensigns, both of which are inherent to Dee's Heptarchic system.

Book H

The next important neo-Enochian document to appear was entitled *Book H,* or *Clavicula Tabularum Enochi.* In fact, I would say that *Book H* is the single most important source document for the neo-Enochian tradition because it would later become the foundation of the Golden Dawn's Enochian system.

Book H focuses entirely upon the Great Table system of angel magick as drawn from Méric Casaubon's publication of Dee's later journals. It contains all of the information recorded by Dee—including the Great Table initiation rite, the functions of the Watchtower angels, and the methods for decrypting their names from the Great Table. Then it considerably expands upon those instructions, seeking to present a fully functional grimoire for the use of the Watchtowers. There are dozens of original prayers and invocations, and the method of extracting the angels' names is altered, thus creating an entirely new hierarchy of spiritual beings that never appear in Dee's records.

There is also a difference in how the author of *Book H* attributed the Watchtowers to the four quarters of the world. As discussed in chapter 2, Dee was told to use the Watchtower associated with the world civilization he wished to influence (Eastern nations, Western nations, etc.). However, *Book H* has changed this so that each Watchtower represents a direction of the compass, with the center point of the world established where the aspirant happens to be working. (This would later have a massive impact on the Golden Dawn system of magick, as well as the systems that followed afterward, from Thelema to Wicca.)

The most significant difference between *Book H* and Dee's system is that *Book H* uses the Reformed Table of Raphael rather than the original Great Table. It would appear that the unknown author of the document had read Casaubon's *A True and Faithful Relation* and found the Reformed Table with Dee's notes in the margin. He read how Dee rejoiced that the Reformed Table solved "a great doubt" and assumed that meant the new version should simply replace the original. (Had the Victorian author known the Reformed Table was associated with the infamous wife-swapping incident, he likely would not have used it.)

This version of the Great Table forms the frontispiece to *Book H*. It is drawn so that the higher divine names on the table are in black ink while most of the angel names are in red.

Book H then provides several quotes from *A True and Faithful Relation* that outline the sacred mythos behind the magick—especially the transgression and fall of Adam and God's establishment of four great overseers to protect humanity from Satan's attacks. This is followed by an outline of "The Hierarchy of Angels" (that is, within the Watchtowers) that is adapted from descriptions of Edward Kelley's first vision of the Watchtower angels.

Next, it presents exhaustive and highly repetitive instructions for decrypting the names of God and the angels from each Watchtower. This is followed by an outline of the functions of each group of angels in the Watchtowers—which mirrors Dee's original version exactly.

The next section contains the instructions for the Great Table initiation ritual, which are largely unchanged from Dee's instructions. It mainly concerns the construction and use of a book containing prayers and invocations for all the names upon the Great Table. A white robe that will be used only once is also mentioned.

The final three sections provide lengthy invocations to the Watchtower angels: the first and third sections seem to contain actual conjurations intended to compel the angels to appear and speak. The second section includes "invocations by way of humble supplication" to all the same angels. The prayers in this second section are not outright conjurations. Instead, they appear to be the invitational prayers that should be written in the special book and used during the Great Table initiation rite.[30]

We do not know exactly when *Book H* was written, nor who authored it. I have heard speculation that it was written by someone involved with the founding of the Golden Dawn, such as W. Wynn Westcott. If so, that would make it a late nineteenth-century text. In the end, however, we simply do not know the true origin of *Book H*. We can only be certain that it was written sometime between the publication of *A True and Faithful Relation* and the establishment of the Golden Dawn in the very late 1800s—a window of two centuries. We know that it could not have been written by Dee or anyone who had seen the journals or grimoire hidden in the cedar chest, because *Book H* contains absolutely no references to information found in those books.[31]

It is most likely that someone sat down in the British Museum with a copy of *A True and Faithful Relation* and did their best to mine the dense tome for useful magickal information. Because they did not know about Dee's hidden journals, they saw in Dee's records (as "Rudd" had seen) some interesting but incomplete ideas about angel magick. *Book H* was this person's attempt to create a complete system for working with the angels of the Great Table.

The Hermetic Order of the Golden Dawn and The Book of the Concourse of the Forces

After *Book H*, the next major contribution to the neo-Enochian tradition came from the Hermetic Order of the Golden Dawn in the late 1800s. This contribution is contained in one of their inner-Order documents entitled *The Book of the Concourse of the Forces*. This document outlines, in exhaustive detail, the Golden Dawn's unique system of Enochian magick as taught in their Adept grades. It focuses entirely upon the Reformed Table of Raphael, apparently drawn from *Book H* itself. There is nothing of the Heptarchia or Gebofal in the Golden Dawn's original system of neo-Enochiana because those parts of Dee's system were still largely unknown.

Meanwhile, *The Book of the Concourse of the Forces* incorporates nearly every scrap of occult symbolism and correspondences taught throughout the rest of the Order's curriculum. Thus we find information here about geomancy, tarot, astrology, the Qabalistic Tree of Life, Coptic-Egyptian godforms, and (of course!) a central focus upon the four philosophical elements—Fire, Water, Air, and Earth. The Great Table became a symbolic compendium of the entire Golden Dawn cosmology.[32]

The most accessible source for *The Book of the Concourse of the Forces* is probably *The Golden Dawn* (Book Nine) by Israel Regardie. Additional Golden Dawn Enochian material can also be found in Regardie's later publication *The Complete Golden Dawn System of Magic*. Plus, if you search the Internet for "Concourse of the Forces," you will discover that some of the material—along with commentary about it—is available for free viewing or download. Here I will simply give a brief overview of the contents of the book as presented in Regardie's *Golden Dawn*.

First, Regardie wrote his own introduction to the Enochian system as a preface to the older Golden Dawn text. This was one of my first introductions to the system, and I dare say the same is true for most Enochian scholars and practitioners today (even those who eventually turned toward the Dee-purist system instead). Sadly, this introduction is overflowing with inaccuracies and outright mythologies that have been repeated over and over again by students and authors ever since its publication.

For example, have you ever heard that the Enochian language and system of magick are remnants of the primordial religion of Atlantis? Or that bits and pieces of the language have been found in ancient—pre-Sanskrit—words and phrases? This introduction is the primary source for that myth as popularized in modern texts. Somewhat less outlandish (yet still incorrect) is the assertion that Dee and Kelley merely presented a skeletal framework for a magickal system that was never completed, and was therefore unworkable. The Golden Dawn, claims Regardie, took that skeleton and gave it flesh, transforming it into a fully formed system of ceremonial magick and the crown jewel of the Golden Dawn's curriculum. Regardie also states that the origins of the system are largely unknown, basically dismissing the work of Dee and Kelley as merely recovering a few bits of an older system (perhaps from subconscious memories of past lives).

All of this we now know to be untrue—and we are well aware of the origins of the system through Dee and Kelley, as well as their source materials. We also know that Dee and Kelley recorded an elaborate and quite complete system of angel magick without need of inclusions from other traditions to make it "workable." However, keep in mind that these inaccuracies are not Regardie's fault, as he was merely presenting what he himself had been taught, and he did not have access to the wealth of historical material we now enjoy about Dee, Kelley, and the system of magick they recorded. It is unfortunate, though, that so many modern authors on the subject of Enochiana have parroted portions of Regardie's introduction as if they were fact.

After this introduction, Regardie presents the proper *Book of the Concourse of the Forces*, which is divided into four parts:

Part One

The first part begins by presenting the four Watchtower tablets and a Table of Union[33] drawn from *Book H*. However, they are never presented together as a unified Great Table. The Golden Dawn prefers to keep the Watchtowers separated in the four quarters of the universe, as well as the four quarters of their hall, with the Table of Union residing in the center upon the altar.

These Watchtowers are directly attributed to the four elements (and the Table of Union to Spirit)—which was not seen in either Dee's work or even *Book H*. This is the first time in history where it was considered that the Eastern Watchtower contained Air angels, the Southern Watchtower contained Fire angels, the Western Watchtower contained Water angels, and the Northern Watchtower contained Earth angels. The functions of the angels in each Watchtower—recorded by Dee and preserved in *Book H*—are not entirely missing from this document, but they are buried within it as a side comment. The main focus has instead shifted to the Golden Dawn's elemental correspondences.

Also, the Golden Dawn's original versions of the Watchtowers had many cells containing more than one letter. This arose from the Order's early adepts' uncertainty about what they were seeing in *A True and Faithful Relation*. So you will often find a cell occupied by several similarly shaped letters: "u" and "v," or "v" and "y," or even "u" and "a." In other cases, you will find letters from the original Great Table mixed in with those from the Reformed Great Table where they differed. I suspect the Order never intended for these cells to actually contain more than one letter, but they wanted to present every possibility in places where they were unsure. (The modern incarnations of the Golden Dawn, having better access to Dee's material, have dispensed with the multilettered squares entirely. This is what I have illustrated in this book as well.)

This first part of the book also outlines the elemental color schemes applied by the Order to the Watchtowers. Originally only black and red lettering on a white background (as seen in *Book H*) was presented to the candidate as he worked his way up the grades of the Outer Order. Upon reaching the Adept grades, he would learn the secret color scales used within the Inner Order and see for the first time the Watchtowers in vibrant color. Today the modern incarnations of the Order tend to utilize the full-color versions even in the Outer Order, though the occult meaning of the colors is reserved for the Inner grades.[34]

Next we are given detailed instructions for decrypting the divine and angelic names from the Watchtowers, again drawn largely from the methods outlined in *Book H* along with several inclusions of Golden Dawn attributions. This is where the central name of God in each Watchtower is demoted to the status of an "angelic king" and attributed to the sun, while the six elders (now called "seniors") are associated with the remaining six planets. These planetary attributions appear nowhere previous to this document.

After these names taken from the central Great Cross of each Watchtower are outlined, the book turns its attention to the four subdivisions of each tablet. Again, the original functions of the angels in these subquadrants have been replaced with elemental correspondences. They are presented as four sub-elements: so, for example, the Watchtower of Air in the east contains Air of Air, Fire of Air, Water of Air, and Earth of Air.

This is all then associated with the Golden Dawn's attributions of the Tetragrammaton (YHVH, the highest Hebrew name of God) to the four classical elements. Each letter of this divine name is assigned to one of the Watchtowers, its subquadrants, and even to each individual cell in the table. This gives the Watchtowers several layers of interlocking elemental symbolism, which then extends to tarot, astrological, geomantic, and other correspondences for each cell as well.

By now it should be obvious just how deep and complex this system of correspondence became and perhaps why the adepts of the Golden Dawn felt they had created (or discovered) something that went beyond what Dee had recorded. And the above merely scratches the surface of the possible correspondences! There is certainly nothing inherently wrong with this system, though Dee purists (and those who make use of the original Great Table over that of the Reformed Great Table of Raphael) may take issue with the particular arrangement of elements and astrology in this scheme.

As for the Golden Dawn, they created an interesting manner of working with this complex system in a practical manner. As you may or may not know, the symbol of the truncated pyramid (a four-sided Egyptian pyramid that appears unfinished because it has a flat top rather than coming to a proper point) is quite sacred within Masonic lodges, which is where the Golden Dawn was, quite literally, born. If you are unaware of the symbol of the truncated pyramid, simply take out a dollar bill and look on the back. You will see such a pyramid preserved there, with the all-seeing Eye of God enthroned at its summit.

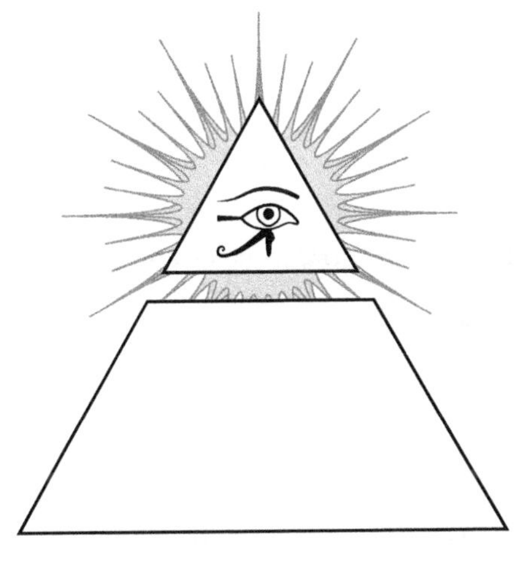

Figure 6: *The Pyramid and the All-Seeing Eye*

The Golden Dawn made use of this symbol in relation to each and every cell of each and every Watchtower. Upon the summit of the pyramid was written the letter from the Watchtower cell, most often transliterated into the Angelical character for that letter. Within the four sides were written the various correspondences for the cell as figured by the above-explained system. Thus, such a pyramid would display symbols for the element(s), tarot card, zodiac sign, planetary symbol, Hebrew letter, and geomantic symbol, all colored according to the Inner Order's color schemes. As you might imagine, this created very intricate and beautiful talismanic images.

Part one of the *Concourse of the Forces* actually goes on for several more pages, covering everything from the Golden Dawn's peculiar system for pronouncing Angelical names to their own take on the four seals of the Watchtowers as recorded by Dee and reinterpreted through Golden Dawn symbolism and even some rather disjointed information about the Seal of the True God. For brevity's sake, however, I will pass over these subjects here.

Part Two

The second part of the *Concourse of the Forces* is much shorter and less complex, mainly because it focuses entirely on the practical application of the above system. It is written in two distinct halves. The first half outlines the specific Golden Dawn hierarchies the Order associated with each cell of the Watchtowers. The second half describes the ceremonies used to invoke them.

First, it explains how to construct a semi-Egyptian figure called a sphinx, based upon the elemental associations of the square's pyramid and the Order's methods of talismanic imaging (constructing the image of a god or angel based upon its occult correspondences). Because the Order associated the four elements with the four biblical kherubim—the lion, eagle, man, and bull described in the first chapter of Ezekiel and the fourth chapter of the Revelation of St. John—it was possible to relate those same biblical figures to the different sides of the pyramids. By taking the head of one kherub, the body of another, the legs of another, etc., a composite sphinxlike figure could be created for every cell of the Watchtowers.

Besides the sphinx, this part of the text also outlines a set of deities—which it calls Egyptian but which are, in fact, Coptic-Egyptian—that are associated with the pyramids. Like the sphinxes, the god associated with any given cell of the Watchtowers is determined by the pyramid's elemental correspondences. For example, if all four elements are equally divided among the sides, then the god Osiris is the deity of the cell. If Water is the dominant element, then Isis is the associated deity. The text gives a list of fifteen Coptic-Egyptian gods and which combination of elements determines the rulership of each.

The rest of this part of the *Concourse of the Forces* is dedicated to outlining the ritual methods of invoking and working with the hierarchies of the Watchtower squares. (This will all be covered in more detail in part two, the neo-Enochian section of this grimoire.)

This part of the text ends with several examples of skryings based upon the above pattern, given as examples of how the system should work in practice. It also mentions the original functions of the Watchtower angels as recorded by Dee and preserved in *Book H*. However, as I stated previously, they are given only as a kind of afterthought and have been overlooked by the greater majority of Golden Dawn adepts and neo-Enochian authors.

Part Three

The third part of the *Concourse of the Forces* outlines the Golden Dawn's method of using the forty-eight Angelical Callings. If you have read my *Angelical Language, Volume I,* you are aware of what Dee himself recorded about the calls and how to use them. They were presented by the angels as keys to unlock the forty-eight gates of heaven represented by the tables of the *Book of Loagaeth*. That holy book and the calls were used in a forty-nine-day initiation ritual the angels called Gebofal.

However, most of the information about the *Book of Loagaeth* is contained in *John Dee's Five Books of Mystery*,[35] while the calls themselves are found later in the journals and preserved in *A True and Faithful Relation*. The early Golden Dawn adepts had ready access to the later records but were largely unaware of the contents of the *Five Books*. They did not know about the *Book of Loagaeth* nor about Gebofal. Instead, they had found the Watchtowers, the forty-eight Angelical Callings, and the Parts of the Earth, all presented outside of their proper context and without much in the way of explanation. (It is no wonder, then, why they assumed Dee's system was incomplete.)

Because of this, the early Golden Dawn adepts developed their own method of using the forty-eight calls. They applied them as keys to unlock the various portions of the Watchtowers—including the Table of Union—and to access the Parts of the Earth. (They were correct about the Parts of the Earth, because that system is contained in *A True and Faithful Relation*.) Along with the use of the Reformed Great Table of Raphael and the association of the four elements to the Watchtowers, this application of the forty-eight callings to the Watchtowers is a hallmark of the neo-Enochian tradition (as opposed to Dee purism).

Dee purists entirely reject this manner of using the forty-eight Angelical Callings. On the other hand, those who defend the Golden Dawn's methods have pointed out that the Great Table of the Earth is formed from the names of the Parts of the Earth, and the Parts of the Earth are associated with the final thirty tables of the *Book of Loagaeth*. Thus, there is a direct line of descent from *Loagaeth* to the Great Table, and thus the callings should be used to invoke the angels of the Watchtowers. I am not here to settle this debate, only to provide you with both sides of the story. There is no arguing against the fact that both systems are firmly established within their own traditions.

Later in this book, I will outline exactly how the calls are used in the Golden Dawn's Watchtower magick. For now, let us move on to the fourth and final portion of the *Concourse of the Forces*.

Part Four

The final section concerns an obscure Golden Dawn form of divination called either Enochian chess or Rosicrucian chess. Entire books can be filled with the history behind this game, the rules for its play, and the manner of using it for divination or magick. However, all of that is beyond this introductory material, so I will not go into much detail here.

I will, however, discuss how this game is related to the greater system of Golden Dawn Enochiana. Every scrap of information outlined in the previous three parts of the *Concourse* is brought together in the construction of the chessboards, movable pieces, game play, and the manner of interpreting the result of the divination.

There are four boards, one for every element and related to the corresponding suit of the tarot. Thus, for example, if one is performing a divination for a question involving passion or aggression, the board of Fire would be used. If the question is about happiness and creativity, the board of Water would be used. If the question is about strife or sickness, the board of Air would be most appropriate. And for questions of home, job, family, etc., the board of Earth should be chosen.

Each board contains sixty-four squares, just like a regular chessboard. However, these squares are equated with the cells of the four Watchtowers, not including the Great Crosses, the Calvary Crosses, or the four cells found above each Calvary Cross. That leaves only the sixteen cells found beneath the arms of each Calvary Cross, which the Golden Dawn calls "servient squares" and recognizes as the forces closest to the physical world. Each square is colored according to the elemental associations I described previously in the construction of truncated pyramids. The only difference is that the pyramids on the Enochian chessboards are not truncated but appear to come to a definite point.

The chess pieces are those of the Order's Coptic godforms: Osiris (= the king), Isis (= the queen), Nephthys (= the rook), Horus (= the knight), and Aroueris (aka Horus the Elder = the bishop). There are also four pawns that take the forms of the four sons of Horus described in the Egyptian Book of the Dead and in the Order's temple symbolism. All of these pieces are colored according to the elemental symbolism of the board one is using for the game. There must be four sets of them on the board, for a total of thirty-six pieces. They represent the divine forces moving upon the elemental foundations of the world.

The game is played by four players, each moving one set of the above godform chess pieces. Each player begins with his pieces on one of the four sub-elemental quadrants of the board and moves outward from there. How each piece is allowed to move, the direction in which the player moves them, and how the pieces interact with one another during game play determines the nature of the divination. It indicates which occult forces will oppose, dominate, or support the other occult forces active in any given situation. The element that "wins" the game, along with how the game was won, will determine the outcome of the question.

The Book of the Concourse of the Forces was not the only Golden Dawn–based Enochian document, so let us now take a look at another important text that has influenced the neo-Enochian tradition.

Liber Vel Chanokh[36]

At this point, mention must be made of Aleister Crowley and the role he has played in the establishment of the neo-Enochian tradition. Crowley was a member of the original Golden Dawn for a time, and it was from them he received his basic magickal instruction. He eventually left the Order on less than pleasant terms and developed his own unique system of mysticism called Thelema (Greek for "true will"). However, it always bore the unmistakable mark of the Golden Dawn, and this is certainly true of his Enochian work as well.

One of his most important neo-Enochian contributions is a document entitled *Liber Vel Chanokh* ("book of Enoch"), *or A Brief Abstract of the Symbolic Representation of the Universe Derived by Doctor John Dee Through the Skrying of Sir Edward Kelley*. The text is part of a long catalog of documents he wrote for his students, this one numbered LXXXIV (eighty-four).

Most of the Enochiana contained in the document is similar to what was explained in the *Concourse of the Forces*. The basic Golden Dawn correspondences are all here, using the Reformed Great Table of Raphael. Interestingly, Crowley has restored the Watchtowers into the Great Table of the Earth form, complete with the Black Cross joining them together.

Later, Crowley provides full diagrams of the individual Watchtowers with every single cell in truncated pyramid form, including the elemental or astrological symbols on each side of every pyramid. This also includes the Table of Union, proving that Crowley felt both this and the Black Cross arrangement of these letters were equally significant.

He then goes on to explain the basic Golden Dawn method of decrypting the divine and angelic names from the Watchtowers, a list of the thirty Aethyrs and their ninety-one Parts of the Earth, and the manner of applying the forty-eight Callings to the Watchtowers.

For me, there are two things that make this document stand out from previous Golden Dawn neo-Enochiana. First, Crowley begins the document with diagrams of the Holy Table and the Seal of the True God, followed by an analysis of the divine and angelic names found upon the seal. He also makes a brief mention of the Heptarchic system and the *Book of Loagaeth* (promising more about them in a future publication that never came). That and his listing of the thirty Aethyrs and the ninety-one parts (including a map of the parts' names upon the Great Table) make me suspect that Crowley had studied Dee's personal grimoire, which the author of the *Concourse of the Forces* does not seem to have done. However, he makes no mention of Gebofal or the proper application of the forty-eight Callings to the tables of *Loagaeth*, so I am fairly certain he did not study—or did not study very deeply—Dee's original *Five Books of Mystery*.

The second thing that stands out about *Liber Vel Chanokh* is the fact that Crowley published this material to a wider audience, where the Golden Dawn's documents would not see publication until Israel Regardie did so in the mid-1900s. Crowley released *Liber Vel Chanokh* (under the longer title: *A Brief Abstract...*) in two issues of his *Equinox* magazine: volume 1, numbers 7 and 8, in the year 1912. Because of this, *Liber Vel Chanokh* was, for some time, one of the standard neo-Enochian documents available to Western students.

The Vision and the Voice

Finally, this historical overview of neo-Enochian documents would not be complete without a mention of Crowley's later publication of *The Vision and the Voice*. This book is essentially a record of Crowley's astral travels through the thirty Aethyrs, and it presents many of the central tenets of his system of Thelema. He and his students, to this very day, consider this book to be one of his most important works, second only to his *Book of the Law*, the primary Thelemic holy book. (You might say that if the *Book of the Law* were Thelema's Torah, then *The Vision and the Voice* would be Thelema's Talmud.)

While it is true that Crowley did not seem to relate the Aethyrs to the tables of *Loagaeth* or the Angelical Callings, he was still closer to the mark than most by simply understanding that the Aethyrs could be spiritually entered and explored as a kind of initiation. (Though I should point out that he entered the lowest Aethyr first and moved upward, which is backward from the Gebofal system recorded by Dee.) What he found there was geared toward his own Thelemic material, and I doubt non-Thelemites will experience anything close to the same visions. Thus I will not take space here to outline what Crowley saw or what his angelic contacts told him.

Since these publications, an abundance of material has been published concerning both the Dee-purist and the neo-Enochian traditions. Some of it has been good, and much of it—sadly—has been full of errors and misconceptions mostly parroted from earlier sources. I am happy to say, however, that this is changing today. Golden Dawners and Thelemites are finally becoming aware of Dee's original journals, and Dee purists are (in some cases) more willing to view neo-Enochiana as a legitimate tradition in its own right.

Some practitioners choose to view the two systems as entirely unrelated, while others (mostly on the neo-Enochian side) have begun to mix the two to various degrees. What is important is that the student understand that there are two distinct traditions at work here and how each of them developed independently. Only then will it be possible to judge the material—especially where the two traditions conflict—and make informed decisions on how, or if, one should import aspects of one tradition into the other.

Further Reading

A Treatise on Angel Magic edited by Adam McLean (this is the "Treatises of Dr. Rudd")

The Practical Angel Magic of Dr. John Dee's Enochian Tables: Tabularum Bonorum Angelorum Invocationes by Stephen Skinner and David Rankine (this is *Book H*)

The Golden Dawn by Israel Regardie (see *Book Nine: The Angelic Tablets*, which includes *The Book of the Concourse of the Forces*)

The Complete Golden Dawn System of Magic by Israel Regardie

Liber LXXXIV Vel Chanokh: A Brief Abstract of the Symbolic Representation of the Universe by Doctor John Dee Through the Skrying of Sir Edward Kelley by Aleister Crowley

The Vision and the Voice, with Commentary and Other Papers: The Collected Diaries of Aleister Crowley, 1909–1914 E. V. by Aleister Crowley

Enochian Vision Magick: An Introduction and Practical Guide to the Magick of Dr. John Dee and Edward Kelley by Lon Milo DuQuette

Enochian World of Aleister Crowley by Lon Milo DuQuette and Christopher Hyatt

Enochian Magic in Theory by Dean F. Wilson

An Enochian Grimoire

*"Now you touch the world and the doings upon earth.
Now we show you the lower world: the governors
that work and rule under God."*
(Archangel Michael)

Chapter Five

The Enochian Universe

Over the years, there has been much confusion over the cosmology behind Dee's magickal system. Exactly how the universe is structured is an important thing to understand when studying any occult tradition. Unfortunately, many occultists have assumed that no cosmology at all is presented in Dee's journals, leading them to simply lay his magick over their own chosen system. Some have attempted to force-fit the Enochian heavens and angels onto the Qabalistic Tree of Life. Others have attempted to interpret Dee's material through the cosmology of Theosophy. Even the Golden Dawn arranged the Enochian Watchtowers within their own fourfold directional and elemental universe.

In fact, Dee *did* record the nature of the "Enochian universe" in his journals, which were outlined in several visions and diagrams that I will explain below. In the end, there is no specific cosmology that is unique to the Enochian system. Instead, Dee recorded the same universe described in the Bible, by ancient Jewish Merkavah mystics, by astrology, and by grimoiric authors such as Agrippa. It was, in fact, the same basic geocentric universe that was commonly accepted as scientific reality during Dee's lifetime and for thousands of years previously.

The Merkavah

"And, behold, a throne was set in heaven, and one sat on the throne.... And round about the throne were four and twenty seats: and upon the seats I saw four and twenty elders sitting.... And there were seven lamps of fire burning before the throne, which are the seven Spirits of God. And before the throne there was a sea of glass like unto crystal: and in the midst of the throne, and round about the throne, were four beasts full of eyes before and behind. And the first beast was like a lion, and the second beast like a calf, and the third beast had a face as a man, and the fourth beast was like a flying eagle."

(Revelation 4: 2–7)

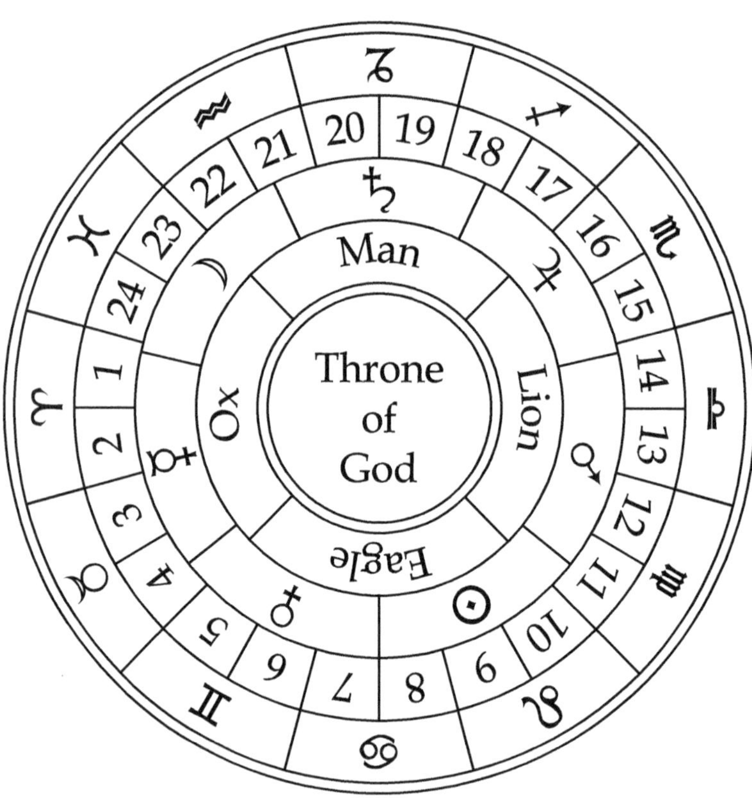

Figure 7: *The Merkavah as Astrological Model*

The basic concept of the Enochian universe is illustrated in chapter 4 of the biblical book of Revelation. Here, St. John has a "Merkavah vision"—a vision of the divine throne—as well as a vision of the entire divine court. The Merkavah itself occupies the center of the vision.

Upon its four sides are the Holy Living Beasts, also known as the kherubim: the lion, eagle, man, and bull. They represent the four elemental triplicities of the zodiac, which, in turn, govern the four elements upon earth. In other sources, these kherubim are represented by the archangels Michael, Gabriel, Raphael, and Uriel.

Also surrounding the throne are the "seven spirits who stand before God." Appearing in John's vision as seven "lamps of fire," they are seven archangels who embody the forces of the ancient planets and represent the seven aspects of God's actions upon earth.

Surrounding the whole scene are the twenty-four elders who collectively represent the forces of the zodiac, governed by the four kherubim and the seven archangels. They are advisers to the king (God). Two elders represent each of the twelve tribes of Israel, which are associated with the twelve signs of the zodiac.

Students of astrology will recognize in this vision a depiction of an astrological chart. Such a chart is encircled by the signs of the zodiac, which are divided into four elemental triplicities. The seven planets that rule them are placed within the circle. In the very center is the earth, which is the throne of God. (The "sea of glass" mentioned in St. John's vision is the firmament, or sky, that surrounds the earth itself.)

The Holy Celestial City

"And [the angel] carried me away in the spirit to a great and high mountain, and shewed me that great city, the holy Jerusalem... And had a wall great and high, and had twelve gates, and at the gates twelve angels, and names written thereon, which are the names of the twelve tribes of the children of Israel: On the east three gates; on the north three gates; on the south three gates; and on the west three gates." (Revelation 21: 10–13)

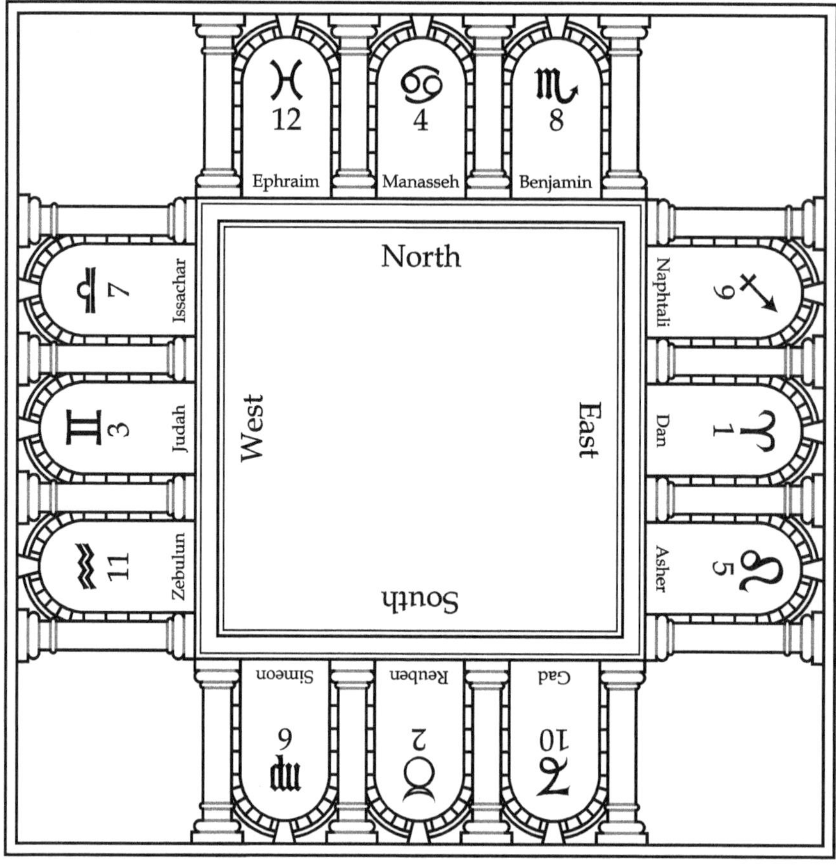

Figure 8: *Dee's Diagram of the Holy City*

The above diagram is taken from Dee's journals and is based upon the end of St. John's vision. Like the previous vision, this illustrates the structure of the universe. This time we see a great city established by God, surrounded by a wall with twelve gates representing the twelve signs of the zodiac. Each gate has an angelic guardian and is also associated with a tribe of Israel.

Dee included the names of the twelve tribes and also assigned each gate a number. These numbers indicate which sign of the zodiac applies to each gate: Aries = 1, Taurus = 2, Gemini = 3, all the way to Pisces = 12. Students should note that these associations are drawn from

Agrippa's *Three Books of Occult Philosophy*, book 2, chapter 14, where we find the "Scale of the Number Twelve." Here Agrippa lists the twelve tribes and the zodiacal sign for each. He also gives names to the twelve angelic gatekeepers, but Dee received different names for these angels.

Also note that Dee has grouped the signs of the zodiac into their elemental triplicities. The three Fire signs are together in the east, the Earth signs are positioned in the south, the Air signs are placed in the west, and the Water triplicity is found in the north.

The Vision of the Watchtowers

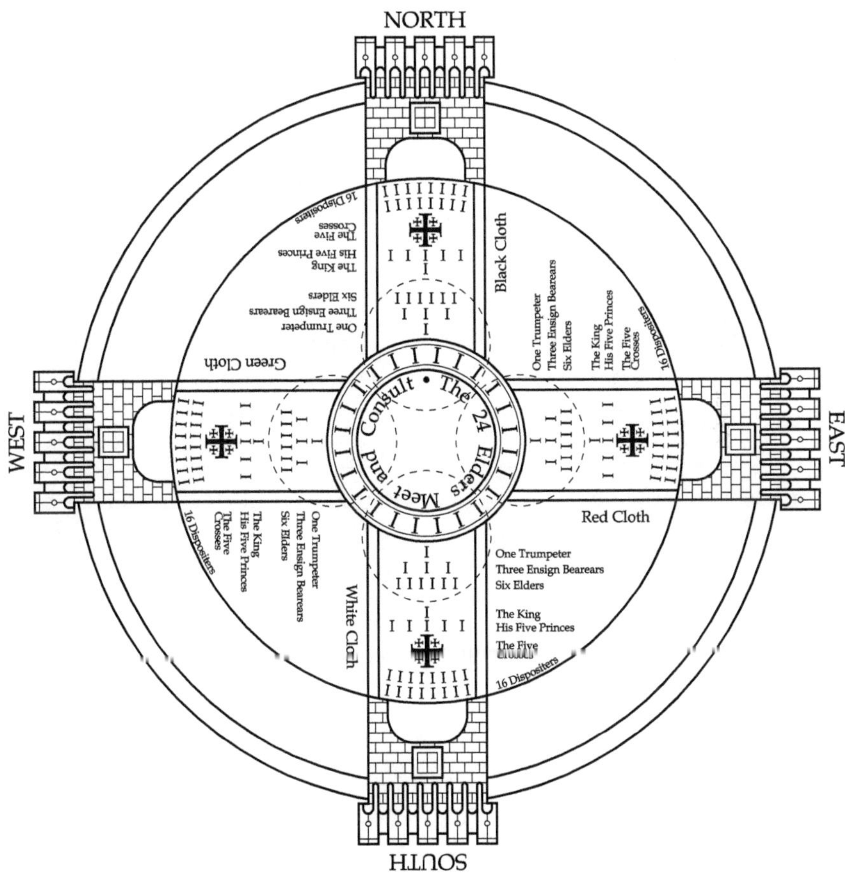

Figure 9: *Diagram of the Vision of the Watchtowers*

Figure 9 was created by (or for) Méric Casaubon to illustrate the vision of the four Watchtowers described by Edward Kelley.[37] This embodies the angelic hierarchies beneath the four kherubim, which Dee's angels referred to as "Watchmen" who protect the universe from the forces of chaos.

The Watchtowers are depicted here as fortified castle towers at the four points of the compass. Trumpets then sounded from the towers, blown three times each. After a pause, the trumpets sounded once more, signaling the opening of the towers' gates.

Then from each gate was rolled a colored carpet: a red one from the east, a white one from the south, a green one from the west, and a black one from the north. These colors appear in many different occult traditions, representing everything from the four seasons upon earth to four layers of heaven and even to four stages of alchemy.

Next the angelic hierarchies of the four Watchtowers proceeded from each gate, walking upon the carpets. First appeared the four angels who blew the trumpets. These trumpets were described as composed of six cones bound together into one instrument. There has been much speculation as to the identity of these four trumpeter angels, as their names are not included in the Watchtowers. Personally, I suspect these may be the four kherubim themselves—Michael, Gabriel, Raphael, and Uriel. (Note that Gabriel is often depicted in religious art with a trumpet. Michael appears with one in some versions of the tarot. Also, both Hebrew tradition and the book of Revelation describe the archangels as possessing six wings, and these four angels carry trumpets made of six cones.)

Following the trumpeters were twelve angels—three from each gate—holding ensigns (flags) as if going into battle. Each ensign displayed one of the twelve names of God that govern the Watchtowers. These twelve angels are not given names in the Watchtower tablets, and, like the trumpeters, there has been much speculation as to their identity. I suspect they are the twelve angels of the zodiac who otherwise guard the gates of the Holy City.

Following these, six elders emerged from each gate, totaling the twenty-four from the book of Revelation. Then appeared a "great king," representing the name of God found in a spiral in the center of each Watchtower. Five princes held up the train of each king. Like the trumpeters and ensign bearers, these princes are given no names in the Watchtowers—at least so far as we know—and I have no idea who they may be.

After each of the four kings appeared a large cross surrounded by four lesser crosses, representing the Great Cross and four Calvary Crosses found in each Watchtower. The sixteen Calvary Crosses were each attended by ten angels whose identities are unclear. There are only four angels set above each Calvary Cross in the Watchtower tables. However, the Crosses themselves are each composed of ten letters, so these ten angels possibly represent those letters.

Finally, from each gate proceeded sixteen angels, called the "dispositors of the will of those that govern the castles." Each Watchtower table actually contains two groups of sixteen angels who fit this description, commonly called the kherubic and servient angels. I suspect the sixteen angels in the vision are intended to represent the servient angels, as they are the ones who act most directly upon the earth.

At the end of the vision, the twelve ensign bearers march to the center point where the four carpets meet, which I assume is the physical world. The twenty-four elders converge at this point and form a circle, where they appear to confer with one another, as would be expected of tribal elders.

The Twelve-Banner Diagram

Figure 10, adapted from Dee's records, is a simplified illustration of the Great Table of the Earth (aka the Watchtowers). It has often been confused as a depiction of an Enochian magickal circle, though no such thing is mentioned by Dee.

In the center of the diagram is a square divided into four portions and marked "Terra"—earth. This is the Great Table of the Earth itself. Each corner is marked by three banners depicting the three names of God that appear in the associated Watchtower: Oro, Ibah, and Aozpi in the east; Mor, Dial, and Hctga in the south; Mph, Arsl, and Gaiol in the west; and Oip, Teaa, and Pdoce in the north.

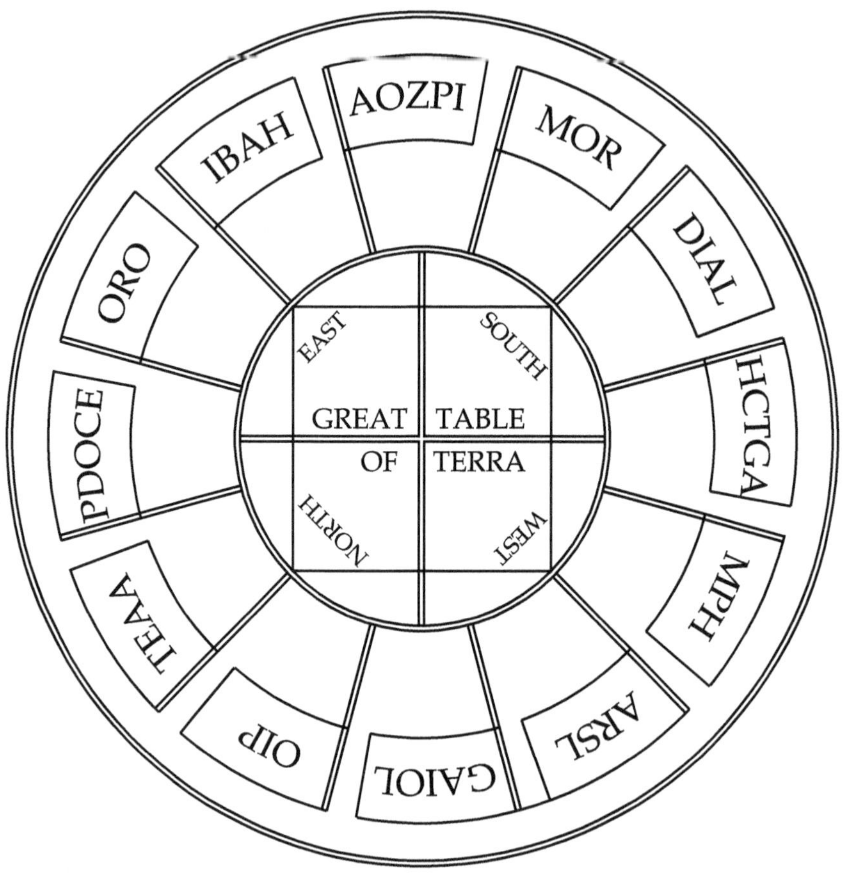

Figure 10: *Twelve-Banner Diagram (Corrected)*

Note: This diagram as it appears in Dee's journals includes an error. When Dee first received the Great Table from the angels, he switched the positions of the western and northern Watchtowers. The angels later corrected the error, but Dee seems to have drawn the banner diagram before the correction. His version places Mph, Arsl, and Gaiol in the north and Oip, Teaa, and Pdoce in the west. For some reason he never bothered to redraw the diagram after the angels corrected his error. Because the error has caused confusion for many students, I have redrawn the diagram myself to show the northern and western names of God in their proper places.[38]

Chapter Six

The Heptarchia

"And out of the throne proceeded lightnings and thunderings and voices: and there were seven lamps of fire burning before the throne, which are the seven Spirits of God." (Revelation 4:5)

The Seven Spirits of God: The Sephiroth

The above-quoted passage from the book of Revelation mentions seven "lamps of fire" that are actually seven "spirits" of God. Exactly what, or who, these spirits are has been a subject of some debate. There are those who insist they are merely metaphorical representations of a sevenfold power of God. However, history suggests they descend from ancient Pagan traditions that worshiped the seven planets, known in later monotheistic traditions as the Secondary Causes. On this basis, occultists have considered the seven spirits to be mighty archangels who "stand eternally before the face of God" and represent divine power as divided into the virtues of the seven planets.

The ancient Gnostics called them Aeons. An Aeon (in this sense) is a kind of "superarchangel" that exists above and beyond the created realm. Not only are they divine beings, but they are also cosmic archetypes that provide the blueprints for all things here in the physical universe. Seven of the Aeons are the divine models upon which the seven planets are based, along with all the angels and intelligences associated with them.

This idea would later be adopted into the Hebrew Qabalah, where the Aeons became the Sephiroth. Today, students generally know the Sephiroth as vast divine realms, but many have forgotten they were originally described as archangelic beings in their own right.[39] A common Hebrew convention was to add "El," the name of God, to the end of a Sephirah's name in order to create the name of an angel; thus, the Sephirah named Binah (Understanding) becomes an archangel named Binael, the Sephirah Chesed (Mercy) becomes an archangel named Chesedel, etc.

Later traditions would instead assign groups of known planetary archangels to represent the active forces of the Sephiroth.[40] One example can be found in Agrippa's *Three Books of Occult Philosophy*,[41] where he outlines the "seven angels which stand in the presence of God." Following are their names and planetary associations as given by Agrippa, along with the Hebrew Sephirah each one represents:

Table 1: *Seven Archangels of the Sephiroth*

	ARCHANGEL	SEPHIRAH	PLANET
1	Zaphkiel	Understanding (Binah)	Saturn
2	Zadkiel	Mercy (Chesed)	Jupiter
3	Cumael[42]	Severity (Gevurah)	Mars
4	Raphael	Majesty (Tiphareth)	Sol
5	Haniel	Victory (Netzach)	Venus
6	Michael	Glory (Hod)	Mercury
7	Gabriel	Foundation (Yesod)	Luna

As a group, these seven archangels never appeared to Dee and Kelley, and seem to play no active role in the Heptarchic system of magick. This makes sense if we consider them to exist far beyond the created realm. They are not the planets but the divine *source* of the planetary forces wielded by the angels of the Heptarchia. They certainly have a place in the cosmology of the Enochian system.

According to Dee's journals, there are seven names of God from which these seven archangels are born. He did not record a one-to-one relationship between the seven names and the archangels; instead, the group seems to share in the power of all seven names. Because these names appear upon an important Enochian magickal tool (which I will explain in detail in chapter 7), I will include them here: ZllRHia, aZCaacb, paupnhr, hdmhiai, kkaaeee, iieelll, and eellMG✠. The mysteries behind these names will be explored in later advanced texts.

The Seven Archangels of Creation

The universe was created over seven ages, or "days" (see Genesis 1). However, this work was not accomplished by God alone. Instead, he dispatched seven archangelic governors, along with their ministers, to perform the actual work of cosmic construction. Their number and mystery is mirrored in the seven celestial heavens, the seven days of our week, and the seven classical planets, all of which are governed by these angels. All things in creation can be classified under the headings of the seven planets, and therefore the angels of the planets can be invoked for any purpose.

Here are the names of the seven archangels who govern all of creation[43]:

Table 2: *The Seven Archangels of Creation*

Cassiel	Saturn and Saturday
Sachiel	Jupiter and Thursday
Samael	Mars and Tuesday
Michael	Sol and Sunday[44]
Annael[45]	Venus and Friday
Raphael	Mercury and Wednesday
Gabriel	Luna and Monday

These seven archangels govern the world in shifts, or universal ages, of 490 years.[46] During Dee's lifetime, the archangel Annael was in power, and should have remained so until the year 1900 CE. The age of Venus saw the Renaissance and Enlightenment, an explosion of artistic expression, invention, and exploration. Early in this age, the printing press was invented by Gutenberg. Toward its end we saw the Industrial Revolution and the first stirrings of massive social changes that would unfold in the next age—women's rights, civil rights, the sexual revolution, and much more.

From 1900 until 2390 CE, we should be under the governance of Raphael and Mercury. These past decades have seen technological (and the above-mentioned social) revolutions that are awe-inspiring in scope. In the early twentieth century, the focus was largely upon faster modes of transportation. Within fifty years we were jetting and orbiting around the planet at will, so our attentions turned to advances in communication technology. We passed quickly from steam-powered machines to vacuum tubes, transistors, and finally microchips. We have seen the invention of the Internet along with cell technology, the common use of satellite GPS devices and smartphones. Scientists stumbled upon the microscopic realm, then the atomic and subatomic realms, and *then* the quantum realm. Meanwhile others were busy discovering and cracking the human genetic code. Today we are developing microscopic robots to patrol your bloodstream and attack diseases and blockages. All of this and much, much more—and we are only slightly over one hundred years into the age of Raphael.

After Raphael's 490 years pass, it will be Gabriel's turn to rule, followed by Cassiel, Sachiel, Camael, Michael, Annael, and so on, in an endless cycle of cosmic ages.

The Seven Ensigns of Creation[47]

Each archangel bears a standard called an Ensign of Creation. This ensign, or emblem, represents the day of creation, the ruling planet, the day of the week, the archangel himself, as well as those angels he governs. The seven ensigns are as follows:

<table>
<tr><td>2 b
b 3</td><td>G
b b</td><td>g.</td><td>B
2 2</td><td>2.4.6
b b b
2 4 6</td><td>b b
L
b</td><td>B
r o g</td><td>Ⓑ</td></tr>
<tr><td>8 b
b
b 2</td><td>b b
8</td><td>G
b</td><td>GG
b</td><td>1 5 2
b</td><td>1 5 2
b</td><td>5 2
B B B</td><td>B
B</td></tr>
<tr><td>☽
q B
q</td><td>b o
o o</td><td>B
7 9</td><td>b b b
b b b
b b b</td><td>11
B
5</td><td>b b
b
b b</td><td>b b
b</td><td>b
8 b 3
b</td></tr>
<tr><td>b b
b b
b b</td><td>b b
15
b b
b b b</td><td>b M
166</td><td>7
bb</td><td>b
5</td><td>G
M</td><td>B</td><td>b A
1556</td></tr>
<tr><td>1
b</td><td>2
B
1 2 3</td><td>3
b</td><td>b
T
b</td><td>4
B
9</td><td>BBB
6
b</td><td>b b
72
F</td><td>b</td></tr>
</table>

Figure 11: *Ensign of Venus (Annael)*

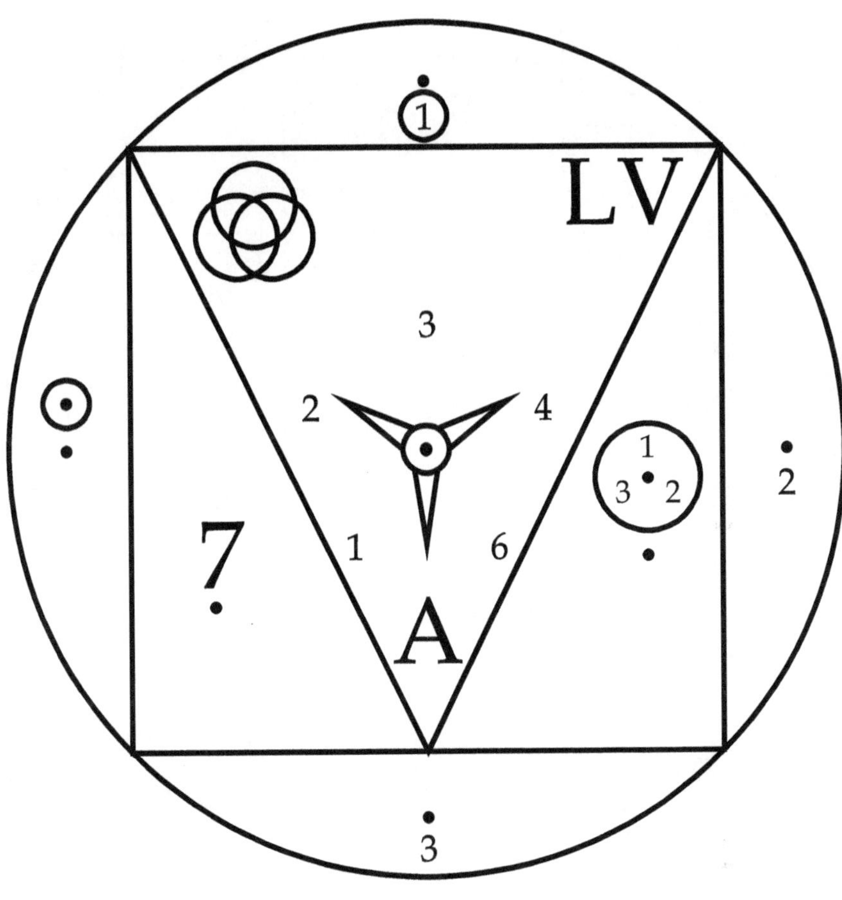

Figure 12: *Ensign of Sol (Michael)*

G B 23	m · 30 q B .9. d · 4 ·	q · q · q Q B o · g og
J 30̣ B G 33· A	B A 9 O	E get B h go
5 ☾ b	d2 id b d 2A	L 30 b pp
V H b 9 22	q·q · q Q b og a	25 L b d

Figure 13: *Ensign of Mars (Samael)*

2 bb 2	b b o	5 3 7 b b b	b B G 11	T • 13 b b b	• b 9
b • 2 B	o 4 BB	B 14 a	b b.b P.3.	b GO	b b C:V 3
8 e b	Q • o 7 b b	5	q q b 3	q • 9 B	L b: 8:
go • 30 B	9 • 3 b b	q q 5 •b•b•	d b b A	7 • 2 b • B	B B •Λ• 8 3

Figure 14: *Ensign of Jupiter (Sachiel)*

g D 2 g	B ((30	B B 8 2	B 22	B.O p d 30	L o B·q q·29	B 8 2	9 6 B
o p B 98	9 B	bb 2. 8.G	bb 9 F	b 3 Q	bbb 9 Q	b ii Q	B B 12 T
B B b 8	M 2 b b	M 5 b	M b b b 20	M b.89 F	d B 17	A b 3	B B B 2 H
M b 99 L	b 6 4 b	b 9 1 b	b b 9 6	6 B 2 4	I B 38	N B 9	b b 4 b

Figure 15: *Ensign of Mercury (Raphael)*

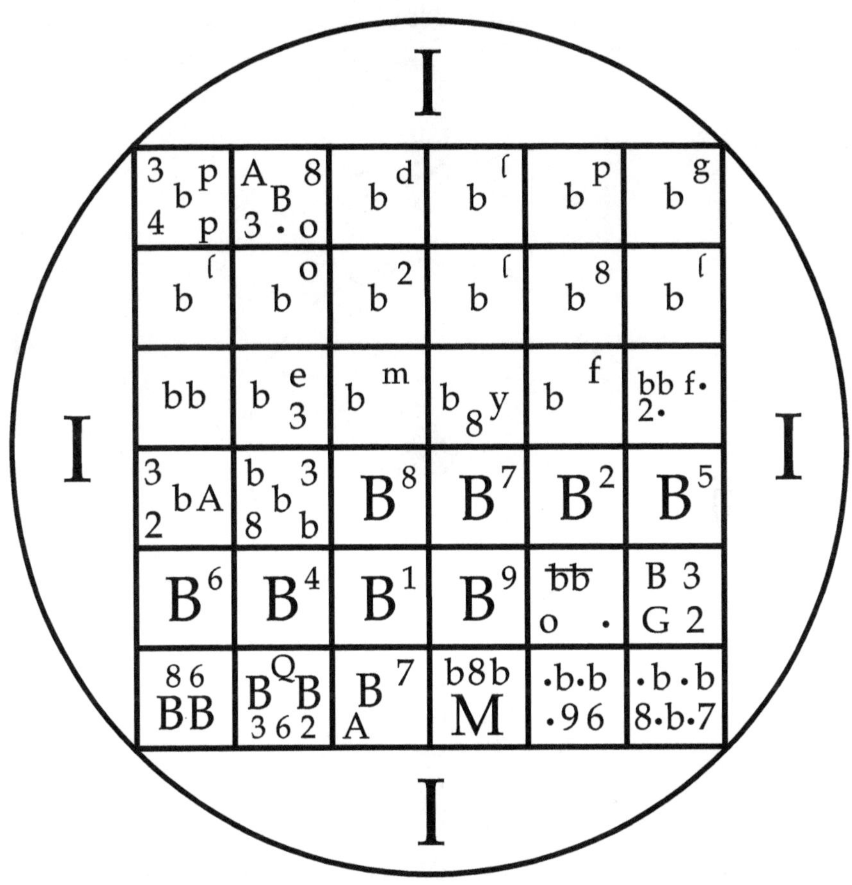

Figure 16: *Ensign of Saturn (Cassiel)*

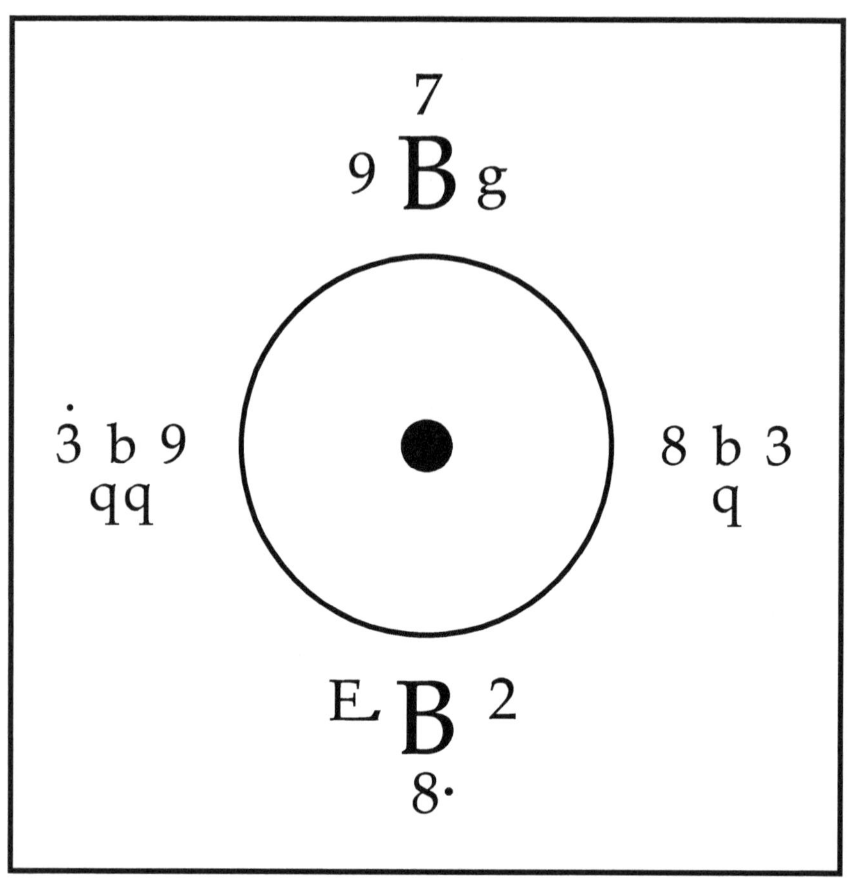

Figure 17: *Ensign of Luna (Gabriel)*

The Seven Archangels of the Planetary Spheres

Next in authority to the seven archangels of Creation are those who govern the seven planets seen in the night sky. Each planet is supposed to be conscious and intelligent in its own right—an angel who transmits his planetary force directly to the earth. This is similar to the Planetary Intelligences described by Agrippa in his *Three Books of Occult Philosophy*,[48] as well as the Olympian Spirits described in the *Arbatel of Magic*. Therefore, this group of angels works more directly with the physical realm than the greater archangels.

The names of the archangels of the planetary spheres are formed from the Hebrew names of the planets themselves, with the name of God "El" added to the end:

Table 3: *The Seven Archangels of the Planetary Spheres*

1	Zabathiel[49]	Saturn (Sabbathai)
2	Zedekiel	Jupiter (Zedek)
3	Madimiel	Mars (Madim)
4	Semeliel[50]	Sol (Shemesh)
5	Nogahel	Venus (Nogah)
6	Corabiel[51]	Mercury (Kokab)
7	Levanael	Luna (Levanah)

Just one of these angels—Levanael—made an appearance in Dee's journals. Otherwise, they seem to play no direct role in the Heptarchic system of magick. However, there are seven names of God recorded in Dee's journals that the angels claimed gave birth to the seven planetary angels. These seven names also appear on an important Enochian magickal tool, so I will include them here: SAAI(21/8.)EME(8.), BTZKASE(30), HEIDENE, DEIMO30A, I(26)MEGCBE, ILAOI(21/8.)VN, and IHRLAA21/8..

Notice the numbers and periods—some attached to letters (in which cases I have placed them in parentheses) and some standing alone. These numbers are, in fact, part of the names, and they are why Dee's angels insisted these names of God cannot be pronounced at all. The mysteries behind these names will be explored in later advanced texts. Also see chapter 7's section on the Seal of the True God.

The Forty-Nine Good Angels of the Heptarchia

Under the command of the seven archangels of Creation are the angels of the Heptarchic royalty. *Heptarchia* literally means "sevenfold rulership," because these are the angels in charge of all created things. There are forty-nine primary angels of the Heptarchia: a king, a prince, and five governors for each planetary force. Their names are as follows:

Table 4: *The Forty-Nine Heptarchic Royal Angels*

VENUS/ FRIDAY	SOL/ SUNDAY	MARS/ TUESDAY	JUPITER/ THURSDAY
King Baligon	King Bobogel	King Babalel	King Bynepor
Prince Bagenol	Prince Bornogo	Prince Befafes	Prince Butmono
Bormila	Bablibo	Bapnido	Basmelo
Binodab	Buscnab	Busduna	Besgeme
Benpagi	Bariges	Bminpol	Blingef
Bermale	Barnafa	Binofon	Bartiro
Bnagole	Bonefon	Bmilges	Baldago

MERCURY / WEDNESDAY	SATURN / SATURDAY	LUNA / MONDAY
King Bnaspol	King Bnapsen	King Blumaza
Prince Blisdon	Prince Brorges	Prince Bralges
Bazpama	Balceor	Baspalo
Bernole	Blintom	Belmara
Blumapo	Branglo	Bragiop
Barfort	Bmamgal	Brisfli
Bliigan	Bamnode	Basledf

King Carmara and Prince Hagonel

Of the seven planetary kings and their princes, one pair is given supreme command of the Heptarchia. During the 1500s (the age of Annael), the king and prince of Venus (Baligon and Bagenol) were in command. When acting in this role, they took on new names (or perhaps honorary titles): King Baligon was called Carmara (or Marmara), and Prince Bagenol was called Hagonel.[52]

Today we are in the age of the archangel Raphael, which suggests the king and prince of Mercury (Bnaspol and Blisdon) should be in command of the Heptarchic angels. However, it is not clear from Dee's records whether these two angels should take on the titles of "Carmara" and "Hagonel" or if they have their own unique titles.

The 294 Ministers

The Heptarchic kings and their princes are served by 294 servient angels, or ministers. The names of the ministers are formed from the letters of *most* of the forty-nine royal angels. (The methods are rather complex and unnecessary to cover here.) Of all the angels of the Heptarchia, these appear to be closest to the physical world. They are the beings who manifest the directives of the forty-nine royal angels here on earth.

Each prince is given command of forty-two ministers, who are divided into six groups of seven angels: a primary minister and six general servants. These six groups are each given power for four hours of the day ruled by their prince, beginning at midnight. The six primary ministers collectively rule the entire day. The remaining servants merely act upon the general orders given to them by the six primary ministers and are not directly invoked in the Heptarchic system.[53] (See the following section for the names and functions of the 294 ministers.)

The Offices, Appearances, and Seals of the Heptarchic Royalty

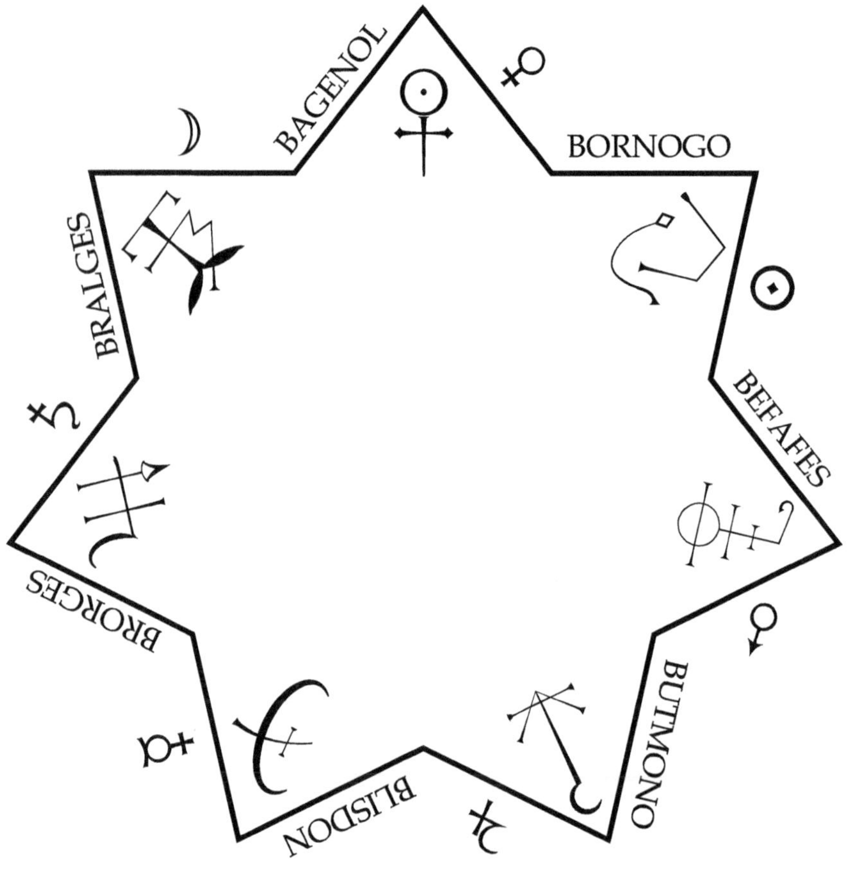

Figure 18: *The Heptagon of the Heptarchic Princes*

"Are they not all ministering spirits, sent forth to minister for them who shall be heirs of salvation?" (Hebrews 1:14)

The following information has been gathered from several places in Dee's journals. Some of it was corrupted (Dee suspected the intrusion of an evil spirit) so that the offices of several of the kings and princes were either switched or missing.[54] Thankfully, Dee left certain marginal notations that have allowed the information to be restored.

King Baligon (Carmara) and Prince Bagenol (Hagonel)—Friday/Venus: Spirits of the Air[55]

The king and prince of Friday are given charge over the air and all aerial spirits and creatures.[56]

In Dee's lifetime, King Baligon appeared as a large man wearing a long purple robe and a golden triple crown upon his head. This represented his position as Carmara, the supreme ruler of the Heptarchic angels. However, his time of rule was limited,[57] and it is unlikely he would take this form today (see King Bnaspol, p. 108). He should, however, still appear as a king wearing a slightly shorter robe (of a color other than purple) and a simpler crown. His seal is as follows:[58]

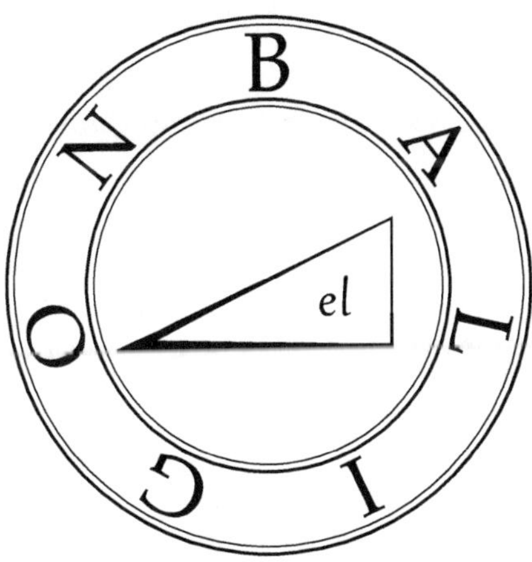

Figure 19: *Seal of Baligon*

Prince Bagenol appeared in a red robe (somewhat shorter than the other princes) and a golden circlet upon his brow.[59] His shorter robe was likely to distinguish him as Hagonel, the ruling prince of the Heptarchic angels.[60] However, like King Baligon/Carmara, the time of his government was limited,[61] and thus his robe would likely be longer now (see Prince Blisdon). His seal was the only one to be given its own name—Barees[62]—and it appears as follows:

Figure 20: *Seal of Bagenol*

The forty-two ministers who serve Prince Bagenol, and their times, are as follows:

Table 5: *Ministers of Prince Bagenol—Friday (Venus)*

12 AM–4 AM	4 AM–8 AM	8 AM–12 PM	12 PM–4 PM	4 PM–8 PM	8 PM–12 AM
Aoaynnl	Lbbnaav	Ioaespm	Gglppsa	Oeeooez	Nllrlna
Oaynnla	Bbnaavl	Oaespmi	Glppsag	Eeooezo	Llrlnan
Aynnlao	Bnaavlb	Aespmio	Lppsagg	Eooezoe	Lrlnanl
Ynnlaoa	Naavlbb	Espmioa	Ppsaggl	Ooezoee	Rlnanll
Nnlaoay	Aavlbbn	Spmioae	Psagglp	Oezoeeo	Lnanllr
Nloaoyn	Avlbbna	Pmioaes	Sagglpp	Ezoeeoo	Nanllrl
Loaoynn	Vlbbnaa	Mioaesp	Agglpps	Zoeeooe	Anllrln

The ministers of Bagenol can work all operations concerning the air or aerial creatures.

Dee's journals do not specify their appearance, though it is likely the seven ministers active from midnight to 4 AM will appear more regal than the rest, wearing apparel similar to their prince. Any of them may also arrive with swarms of aerial creatures about them.[63]

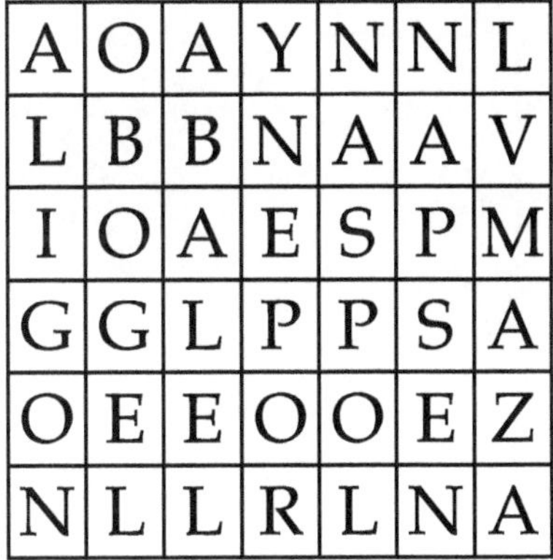

A	O	A	Y	N	N	L
L	B	B	N	A	A	V
I	O	A	E	S	P	M
G	G	L	P	P	S	A
O	E	E	O	O	E	Z
N	L	L	R	L	N	A

Figure 21: *The Ministers of Venus (left) and the Seal of the Ministers (right)*

King Bobogel and Prince Bornogo— Sunday/Sol: Wisdom and Science

The king and prince of Sunday can bestow wisdom and scientific learning. Prince Bornogo, especially, teaches the altering of nature and the knowledge of metals, which likely includes both metallurgy and alchemy.[64]

King Bobogel appears as a stately and handsome noble with a long beard, wearing a black velvet coat and stockings trimmed with golden lace. He wears a velvet cap with a black feather in it and a cape that hangs from one shoulder. He has a purse hanging around his neck and tucked into his girdle. He carries a gilt (or gold-encrusted) rapier.[65] He may also appear with seven jester angels playing a sweet melody on seven horns.[66] The horns appear to be a cross between a Renaissance recorder (with a flared end) and a *pungi*—an Indian wind instrument often made from a dried gourd and used by snake charmers.

Figure 22: *The Pungi Played by Bobgel's Musicians*

The recorders/pungis played by Bobogel's seven musicians each have forty-nine (or 7×7) holes, implying these angels are playing the harmonies of the seven planetary spheres.

His seal is as follows:

Figure 23: *Seal of Bobogel*

Prince Bornogo appears in a red robe with a golden circlet upon his brow. His seal is as follows:

Figure 24: *Seal of Bornogo*

The forty-two ministers who serve Prince Bornogo, and their times, are as follows:

Table 6: *Ministers of Prince Bornogo—Sunday (Sol)*

12 AM–4 AM	4 AM–8 AM	8 AM–12 PM	12 PM–4 PM	4 PM–8 PM	8 PM–12 AM
Leenarb	Lnanaeb	Roemnab	Leaorib	Neiciab	Aoidiab
Eenarbl	Nanaebl	Oemnabr	Eaoribl	Eiciabn	Oidiaba
Enarble	Anaebln	Emnabro	Aorible	Iciabne	Idiabao
Narblee	Naeblna	Mnabroe	Oriblea	Ciabnei	Diabaoi
Arbleen	Aeblnan	Nabroem	Ribleao	Iabniec	Iabaiod
Rbleena	Eblnana	Abroemn	Ibleaor	Abnieci	Abaiodi
Bleenar	Blnanae	Broemna	Bleaori	Bniecia	Baiodia

The Ministers of Bornogo are the "gates of nature." There is no force in nature they cannot manifest nor any wisdom concerning nature they cannot bestow.[67] The first seven, active from midnight to 4 AM, appear to have knowledge of fire. The second seven, active from 4 AM to 8 AM, have knowledge of metals and/or metallurgy. The third group of seven has knowledge of air. The fourth group has knowledge of water. The fifth group has knowledge of storm and hail. The knowledge held by the sixth and final group of seven ministers is not specified.[68]

All of these ministers will appear as handsome noblemen, dressed after the manner of Renaissance nobility, with curled hair and carrying gilt rapiers. The seven ministers who are active from midnight to 4 AM are very sage and stern, and are dressed like King Bobogel. They appear brighter than their fellow ministers. Those remaining thirty-five ministers are darker and more casual in their appearance. Finally, the seven ministers who are active from 8 PM to midnight (whose knowledge was not specified) appear as partly male and partly female or as rather feminine men wearing wide hoop skirts.[69]

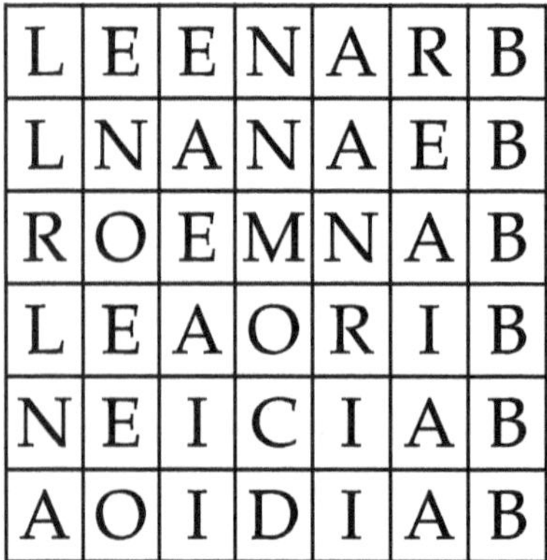

L	E	E	N	A	R	B
L	N	A	N	A	E	B
R	O	E	M	N	A	B
L	E	A	O	R	I	B
N	E	I	C	I	A	B
A	O	I	D	I	A	B

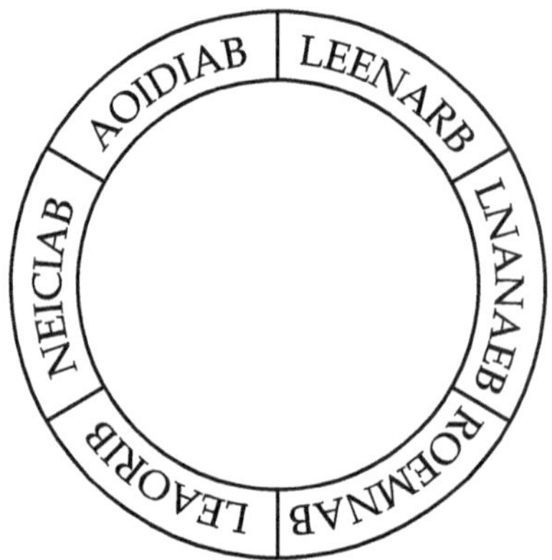

Figure 25: *The Ministers of Sol (left) and the Seal of the Ministers (right)*

King Babalel and Prince Befafes—
Tuesday/Mars: The Waters and Seas[70]

The king and prince of Tuesday are given charge over the waters and seas of the earth. Prince Befafes brought life to the seas (see Genesis 1:20–23), controls the movements of the waters, and has charge over all sea creatures and the mysteries of the deep. He claims credit for having drowned the armies of pharaoh in the Red Sea (see Exodus 14:26–28) and states that Moses knew his name, suggesting he was also the power that parted the waters.[71]

King Babalel appears with a golden crown upon his head and wearing a robe of three colors: the left arm is perfectly white, the right arm is black, and the body of the robe is gray or off-white. He may be preceded by a playful little boy in a green coat, who will identify himself as Multin, the king's minister.[72] Babalel's seal is as follows:

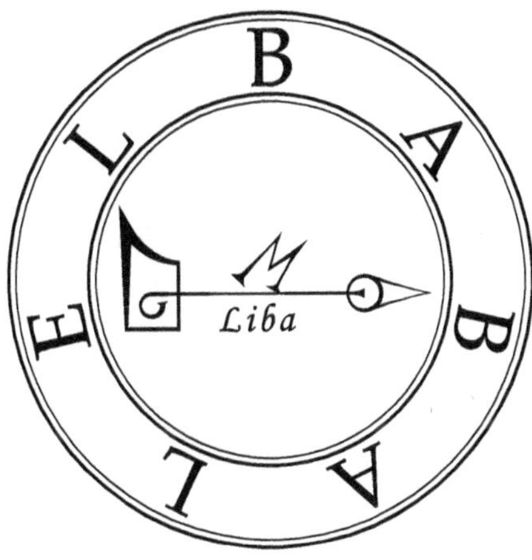

Figure 26: *Seal of Babalel*

Prince Befafes—who is also called Obelison ("a pleasant deliverer")—appears in a red robe with a golden circlet upon his brow. Beneath his robe he wears a golden girdle with his name engraved upon it, and he appears to be covered in feathers.[73] His seal is as follows:

Figure 27: *Seal of Befafes*

The forty-two ministers who serve Prince Befafes, and their times, are as follows:

Table 7: *Ministers of Prince Befafes—Tuesday (Mars)*

12 AM–4 AM	4 AM–8 AM	8 AM–12 PM	12 PM–4 PM	4 PM–8 PM	8 PM–12 AM
Eilomfo	Neotpta	Sagaciy	Onedpon	Noonman	Etevlgl
Ilomfoe	Eotptan	Agaciys	Nedpono	Oonmann	Tevlgle
Lomfoei	Otptane	Gaciysa	Edponon	Onmanno	Evlglet
Omfoeil	Tptaneo	Aciysag	Dponone	Nmannoo	Vlglete
Mfoeilo	Ptaneot	Ciysaga	Pononed	Mannoon	Lgletev
Foeilom	Taneotp	Iysagac	Ononedp	Annoonm	Gletevl
Oeilomf	Aneotpt	Ysagaci	Nonedpo	Nnoonma	Letevlg

The ministers of Befafes can work any operation concerning water. They control the movements of the waters and the saltiness of the seas. They grant victory in naval battles and can sink the ships of one's enemies. All the fish and sea monsters and myriad forms of life in the seas are known to them. They are the "distributors of God's judgments upon the waters that cover the earth."

The first seven ministers, active from midnight to 4 AM, are responsible for manifesting clouds. The second group of seven, active from 4 AM to 8 AM, creates hail and snow. The particular functions of the remaining ministers are not specified, except that they direct the waters throughout the earth and deliver treasures and "unknown substances" from the deep.

The first group of seven ministers wears circlets upon their brows to distinguish them from the rest. No further details of the appearances of these forty-two ministers are recorded.[74]

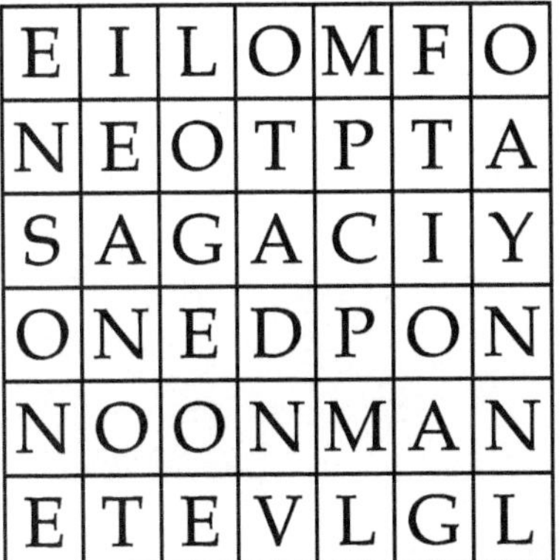

E	I	L	O	M	F	O
N	E	O	T	P	T	A
S	A	G	A	C	I	Y
O	N	E	D	P	O	N
N	O	O	N	M	A	N
E	T	E	V	L	G	L

Figure 28: *The Ministers of Mars (left) and the Seal of the Ministers (right)*

King Bynepor and Prince Butmono— Thursday/Jupiter: Life of All Mortals

The king and prince of Thursday are responsible for the life of all mortal things, especially people and beasts that live on the land (see Genesis 1:24–31).[75] They are in charge of the spread of life on the planet and know the times of birth, lifespan, and death of every creature. King Bynepor, especially, governs the forces of evolution, bringing into existence new worlds, new people, and even new forms of government.[76]

King Bynepor is given no description except that he appears as a king. He likely wears a crown. His seal appears as follows:

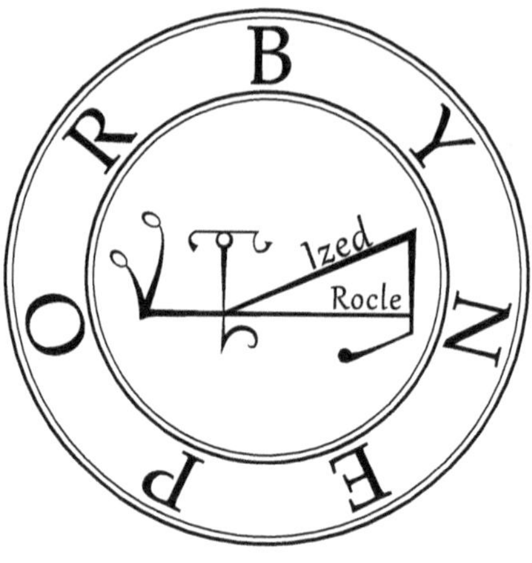

Figure 29: *Seal of Bynepor*

Prince Butmono appears in a red robe with a golden circlet upon his brow. His seal appears as follows:

Figure 30: *Seal of Butmono*

The forty-two ministers who serve Prince Butmono, and their times, are as follows:

Table 8: *Ministers of Prince Butmono—Thursday (Jupiter)*

12 AM–4 AM	4 AM–8 AM	8 AM–12 PM	12 PM–4 PM	4 PM–8 PM	8 PM–12 AM
Bbarnfl	Bbaigao	Bbalpae	Bbanifg	Bbosnia	Bbasnod
Barnflb	Baigaob	Balpaeb	Banifgb	Bosniab	Basnodb
Arnflbb	Aigaobb	Alpaebb	Anifgbb	Osniabb	Asnodbb
Rnflbba	Igaobba	Lpaebba	Nifgbba	Sniabbo	Snodbba
Nflbbar	Gaobbai	Paebbal	Ifgbban	Niabbos	Nodbbas
Flbbarn	Aobbaig	Aebbalp	Fgbbani	Iabbosn	Odbbasn
Lbbarnf	Obbaiga	Ebbalpa	Gbbanif	Abbosni	Dbbasno

The ministers of Butmono aid their prince and King Bynepor in the multiplication and evolution of life throughout the world.

All forty-two of these angels appear as formless apparitions (like smoke), each with a bright spark of fire burning within their center. The first seven ministers, active from midnight to 4 AM, are blood red in color and have brighter sparks than the rest. The second seven, active from 4 AM to 8 AM, are a lighter red color. The third group of seven is "like whitish smoke." The remaining twenty-one ministers are described as having diverse colors.[77]

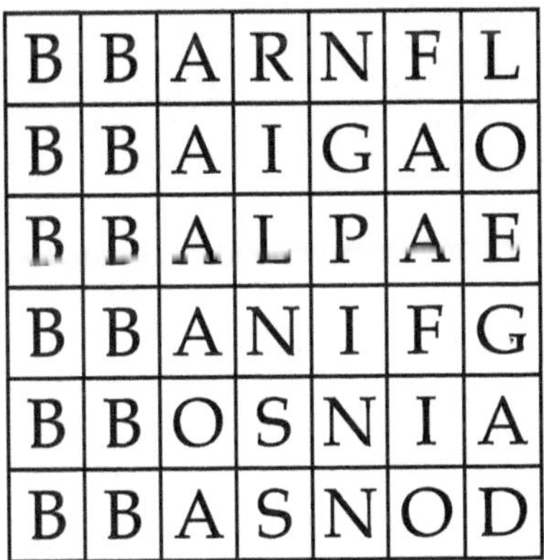

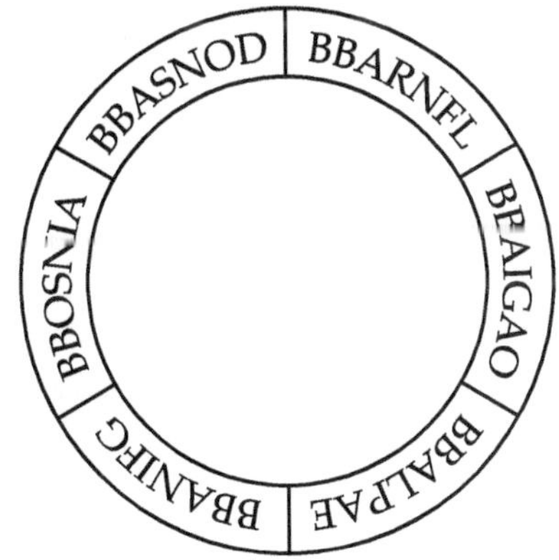

Figure 31: *The Ministers of Jupiter (left) and the Seal of the Ministers (right)*

King Bnaspol and Prince Blisdon—
Wednesday/Mercury: The Spirits and Bowels of the Earth[78]

The king and prince of Wednesday are given charge over the spirits of earth and all that reside beneath the ground. The dead are in their charge, as are all buried treasures, minerals, caverns, etc.[79] This also includes the buried treasures, guarded by evil spirits, that legend claims are stored up for the Antichrist.[80]

During Dee's lifetime, King Bnaspol appeared in a red robe with a crown upon his head.[81] Today he should be the supreme ruler of the Heptarchic angels (taking over in 1900 from King Baligon), thus he should wear a long purple gown and wear a golden triple crown. His seal appears as follows:

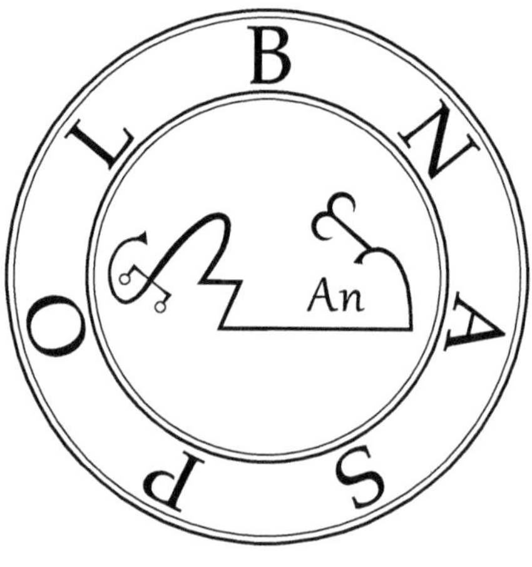

Figure 32: *Seal of Bnaspol*

Prince Blisdon appears in a robe of many colors,[82] with a golden circlet upon his brow.[83] Since inheriting the role of supreme prince of the Heptarchia from Prince Bagenol, Blisdon's robe should be somewhat shorter today. His seal appears as follows:

Figure 33: *Seal of Blisdon*

The forty-two ministers who serve Prince Blisdon, and their times, are as follows:

Table 9: *Ministers of Prince Blisdon—Wednesday (Mercury)*

12 AM–4 AM	4 AM–8 AM	8 AM–12 PM	12 PM–4 PM	4 PM–8 PM	8 PM–12 AM
Elgnseb	Nlinzvb	Sfamllb	Oogosrs	Nrpcrrb	Ergdbab
Lgnsebe	Linzvbn	Famllbs	Ogosrso	Rpcrrbn	Rgdbabe
Gnsebel	Inzvbnl	Amllbsf	Gosrsoo	Pcrrbnr	Gdbaber
Nsebelg	Nzvbnli	Mllbsfa	Osrsoog	Crrbnrp	Dbaberg
Sebelgn	Zvbnlin	Llbsfam	Srsoogo	Rrbnrpc	Babergd
Ebelgns	Vbnlinz	Lbsfaml	Rsoogos	Rbnrpcr	Abergdb
Belgnse	Bnlinzv	Bsfamll	Soogosr	Bnrpcrr	Bergdba

The ministers of Blisdon know all the mysteries of the earth and the bowels of the earth.

The individual appearances of these ministers are not recorded. They may appear with an innumerable multitude of ugly spirits who stand far in the background. These ugly spirits were described as the "spirits of perdition" who guard the buried treasures saved for the Antichrist.[84]

E	L	G	N	S	E	B
N	L	I	N	Z	V	B
S	F	A	M	L	L	B
O	O	G	O	S	R	S
N	R	P	C	R	R	B
e	r	g	d	b	a	b

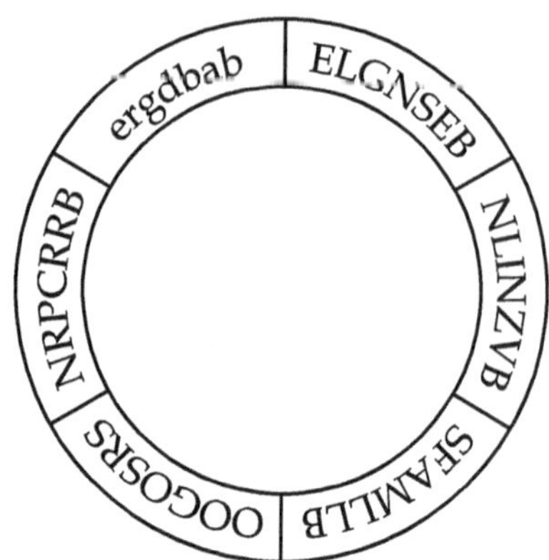

Figure 34: *The Ministers of Mercury (left) and the Seal of the Ministers (right)*

King Bnapsen and Prince Brorges— Saturday/Saturn: Fire, Wicked Spirits, and Evil Men

The king and prince of Saturday are given charge over fire as well as evil spirits and humans. King Bnapsen, especially, governs evil spirits, black witches, and others who live in darkness. By him you may cast out wicked spirits and discover the doings of evil people.[85]

King Bnapsen appears with a crown upon his head.[86] His seal appears as follows:

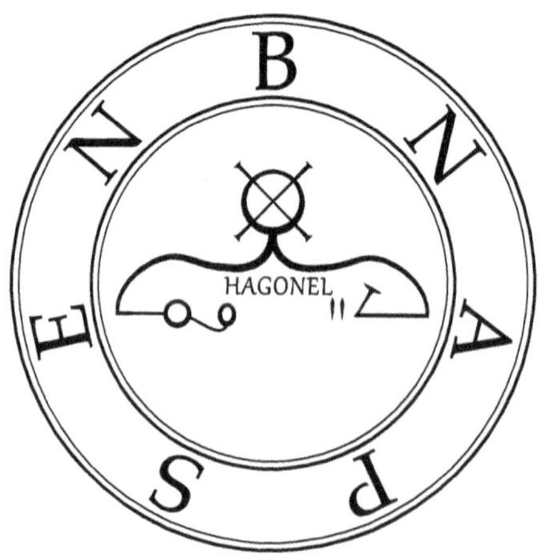

Figure 35: *Seal of Bnapsen*

Prince Brorges appears in "red apparel" (most likely a red robe with a golden circlet upon his brow). Beneath his robes, mighty and terrible flames of fire issue from his sides. His seal appears as follows:

Figure 36: *Seal of Brorges*

The forty-two ministers who serve Prince Brorges, and their times, are as follows:

Table 10: *Ministers of Prince Brorges—Saturday (Saturn)*

12 AM–4 AM	4 AM–8 AM	8 AM–12 PM	12 PM–4 PM	4 PM–8 PM	8 PM–12 AM
Banssze	Byapare	Bnamgen	Bnvages	Blbopoo	Babepen
Ansszeb	Yapareb	Namgenb	Nvagesb	Lbopoob	Abepenb
Nsszeba	Apareby	Amgenbn	Vagesbn	Bopoobl	Bepenba
Sszeban	Parebya	Mgenbna	Agesbnv	Opooblb	Epenbab
Szebans	Arebyap	Genbnam	Gesbnva	Pooblbo	Penbabe
Zebanss	Rebyapa	Enbnamg	Esbnvag	Ooblbop	Enbabep
Ebanssz	Ebyapar	Nbnamge	Sbnvage	Oblbopo	Nbabepe

The ministers of Brorges aid their prince and king in the expulsion of evil spirits, revealing the deeds of evil men, the works of fire, etc.

The individual appearances of these ministers are not recorded.[87]

B	A	N	S	S	Z	E
B	Y	A	P	A	R	E
B	N	A	M	G	E	N
B	N	V	A	G	E	S
B	L	B	O	P	O	O
B	A	B	E	P	E	N

Figure 37: *The Ministers of Saturn (left) and the Seal of the Ministers (right)*

King Blumaza and Prince Bralges— Monday/Luna: The Kings of the World

The king and prince of Monday are given charge of all the kings of the world—both physical kings and the spiritual rulers of nature. They can motivate or restrain a king from any action. They can also be called upon to support virtuous kings or do harm to evil and ill-living kings.[88]

King Blumaza is given no description except that he appears as a king. He likely wears a crown. His seal appears as follows:

Figure 38: *Seal of Blumaza*

Prince Bralges appears in a red robe with a golden circlet upon his head. His seal appears as follows:

Figure 39: *Seal of Bralges*

The forty-two ministers who serve Prince Bralges, and their times, are as follows:

Table 11: *Ministers of Prince Bralges—Monday (Luna)*

12 AM– 4 AM	4 AM– 8 AM	8 AM– 12 PM	12 PM– 4 PM	4 PM– 8 PM	8 PM– 12 AM
Oesngle	Avzniln	Yllmafs	Nrsogoo	Nrrcprn	Labdgre
Esngleo	Vznilna	Llmafsy	Rsogoon	Rrcprnn	Abdgrel
Sngleoe	Znilnav	Lmafsyl	Sogoonr	Rcprnnr	Bdgrela
Ngleoes	Nilnavz	Mafsyll	Ogoonrs	Cprnnrr	Dgrelab
Gleoesn	Ilnavzn	Afsyllm	Goonrso	Prnnrrc	Grelabd
Leoesng	Lnavzni	Fsyllma	Oonrsog	Rnnrrcp	Relabdg
Eoesngl	Navznil	Syllmaf	Onrsogo	Nnrrcpr	Elabdgr

The ministers of Bralges[89] are concerned with the estate and condition of all earthly kings, both human and spiritual. The first group of seven, active from midnight to 4 AM, can be invoked for good and beneficial causes. The next group of seven, active from 4 AM to 8 AM, is invoked for harmful or destructive purposes. Any of the forty-two can be invoked to bring harm to the person or government of an evil and lying king.[90] Beyond that, all that is said of the remaining ministers is that they busy themselves with various intents and purposes concerning kings.[91]

The first group of seven ministers appears brighter than the rest. They are distinguished by wearing longer coats, golden circlets upon their brows, and by carrying whole crowns in their hands. The next group of seven carries three-quarter crowns in their hands. The third group of seven carries robes. The rest carry small spheres of gold that they toss back and forth between one another.[92]

O	E	S	N	G	L	E
A	V	Z	N	I	L	N
Y	L	L	M	A	F	S
N	R	S	O	G	O	O
N	R	R	C	P	R	N
L	A	B	D	G	R	E

Figure 40: *The Ministers of Luna (left) and the Seal of the Ministers (right)*

Angels of the Family of Light

The 294 ministers are not the only angels who serve the Heptarchic royalty. Another group of angels who "minister" to the royal angels is listed in Dee's journals, and they had a prominent role to play in the transmission of the Enochian system of magick. They are known today as the Family of Light, consisting of four groups of seven angels: the Daughters of Light, the Daughters of the Daughters of Light, the Sons of Light, and the Sons of the Sons of Light.

Each group gives birth to the group that follows, so that the Sons of the Sons of Light are technically the great-grandchildren of the Daughters of Light. In any case, they are all children of the Mother of Angels, who appeared to Dee and Kelley at various times under the names "I Am," Wisdom, and Galvah (the Omega).[93]

At one point in the journals, the prince of the Heptarchia, Hagonel, states that the Heptarchic King Carmara's "power rules in the Sons."[94] Soon afterward, he claims that he is personally in charge of the Sons of the Sons.[95] In another place they are described as the ministers of all the Heptarchic kings.[96] (This seems to be supported by the fact that each of the kings' seals includes the name of one of the Sons of the Sons, and one of them, oddly, includes a single name from the Daughters of the Daughters.)

However, the exact role these angels play in Dee's magick is not entirely clear. As mentioned above, the seals of the Heptarchic kings include the names of several of the Family of Light angels, and all of their names appear on the Seal of the True God. Yet they do not otherwise seem to play a direct role in the Heptarchic invocations.

Meanwhile, the Family of Light angels were quite active in the transmission of the Enochian system to Dee and Kelley. One of the Daughters of the Daughters, named Madimi, became one of the men's primary angelic contacts and worked with them on a regular basis. (Dee was especially fond of Madimi and would later name his daughter after her.) She often helped by fetching other angels or bearing messages to and from her Mother. Others such as Ave, Aath, and Ilemese would make semi-regular appearances throughout the journals, being charged to reveal specific aspects of the system. The seven Daughters revealed the seven Ensigns of Creation. Illemese had some interaction with Mother Galvah and helped reveal the mysteries of *Loagaeth* (including revealing the thirty Aethyrs and their call). Ave revealed the instructions for Gebofal and the Great Table of the Earth.

The names of the Family of Light angels are as follows:

Table 12: *Angels of the Family of Light*

DAUGHTERS OF LIGHT	DAUGHTERS OF THE DAUGHTERS OF LIGHT	SONS OF LIGHT	SONS OF THE SONS OF LIGHT
El	S	I	El
Me	Ab	Ih	An
Ese	Ath	Ilr	Ave
Iana	Ized	Dmal	Liba
Akele	Ekiei	Heeoa	Rocle
Azdobn	Madimi	Beigia	Hagonel[97]
Stimcul	Esemeli	Stimcul	Ilemese

Chapter Seven

The Angelic Magickal Tools

"Go forward. God hath blessed thee. I will be thy guide. Thou shalt attain unto thy searching. The world begins with thy doings. Praise God. The angels under my power shall be at thy commandment." (Archangel Michael, March 11, 1582)

The Seal of the True God[98]

"And I saw another angel ascending from the east, having the seal of the living God….And I heard the number of them which were sealed: and there were sealed an hundred and forty and four thousand of all the tribes of the children of Israel." (Revelation 7:2, 4)

Figure 41: *Seal of the True God*

The above figure is the central glyph of Dee's system of angel magick. He referred to it as the *Sigillum Dei Aemeth*, which literally translates as "Seal-God-Truth." The figure is based upon earlier versions found in grimoires like *Liber Juratis*, where it is called the "Seal of the True and Living God." Therefore, I suggest the intended translation for *Sigillum Dei Aemeth* in Dee's journals is "Seal of the True God." In some cases, Dee shortened this name to *Sigillum Dei* (Seal of God) or *Sigillum Aemeth* (Seal of Truth), the latter of which has become the most common name for the seal today.

The Seal of the True God is a Qabalistic compendium of the sevenfold power of God expressed as a group of Hebrew archangels. However, you will not find governors Annael, Cassiel, Sachiel, and their brothers here. Instead, this glyph is the central powerhouse from which those archangels—and indeed the entire Heptarchic royalty—draw their power. (They do not lend their own power *to* it.) This image truly represents the seven "Spirits" that stand eternally before the Face of God (Revelation 4).

The Seal of the True God is fashioned of wax and placed in the center of the Holy Table (described in the next section) so that one of the Ensigns of Creation rests just beyond each point of the seven-pointed star. Also, four smaller wax seals are to be placed under the feet of the Holy Table.

The Secret Names of God

In chapter 6's sections on the seven Spirits of God and the seven archangels of the planets, I revealed fourteen secret and unpronounceable names of God—found in Dee's journals—that give birth to and govern the two groups of Hebrew planetary archangels. These divine names and their archangels are the true heart and soul of the seal. Nearly every angelic name upon it arises in some fashion from these fourteen names of God.

The first seven names appear in the cells of the large heptagon surrounding the seven-pointed star; they are ZllRHia, aZCaacb, paupnhr, hdmhiai, kkaaeee, iieelll, and eellMG✠. They are the divine source of the archangels of the Sephiroth: Zaphkiel, Zadkiel, Cumael, Raphael, Haniel, Michael, and Gabriel. Remember, the Sephiroth are not the planets but the divine wellsprings from which the planetary forces arise. It is from these seven Sephiroth that the Heptarchia ultimately derives its power and authority.

Just inside the large heptagon, between the points of the seven-pointed star, you will find the remaining seven secret names of God: SAAI(21/8.)EME(8.), BTZKASE(30), HEIDENE, DEIMO30A, I(26)MEGCBE, ILAOI(21/8.)VN, and IHRLAA21/8.. They are the divine source of the archangels of the physical planets: Sabathiel,

Zedekiel, Madimiel, Semeliel, Nogahel, Corabiel, and Levanael. They are the opposite end of the scale from the archangels of the Sephiroth. They work very close to the physical realm, where they transmit the forces of the seven planets directly to earth.

You will note the names of the planetary angels are found in the very center of the seal, arranged to mirror an earth-central solar system. In the very heart of the symbol is a cross, representing earth. Directly surrounding the cross is the name Levanael, just as the moon closely orbits the earth. Farther out, in the angles of the pentagram, are the names of the angels from Mercury to Jupiter: Corabiel, Nogahel, Semeliel, Madimiel, and Zedekiel.[99] Finally, surrounding all of this is the name "Zabathiel" (changed from Sabathiel, as "Z" and "S" seem to be interchangeable), just as Saturn is the furthest planet whose orbit encompasses the solar system.

The Family of Light

Most of the remaining names on the seal—found within the seven-pointed star and the smaller heptagon within it—are those of the twenty-eight angels of the Family of Light. Remember, they are ministers to the Heptarchic kings. Their names are born from the same seven names of God that give rise to the planetary angels (Sabatheil, Zedekiel, etc.)—a mystery I will explore in a later publication.

Because I gave the names of these angels in the previous chapter, I will not repeat them here. Besides the appearance of a few of their names in the talismans of the Heptarchic kings, they appear to play no direct role in the Heptarchic invocations recorded by Dee.

The Seven Secret Angels of the Circumference

> *"And I saw in the right hand of him that sat on the throne a book written within and on the backside, sealed with seven seals. And I saw a strong angel proclaiming with a loud voice, Who is worthy to open the book, and to loose the seals thereof?"* (Revelation 5:1–2)

> *"And I saw the seven angels which stood before God; and to them were given seven trumpets."* (Revelation 8:2)

Dee's angels explained that the forty characters (the combined letters and numbers) found in the circumference of the seal form the greatest name of God.[100] This great name of God, then, gives birth to seven (actually eight)[101] secret angels. However, these angels are not found among the fourteen Hebrew archangels that govern the rest of the seal. The primary seven names, as recorded in Dee's journals, are as follows:

Table 13: *The Seven Secret Angels of the Circumference*

1	Galas
2	Gethog
3	Thaoth
4	Horlon
5	Innon
6	Aaoth
7	Galethog

Dee did not indicate what function these angels serve. However, we are given a few clues concerning the angel Galethog, who is apparently the leader of the group. If you look again at the Seal of the True God, you'll notice that Galethog's name appears just inside the circumference, surrounding the entire figure. Each letter of his name (the final "og" being counted as a single character) has a cross and a number appended to it:

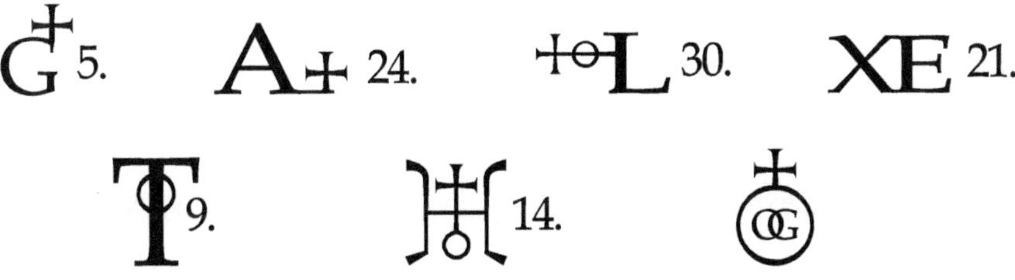

Figure 42: *The Seven Sigils of Galethog*

According to the archangel Michael, these letters are "the seven Seats of the One and everlasting God," which represent the Father, Son, and Holy Spirit. The name Galethog is said to banish or destroy the wicked, expel evil spirits, calm rough waters, strengthen the just, and exalt the righteous. (Interestingly, these are some of the very powers attributed to the angels of the Heptarchic royalty.)

Creating the Seal of the True God

The seal must be inscribed upon a disk of pure beeswax. The wax should not be bleached or dyed, merely strained to remove debris. (The angels informed Dee that they "have no respect of color," at least in relation to the seal.) You can find beeswax in many locations, from health food stores to metaphysical shops to art suppliers. Otherwise, you can search the Internet and easily find suitable beeswax or (best of all) even discover a local apiary (beekeeper) who will sell you wax taken fresh from an active hive.

The disk must be 9 inches in diameter (about 27 inches around the circumference) and it must be 1⅛ inches thick. You can either make a mold using a clay disk and plaster or silicon, or you can improvise a mold with a 9-inch cake pan. (Make sure you coat the mold with cooking spray before pouring in the wax!) My wife and I went as far as using clay to carve a complete seal, then formed a mold with silicon; that way, we can easily cast a new seal anytime we need one.

The front of the seal should, of course, display the names and figures as shown at the start of this chapter. Upon the back, the following character must be inscribed:

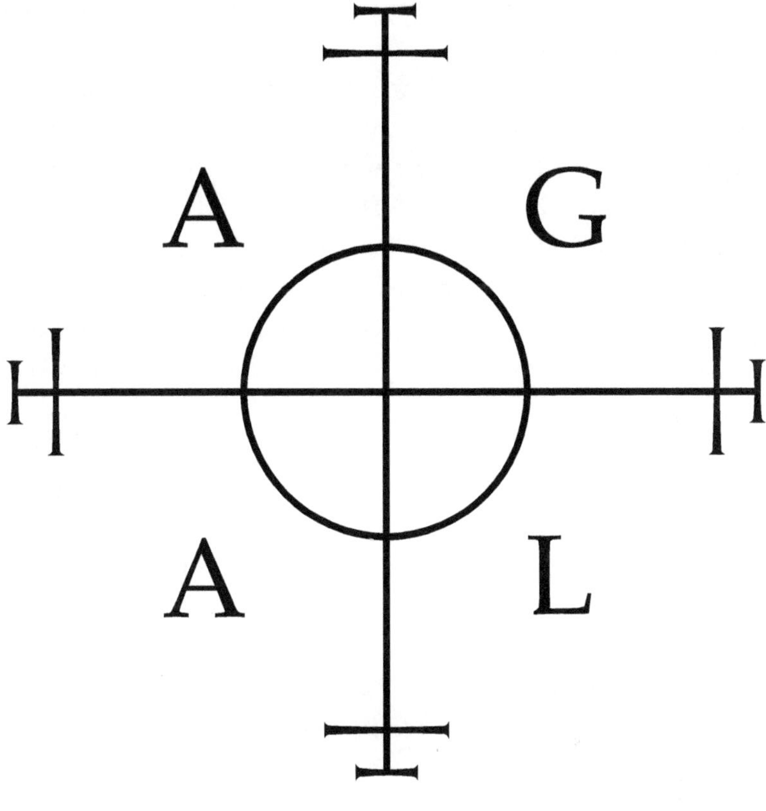

Figure 43: *The "AGLA Cross"*

This kind of wax tablet has a long tradition in Western occultism, where it is usually known as an almadel or almandel. The tradition seems to extend (at least) as far back as ancient Egypt, where sacred pools of water were used for the purpose of skrying. As it developed over the centuries, many different kinds of reflective surfaces were used—from plates of silver to pools of ink and, eventually, non-reflective tablets of wax. The almadel tradition has also been associated with the use of children, virgins, or even pregnant women as skryers while the conjuror focuses upon the invocations used to call the spirits. The tradition comes to us today in various popular forms, including the use of the "Lamen of

Silver" and a child skryer in the *Book of Abramelin*, the book in the *Lemegeton* entitled the *Art Almadel of Solomon*, and (of course) the work of John Dee and Edward Kelley.

Dee seems to have been greatly influenced by the *Art Almadel of Solomon* in the construction of his skrying furniture. The geometric figures painted on the Holy Table (see next section) are apparently adopted from the almadel itself. However, the table is made of wood rather than wax, so the Seal of the True God becomes the actual almadel of this setup. Like the Solomonic almadel, the seal is essentially a miniature altar, providing a sacred and pure place where angels can be evoked. If you use a crystal ball or other skrying device, it must be placed upon the seal.

Further, the archangel Michael hinted to Dee that the circumference of the seal could be inscribed upon the ground as a kind of magickal circle. Remember that the forty characters of the circumference, taken altogether, represent an exalted name of God. According to Michael, no "defiled" creature can cross that boundary after having entered it, which suggests it is not intended for the magician to stand within but for a spirit to be summoned into (much like the Triangle of the Art described in the *Goetia*). Most modern Enochian practitioners consider this to be true of the seal's circumference whether it is inscribed upon the ground or carved into wax and placed on the Holy Table.

Finally, you will need to make five of these seals in total. One, full sized (9 inches in diameter), is placed upon the Holy Table. The other four, made much smaller (Dee's were about 5 inches in diameter), are to be placed on the ground so the legs of the Holy Table can rest upon them.

The Holy Table of Practice[102]

"And thou shalt make an altar of shittim wood, five cubits long, and five cubits broad; the altar shall be foursquare: and the height thereof shall be three cubits." (Exodus 27:1)

Figure 44: *The Top of the Holy Table*

The Enochian Holy Table or Table of Practice (or Table of the Covenant) provides a sacred space for the invocation of angels. According to Dee's records, it is an "instrument of conciliation"—which means that it reconciles the human/earthly state with the pure state of the angels.

Along with the other Enochian magickal tools, it creates a pocket of shared space within which both human and angel can exist and hold a conversation.

Such tables were not uncommon to Western occult literature, where they were routinely used for the invocation and skrying of angels and other spirits. Skrying tables very similar to Dee's version can be found in the *Almadel of Solomon*, the *Pauline Arts,* and even Trithemius's *Art of Drawing Spirits into Crystals*, all of which seem to have had a direct influence upon the design and use of the Enochian holy table.

There is also, as we shall see, a notable relationship between this table and the force of Mercury. Mercury is the traditional planet of both magicians and angels (who are messengers, after all). Thus, one finds a similar focus upon Mercury in the *Key of Solomon the King,* where it is described as the force of all communication, magick, divination, and summoning of spiritual entities.[103] It has just this meaning in relation to the Enochian Holy Table as well.

There are, in fact, two Holy Tables found in Dee's journals. The second version is the one pictured in figure 44. The original design is missing from Dee's records. We only know that its border contained both "characters and names"[104]—which suggests it was similar to the skrying table described by Trithemius.[105] However, an angel later informed Dee that the characters and names were "devilish" and must be removed. He replaced them with the names of the Heptarchic kings and princes—all with the initial letter B removed. (Instead, a single B is written upon each of the four corners.) The letters in the 3 × 4 box in the center of the table are likewise drawn from the names of the kings and princes.[106]

Making and Using the Holy Table

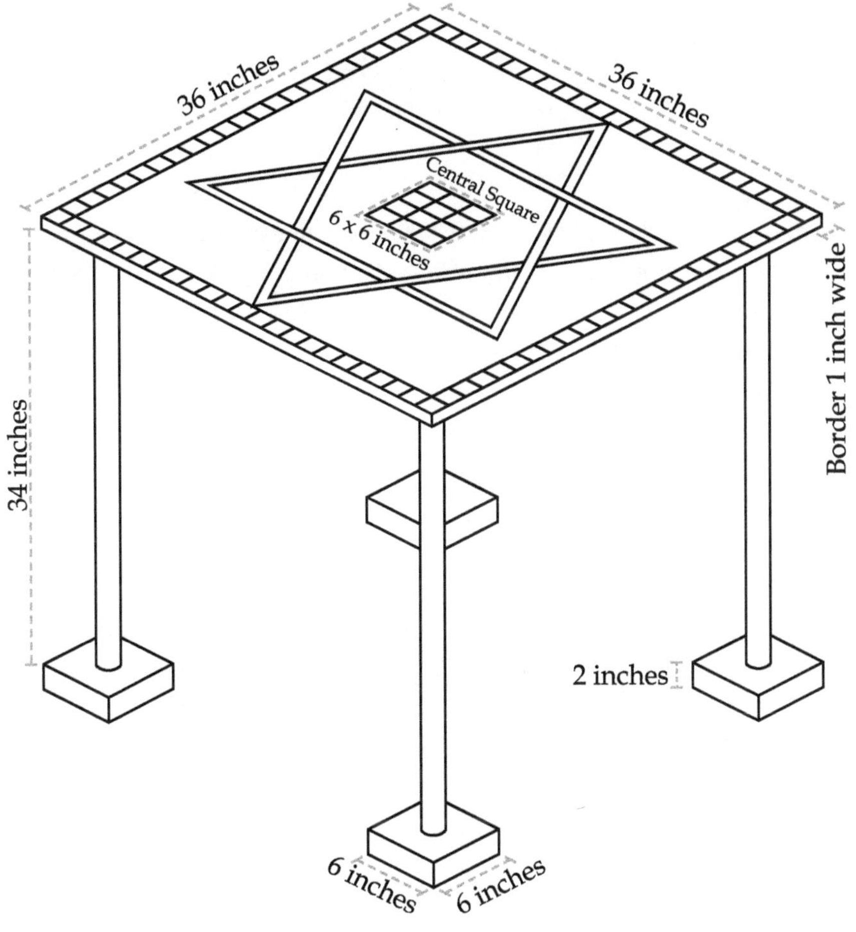

Figure 45: *Dimensions and Measurements of the Holy Table*

The holy table must be 3×3 feet wide and 3 feet tall, thus forming a perfect cube. It must be made of "sweetwood," though there has been some debate over exactly what that term means. In Dee's lifetime (roughly the same as Shakespeare's), the word "sweet" was most commonly used to indicate taste rather than smell. (The term for a pleasant smell was "odoriferous.") Thus, it is possible—perhaps even likely—that the Holy Table should be made with a *sweet-tasting* wood—perhaps a syrup or fruit wood such as maple, apple, or cherry. On the other hand, there are rare instances of the word *sweet* indicating smell at that time (at least one of which appears in Shakespeare), so it remains slightly possible that a *sweet-smelling* wood such as cedar was intended. By the time antiquarians wrote descriptions of Dee's own Holy Table, they noted that it had no scent.

The design and characters on the tabletop must be painted with yellow (or gold) oil paint, using oil that has been used in a church (and thus, we must assume, blessed by a priest). The outer border containing the letters should be one inch broad, and the dimensions of the 3×4 grid in the center should be 6×6 inches.

In the center is placed the large wax Seal of the True God, and four smaller versions of the seal—also waxen—are placed under the boxes to make the "feet" of the table. In fact, the boxes are optional, and the legs of the table can stand directly upon the smaller seals, keeping it from touching the ground. However, if you wish to keep the weight of the table from damaging the lesser seals, you may include the square feet as pictured in the diagram. These are simply small boxes with a top and no bottom, placed directly over each of the lesser seals so that the table legs rest upon the boxes instead of on the wax. Just remember to shorten the table's legs by the height of the box-feet so the whole remains three feet tall.

The seven Ensigns of Creation must also be used with the Holy Table. You have a choice between either inscribing them upon plates of purified tin[107] or painting them directly upon the Holy Table with the consecrated yellow or gold paint. If you inscribe them into tin plates, you have the option of leaving them off of the table and only bringing out the one you need to use at any given time. Otherwise, you can place (or paint) all seven of them upon the table, surrounding the Seal of the True God, one at each point of the seal's large heptagram, about seven inches inward from the outer border of the table. They should be placed in proper order, starting with the Ensign of Venus at the top and moving clockwise to the Ensigns of Sol, Mars, Jupiter, Mercury, Saturn, and finally the Ensign of Luna.[108]

At one point, Dee asked if the lettering of the seven ensigns should be transliterated into Angelical characters. The archangel Uriel replied, "Into their proper characters." Elsewhere in the journals, the angels did use the term "proper characters" to refer to Angelical, so it is possible Dee was meant to transliterate the letters on his ensigns. However, the ensigns happen to contain both upper- and lowercase lettering, which Angelical does not recognize. This may be why Dee never bothered to transliterate the letters of his own ensigns. I chose to follow Dee's lead in this, leaving them with English characters.

When the Holy Table is put to use, it should stand upon a red silk cloth that is two yards square. Upon the table rests a long white tablecloth, also made of silk. The Seal of the True God and the seven ensigns are placed upon the white cloth, then the whole is covered with a long mixed-color silk tablecloth with a tassel at each corner.[109] (Such mixed colors—known as pied color, or peacock, in alchemy—are traditionally associated with Mercury, and thus further highlight the table's function of reconciliation and communication with the angels.)

The Angelic Skrying Stone

"One thing yet is wanting: a meet[110] receptacle...There is yet wanting a stone...One there is, most excellent, hid in the secret of the depth... In the uttermost part of the Roman possession." (the angel Carmara, November 21, 1582)

The crystal ball, or shewstone, is perhaps the most famous magickal tool associated with Dee and Kelley. However, there has been some confusion over the skrying receptacles used by the men to skry the angels—not only over which crystals were actually used but also over exactly *how* they were used.

There are, in fact, three skrying receptacles associated with Dee's work. The first was an obsidian mirror (a common magickal mirror of the period) that we still have in the British Museum today. Several books about Dee have claimed he used the obsidian mirror in his Enochian work with Edward Kelley; however, none of Dee's records indicate that this was the case. Instead, Dee seems to have made use of two specific crystals in his Enochian work: one was his own clear crystal shewstone and the other was a crystal lens he claimed to have received from an angel. These two crystals are often confused with one another in texts about Dee's magick.

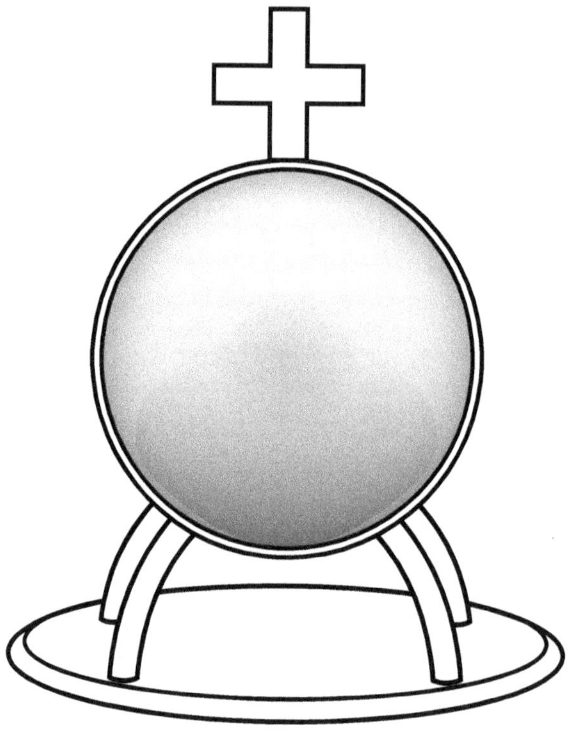

Figure 46: *Dee's Framed Shewstone*

The Framed Shewstone[111]

The first crystal ball we see in Dee's journals is pictured above: a simple crystal sphere set into a metal frame with a cross on the top. Many sources have claimed that Dee received this crystal directly from an angel, but this is not the case.[112] Dee states in the record that he received the shewstone as a gift from a (human) friend.

In the very first skrying session recorded in his *Five Books of Mystery*, Dee used this crystal ball in the invocation of Annael. He asked the archangel if any angel was specifically attached to the crystal and was informed that Michael was bound to it. Later, he learned that there were actually four angels attached to the stone: Michael, Gabriel, Raphael, and Uriel.[113] These four archangels, then, delivered the entire Enochian system of magick via the agency of that shewstone.

What is important here is that Dee did not simply use any old crystal in his magick. His crystal was dedicated strictly to the angels with whom he wished to work. He was instructed to place the shewstone upon the Holy Table, above the silk cloths and directly in the center of the Seal of the True God. Plus, he was to open his window and allow the rays of the sun to shine directly into it.[114]

Having said the above, I should also point out that this shewstone was never listed as an indispensable tool for Enochian magick.[115] The crystal ball was simply the preferred method of skrying for Dee and Kelley, and it was quite traditional in the Solomonic texts known to them. I see little reason why another skrying receptacle couldn't be used—a magick mirror, a chalice of wine, a candle flame, incense smoke, etc., or even no device at all (beyond the Holy Table and its Seal of the True God). It may be a matter of personal preference or something the angels have directed you to use. Still, the crystal ball is certainly traditional to both Solomonic and Enochian angel magick.

The Crystal Lens[116]

The second crystal associated with Dee's Enochian magick is the one famously given to him by an angel. It was first mentioned relatively late in the *Five Books*, on November 21, 1582 (see the quote on page 129), and it has no relationship whatsoever to the framed shewstone that sat on Dee's Holy Table. According to Kelley, the angel Carmara indicated that Dee should look for something near his western window. Kelley saw a small angel (about the height of a child) by the window, holding forth the crystal as if offering it to Dee. When Dee approached the same window, he saw the actual crystal sitting on some mats by his books.

This crystal was described as being the shape of an egg, somewhat less than the size of the palm of Dee's hand. Later, in the appendix to the *Five Books*, it is described as about half an inch thick, so it was really more like a lens than a ball. Dee was instructed to inscribe the names of five planetary angels in a circle upon the back of the Holy Lamen.[117] The crystal lens was to be set (or affixed) within that circle of names. There, Dee was told he would be able to "see the state of God's people through the whole earth," which likely indicates its use with the Parts of the Earth system.

The Holy Lamen[118]

"And thou shalt make the breastplate of judgment with cunning work...And thou shalt put in the breastplate of judgment the Urim and the Thummim; and they shall be upon Aaron's heart when he goeth in before the Lord." (Exodus 28:15, 30)

A lamen is a talisman worn by a mage as a symbol of spiritual authority, usually suspended around the neck. The symbols and/or characters upon such a lamen represent a signature of divine authority, indicating that the mage speaks on behalf of the highest god (not unlike a badge carried by a law enforcement officer). Such lamens were (and are) common in the Western occult tradition; countless grimoires include some form of lamen to be worn or carried by the aspirant in order to encourage obedience from the spirits. In fact, it is perhaps the single most common element shared by Medieval and Renaissance occult texts.

The Enochian Holy Lamen pictured opposite is intimately connected to the Table of Practice. Like the table, it is intended to reconcile the nature of the human operator with the pure state of the angels. Whereas the table is an instrument of "conciliation," the lamen is an instrument of "dignification," elevating the state of the operator to a higher state worthy of angelic communication. Also like the table, the Angelical letters found upon it are taken from the names of the Heptarchic kings and princes. (The method is rather complex and will not be covered here.) Finally, again like the Holy Table, there were two forms of the lamen given in Dee's journals, the original being declared "false and devilish" by Uriel, who replaced it with the version you see here.

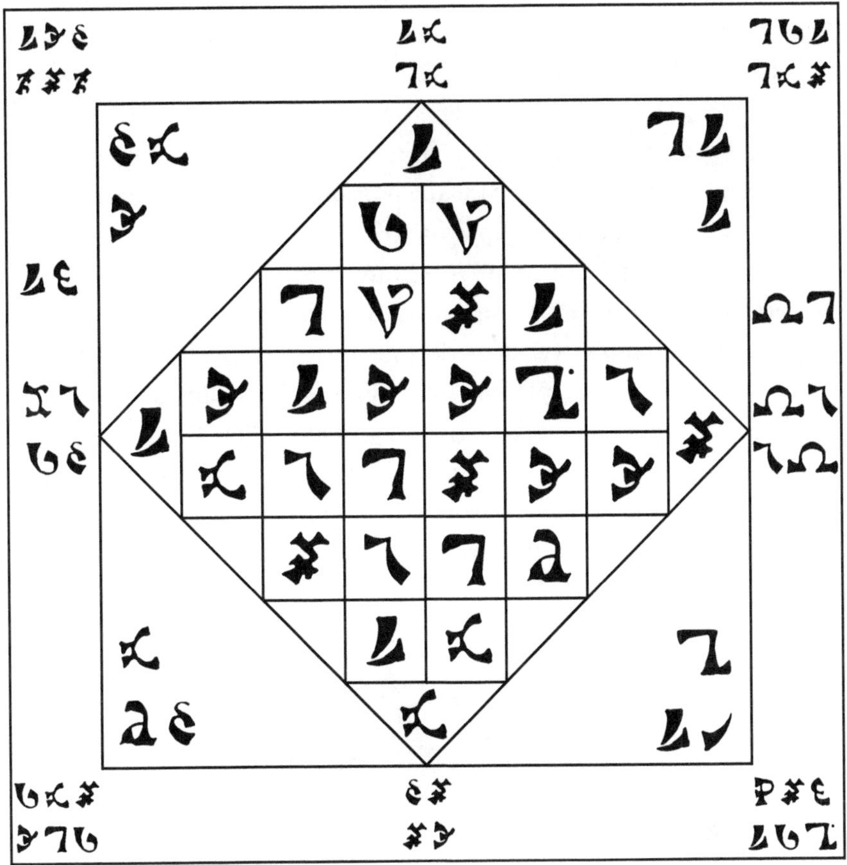

Figure 47: *The Front of the Holy Lamen*

When Dee recorded the original form of the lamen, he was told to wear it upon his chest, likely suspended around his neck—the most common location prescribed for such lamens in the grimoires. More than likely, this convention arose to mimic the breastplate worn by the High Priest of Israel (Exodus 28).

Later, the archangel Michael amended this instruction, telling Dee it must be "hanged unseen in some scarf." This is similar to an instruction found in the *Goetia* where the lamen called the Hexagram of Solomon is pinned to the skirt of one's robe and covered with a linen cloth. Once the infernal spirits appear, the lamen is revealed to compel them to take human form and render obedience. However, nothing is said in Dee's journals about revealing the Holy Lamen once the angels appear. Following the directions as given, one would simply wear the lamen on the chest and cover it with a piece of cloth (such as white linen or silk). However, I admit there still exists the possibility that it was intended to be revealed upon the angels' appearance.

Finally, we have already discussed the small crystal lens that Dee apparently received from an angel and was told to use with the Holy Lamen. He was instructed to inscribe the names of five planetary angels in a circle on the back of the lamen: Zedekiel, Madimiel, Semeliel, Nogahel, and Corabiel (the angels of Jupiter, Mars, Sol, Venus, and Mercury). It is not clear why the angels of Saturn and Luna are excluded. The crystal lens, then, was to be placed or affixed in the center of that circle of names, where the aspirant may "see the state of God's people through the whole earth."[119]

Figure 48: *The Back of the Holy Lamen*

Creating the Holy Lamen

The construction of the Holy Lamen is very simple. It can be drawn on clean white paper—and I would add that such paper should not be recycled or previously used. For durability, I suggest making it on white card stock. Its size is four inches square. No mention is made of color for the lettering; I suggest black to contrast with the white paper, or even gold ink or gold leaf to highlight its lofty, holy nature.

Make sure you obtain your crystal lens before drawing the names upon the back, so that you can measure the size of the circle properly. Rather than attempting to glue the lens onto the lamen, I would keep them separate. For skrying rituals, the lamen can be placed facedown upon the Holy Table and the lens can be placed within the circle of names.

The Ring of Solomon[120]

"Without this, thou shalt do nothing. Blessed be His Name, that compasseth all things: Wonders are in Him, and His Name is WONDERFUL: His Name worketh wonders from generation to generation."
(the archangel Michael, March 14, 1582)

Figure 49: *The Enochian Ring of Solomon*

Legend tells us that King Solomon was given a magickal ring by the archangel Michael. This ring had the power to expel and/or bind demons and allowed the king to fly through the air, speak with animals, and perform any number of miracles. The actual design of the ring seems to change depending on who is telling the story. It was either made of brass and iron or gold or silver. Some say it was set with four powerful stones, one given to Solomon by each of the angels of the four corners of the world. Other legends insist that a mythical worm called the *Shamir* was housed inside the ring. This worm was said to be able to burrow through solid stone and was thus the instrument used to cut the stones of the Holy Temple without iron tools.

Yet other legends attribute the power of the ring to an occult symbol inscribed upon it; older stories identify it as a pentagram, while more recent legends insist it was the hexagram (or Star of David, aka the Seal of Solomon). In the grimoires, such Seals of Solomon take various forms—such as concentric rings, pentagrams, hexagrams, or other geometric symbols—and usually include various sigils and names of God and/or angels. Quite often they are used along with (or are one and the same with) the lamens intended to render the spirits obedient.

When Dee established contact with Michael, one of the first magickal tools revealed by the archangel was the ring that he had once given to King Solomon. He affirmed that Solomon had worked all of his miracles through the agency of the ring and that Dee would do likewise, as you can see in the quote from archangel Michael on page 135.

Michael's words are a direct reference to the divine name PELE that appears on the bezel of the ring. It is a Hebrew word meaning "wonder" or "miracle," and therefore as a title of God it indicates a worker of miracles. It is mentioned in Agrippa's *Three Books*: "The Lord sayeth, My name which is Pele, signifieth with us, a worker of miracles, or causing wonders."[121] This is quite fitting for a magickal ring that promises to help one produce miracles.

Also note the L and V that appear in the design. These letters are taken from the Ensign of Creation attributed to the sun and Sunday, which are governed by Michael. In the Angelical language, L (or El) means "the First" and is a name of God. LV (or Lu) means "from One"—likely indicating something that comes directly from God.

The construction of the ring is very simple. It should be made of gold and needs only a simple band and a square bezel. Dee was told by

Michael to make it of the purest gold available, which in his lifetime was not nearly as pure as we can make it today. Our 24-carat gold is very pure but too soft for wearing as jewelry. Eighteen carats (¾ pure gold) would likely be workable, though 14 carats would be sufficient and more durable. The letters and figures shown in figure 49 should be engraved upon its face. The ring must be worn for *all* magickal operations.

A Note about Consecrations

"But all the silver, and gold, and vessels of brass and iron, are consecrated unto the Lord: they shall come into the treasury of the Lord." (Joshua 6:19)

One thing that is notably missing from Dee's records are instructions for the consecration of the magickal tools and furniture. The angels only mentioned such consecrations once: when they told Dee that all things used in the creation of the *Book of Loagaeth* must be purified beforehand. They gave no instructions for how to do this; however, several details of the Gebofal system suggest a close relationship to the *Key of Solomon*, so it is likely that we can turn to that book for instructions on the consecration of pens, papers, inks, etc.

From there, we could assume that "standard grimoiric procedures" could be followed in the consecration of all the Enochian tools. You can find useful instructions in *The Heptameron*, *Fourth Book of Occult Philosophy*, and *Magus*. I would suggest checking into my own *Secrets of the Magickal Grimoires* (chapters 6, 9, and 11) for comprehensive instructions on the creation and consecration of magickal tools.

To summarize the process briefly here: you will need incense such as frankincense or "church" incense, along with a censer and coals. You will also need to acquire or make a small amount of holy water, and if you have prepared the Solomonic holy water sprinkler (or aspergillum), all the better. You will also need a candle—either a white candle or one made of unbleached beeswax. No consecrations are ever performed without the presence of fire.

You will also need to find psalms or other sacred scripture—or write your own prayers—that are appropriate to each object you will consecrate. For example, in the consecration of the Holy Table, you can mention the altar in the Temple of Solomon. When consecrating the Holy Lamen, you might mention the breastplate of Aaron. (For examples, note the scriptural and other verses I have included at the heads of many chapters and subsections of this book.) Today it is quite easy to use keyword searches in online bibles and other sacred scripture, apocrypha, etc., in order to find prayers suitable for your needs.

You will need to ritually prepare and wash yourself beforehand. Then cense and sprinkle each magickal tool while reciting the related psalms, scripture, or prayers. You should also cense and sprinkle the entire room or sacred space in which you will be working. I have found that Solomon's consecration of the Holy Temple (1 Kings 8: 23–53) is quite appropriate and powerful for blessing a ritual or prayer chamber.

Chapter Eight

Instructions for Heptarchic Invocation[122]

"Request and invoke our appearance with sincerity and humility." (Archangel Uriel, March 10, 1582)

What You Will Need

In order to summon the angels of the Heptarchia, you will first need to prepare the Enochian magickal tools and furniture: the Holy Table of Practice with its five wax seals and seven purified tin ensigns, the Ring of Solomon, and the Holy Lamen of Dignification. Your chosen skrying receptacle is placed upon the Holy Table's multicolored silk tablecloth. I would also suggest wearing a white robe or one colored according to the planet you wish to invoke, as should your skryer if you choose to work with one.

I also recommend finding psalms and creating prayers that are in harmony with your goal. The prayers should ask for the angels to be present when you call and to aid you in your desire.

Incense

Curiously, incenses are mentioned only once in Dee's journals—in relation to the summoning of Archangel Michael. However, they are quite common to Renaissance angel magick. If you choose not to use them in your Enochian magick, you would not be breaking any specific rule. However, I see no harm (and, in fact, much benefit) in making use of them anyway. If you choose to use an incense, I suggest burning a scent appropriate to the planet whose force you wish to invoke.

Incense of Saturn/Saturday

1 part myrrh
1 part asafoetida
¼ part sulfur

Incense of Jupiter/Thursday

1 part cedar
¼ part clove
⅛ part apple pectin
A few drops pine oil

Incense of Mars/Tuesday

1 part pipe tobacco (my favorite is "Black and Mild")
½ part cinnamon
⅛ part crushed red pepper

WARNING: Martian incense is one of the most dangerous substances I've worked with; it is, quite simply, tear gas. If you make this, do not add too much red pepper, and when you burn it, do it in small quantities. Never, for any reason, lean over the censer and inhale or draw in breath! Too much pepper or direct inhalation can burn your throat and lungs.

Incense of Sol/Sunday

1 part frankincense
1 part copal
½ part benzoin

Note: You may also use standard church incense, which can be found in most botanicas or Christian supply stores.

Incense of Venus/Friday
1 part sandalwood
1 part benzoin
½ red rose petals

Incense of Mercury/Wednesday
1 part benzoin
¼ part frankincense
⅛ part lavender blossoms

Incense of Luna/Monday
1 part calamus
½ part juniper berries
¼ part gardenia flower

Generally I find that the various flowers used in the above incenses tend to produce a burnt smell when placed on hot coals. A good solution is to replace the flowers with a couple drops of essential oil instead. Just be careful, as too much flower essence will quickly overpower the other ingredients in the recipe.

Talismans

You will also need to construct three talismans for the angels you will invoke: one for the king, one for his prince, and one for the forty-two ministers of the day in question.[123] These talismans are all included with the descriptions of the appearances and offices of the Heptarchic royalty (see chapter 6). All three must be cut from the same kind of sweetwood used to build the Holy Table. Though Dee's journals do not indicate color, I would suggest using the same yellow or gold oil paint that was used for the Holy Table.

A Note about the Talismans of the Heptarchic Kings

One of the few truly missing pieces of the Enochian system involves the seals and talismans of the Heptarchic kings. In several places throughout *John Dee's Five Books of Mystery*, mention is made of a large globe the angels had revealed to Kelley. Atop the globe stood a human figure that was understood to be Carmara, the ruling king of the Heptarchic royalty. Within the globe appeared the seals of the seven kings along with a series of letters. Some of the letters were written forward and some of them were written backward.[124]

The significance of these letters was never explained, and the globe itself is never pictured. (It is quite possible the information was contained in some of the journal entries that were destroyed.) We do know that the letters were supposed to be included on the talismans of the Heptarchic kings, but only a single example has made it to us:

Figure 50: *Dee's Example Heptarchic Talisman with Annexed Letters (Seal of King Babalel)*

In my opinion, if this mysterious globe and the letters associated with the Heptarchic kings had been vital to the magick, it surely would have survived for us to see. We only have the seals of the Heptarchic kings today because Dee thought to include them in his personal Enochian grimoire, yet he did not find it necessary to include the associated letters from the globe. Therefore, I suggest they are not critical to the creation of the kings' talismans. Even including them upon the single talisman for which we have an example would leave the system unbalanced.

Ritual Preparation

You should undertake a nine-day period of preparation during which you must ritually purify yourself: isolate yourself as much as possible for the entire period, eat a fasting diet that includes no meat, and engage in prayer and washing. During this time, erect and purify your working space and make sure the talismans are properly constructed.[125]

It is also necessary to repeat the Oration to God (see step four below) three times in a row every day.[126]

The nine days must be timed to end the night before the day you wish to work. For example, if you wish to invoke the angels of the sun, you will need to begin preparations on a Friday so they will end on the Saturday night before your chosen Sunday.

Next, consider the time of day you wish to perform the summoning ritual. Remember the day is divided into six segments of four hours, each governed by a group of seven Heptarchic ministers. Decide which group of ministers can accomplish your desire, and work during their four hours. If you would rather invoke the aid of all the ministers in general, then you may work at any time of the day. In that case, I suggest choosing an hour ruled by the planet you wish to invoke.

During the ritual, you will only need to request the appearance of the primary minister who governs his period of the day. (That is, one of the six whose names appear on the ministers' talisman.) Or, if you are working by all the ministers in general, you will need to call upon all six primary minsters to appear.

Summoning

1) Before entering the sacred space, wash thoroughly. Then don the robe, the Holy Lamen, and the Ring of Solomon. Sit—or have your skryer sit—at the Holy Table facing eastward.[127] Remember, the seven Ensigns of Creation may be arranged or painted upon the table at all times; however, you may choose to keep them separate if you wish. If so, you must place the ensign of the archangel who currently governs the universe (which today should be Raphael) upon the table but beneath the multicolored silk tablecloth.[128]

2) Open the ritual by reciting the psalms and prayers you prepared for your goal. Elaborate these prayers as much as possible, as the spirit moves you.

3) The skryer now takes up the talisman of the Heptarchic king, holding it in one hand. Which hand is not specified, but I would recommend the left (receptive) hand.

   The talisman of the prince is set upon the table (above the silk cloths) directly atop the ensign of the ruling archangel.[129]

   Finally, the talisman of the ministers is placed upon the ground so the skryer's feet can rest directly upon their names. I doubt this is intended to show dominance or disrespect. It likely indicates that the ministers are the foundation of the work.

4) Recite the following Oration to God three times in a row:[130]

   O almighty, eternal, true and living God; O King of Glory; O Lord of Hosts. O thou, the creator of heaven and earth, and of all things visible and invisible. Now (even now, at length), among other of thy manifold mercies used, and to be used, toward me, thy simple servant [insert your name here], *I most humbly beseech thee in this, my present petition, to have mercy upon me, to have pity upon me, to have compassion upon me, who faithfully and sincerely, of long time, have sought among men in earth and also by prayer (full oft and pitifully) to have made suit unto thy divine majesty for the obtaining of some convenient portion of true knowledge and understanding of thy laws and ordinances established in the natures and properties of thy creatures.*

   By which knowledge thy divine wisdom, power, and goodness (on thy creatures bestowed and to them imparted) being to me made manifest might abundantly instruct, furnish, and allure me (for the same) incessantly to pronounce thy praises, to render unto thee most hearty thanks, to advance thy true honor, and to win unto thy name some of thy due majestical glory among all people and forever.

And whereas it hath pleased thee, O God, of thy infinite goodness by thy faithful and holy spiritual messengers to deliver unto us long since (through the eye and ear of Edward Kelley and the pen of Dr. John Dee)[131] *an orderly form and manner of exercise Heptarchical. How to thy honor and glory, and the comfort of my own poor soul, and of others thy faithful servants I may, at all times, use very many of thy good angels, their counsels and helps, according to the proprieties of such their functions and offices as to them, by thy divine power, wisdom, and goodness, are assigned and limited. (Which orderly form and manner of exercise, until even now, I never found so urgent opportunity, and extreme necessity, to apply myself unto.)*

Therefore, I, thy poor and simple servant, do most humbly, heartily, and faithfully beseech thy divine majesty, most lovingly and fatherly, to favor. And by thy divine calling[132] *to further this, my present industry, and endeavor to exercise myself according to the aforesaid orderly form and manner.*

And now (at length, but not too late), for thy dearly beloved son Jesus Christ his sake (O Heavenly Father) to grant also unto me this blessing and portion of thy heavenly graces: that thou wilt, forthwith, enable me, make me apt and acceptable (in body, soul, and spirit) to enjoy always the holy and friendly conversation with the sensible, plain, full, and perfect help (in word and deed) of thy mighty, wise, and good spiritual messengers and ministers generally and, namely, of blessed Michael, blessed Gabriel, blessed Raphael, and blessed Uriel. And, also especially, of all those which do appertain unto the Heptarchical Mystery. Isagogically[133] *(as yet), and very briefly unto me declared, under the method of seven mighty kings and their seven faithful and princely ministers, with their subjects and servants to them belonging.*

And in this, thy great mercy and grace, on me bestowed and to me confirmed (O Almighty God), thou shalt (to the great comfort of thy faithful servants) prove, to thy very enemies and mine, the truth and certainty of thy manifold most merciful promises heretofore made unto me. And that thou art the true and almighty God, creator of heaven and earth, upon who I do call and in who I put all my trust. And thy ministers, to be the true and faithful angels of light, which have hitherto, principally, and according to thy divine providence dealt with us.

And also I, thy poor and simple servant, shall then, in and by thee, be better able to serve thee according to thy well pleasing, to thy honor and glory. Yea, even in these most miserable and lamentable days, grant, O grant, O our heavenly Father, grant this (I pray thee) for thy only begotten son Jesus Christ, his sake: amen, amen, amen.

5) Now recite the following Invitation of the Heptarchic King:[134]

O puissant and right Noble King, (name), and by what name else soever thou art called or mayest truly and duly be called, and to whose peculiar government, charge, disposition, and kingly office doth appertain the (________).[135] *In the Name of the King of Kings, the Lord of Hosts, the Almighty God, creator of heaven and earth and of all things visible and invisible. O right Noble King, (name), come now and appear with thy prince and his ministers and subjects to my perfect and sensible eye's judgment, in a godly and friendly manner, to my comfort and help, for the advancing of the honor and glory of our almighty God by my service. As much as by thy wisdom and power, in thy proper kingly office and government, I may be helped*[136] *and enabled unto. Amen.*

Come, O right Noble King, (name). I say come. Amen.

Glory be to the Father, to the Son, and to the Holy Spirit.
As it was in the beginning, is now and ever
shall be, world without end, amen.

6) Now recite the Invitation of the King's Prince:[137]

   O Noble Prince, (name), and by what name else soever thou art called or mayest truly and duly be called, and to whose peculiar government, charge, disposition, office, and princely dignity doth appertain the (________).[138] In the name of Almighty God, the King of Kings, and for his honor and glory to be advanced by my faithful service, I require thee, O Noble Prince, (name), to come presently and to show thyself to my perfect and sensible eye's judgment, with thy ministers, servants, and subjects, to my comfort and help, in wisdom and power, according to the property of thy noble office. Come, O Noble Prince, (name), I say come. Amen.

   Our Father, who art in heaven, hallowed be thy name. Thy kingdom come, thy will be done on earth as it is in heaven. Give us this day our daily bread, and forgive us our debts as we have forgiven our debtors. And lead us not into temptation but deliver us from evil. For thine is the kingdom and the power and the glory forever. Amen.

   If the angels have not appeared to you (or your skryer) after the above two invitations, you may repeat them up to seven times.[139] It is possible the king will appear first, then call upon the prince and ministers, or the king may not appear at all, sending the prince in his stead. In either case, explain to the royal angels what you need and name the minister or ministers who can aid you in your desire. Record what any of these angels have to say, and—very important!—ask them what they require of you in order to achieve your goal.

7) Once you have obtained your vision, thank the angels for speaking with you. Close the ritual with psalms and prayers of thanksgiving.

Chapter Nine

The *Book of Loagaeth* and Gebofal

"And I saw in the right hand of him that sat on the throne a book written within and on the backside, sealed with seven seals... And they sung a new song, saying, Thou art worthy to take the book and to open the seals thereof." (Revelation 5:1, 9)

The *Book of Loagaeth*—the "book of the speech from God"—is an earthly copy of the celestial "Book of Life" that is the divine record of every created thing that ever was, is, or ever will be. It is said that the book contains the very words with which God created the universe, and it is from this book the angels draw their own Angellical tongue. It has only been revealed to humanity twice: once to the prophet Enoch and once again to the scholar and mystic John Dee and his skryer Edward Kelley. This is the Book of the Lamb described in the Revelation, whose seven seals are opened during the world's final days.

The Holy Book was revealed to Dee and Kelley by Raphael, the archangel of wisdom, language, magick, science, and medicine. He referred to the book as a divine elixir or medicine that would heal the world.

Each table in the book is associated with one of the forty-nine gates of heaven; forty-eight of them lead into the twelve kingdoms of heaven (the astrological houses), but the highest gate remains closed at all times. That sealed gate is reserved for the Christos, or Messiah.

The book also encompasses the entire universe from creation to destruction, symbolically represented by the seven biblical days of Creation. By summoning the angels who guard the gates, one can learn about absolutely anything or achieve any goal. There are strong clues in Dee's journals that each leaf of the *Book of Loagaeth* represents a specific astrological force (such as the twelve signs of the zodiac, the four elements, etc.)—however, exactly which force is represented by each leaf was never recorded.[140]

Meanwhile, the angels did reveal a set of invocations, or callings, written in their own Angelical language, to open the gates and call forth the angels who guard them. Likewise, the same invocations can grant one access to spiritually enter the gates and explore the celestial cities beyond them. To accomplish either feat, the angels revealed the system of Gebofal for putting the Holy Book into practice.

The forty-nine-day ritual of Gebofal is devotional mysticism—a method of harmonizing oneself with the greater universe, obtaining prophetic visions, and gaining wisdom from the angels. Put simply, Gebofal is an initiation ceremony that introduces you to the gatekeepers of heaven and grants you access to all the wisdom and knowledge of the universe. Many aspirants have come to view Gebofal as the primary initiation ceremony for all Enochian work.

Once the Gebofal initiation has been accomplished, it appears that the Holy Book and the Angelical Callings can be put to any number of practical uses. Only one was outlined in Dee's journals: the Parts of the Earth system (which will be covered in chapter 10). It made use of the last thirty tables of *Loagaeth*, and the Angelical Call(s) that opened them, to perform remote viewing of any location on earth. Sadly, the exact uses of the first eighteen tables of *Loagaeth* were never recorded.[141]

Unfortunately, available space in this book will not allow me to include the forty-nine massive word-tables of *Loagaeth*. At this time, I am only aware of two sources for the tables[142]—however, I do hope to publish my own edition of the *Book of Loagaeth* in the future.

Below, I will give a brief outline of how to accomplish the Gebofal initiation ritual. For an in-depth exploration of this fascinating system of devotion and mysticism, I strongly recommend my own *Angelical Language, Volume I: The Complete History and Mythos of the Tongue of Angels*, especially chapter 4.

Gebofal: Opening the Gates of Heaven

"And I will give unto thee the keys of the kingdom of heaven..." (Matthew 16:19)

What You Will Need

For this and, in fact, *all* Enochian summoning rituals, you will need the Holy Table (including the five wax seals and seven Ensigns of Creation, the silk cloths, and your chosen skrying receptacle), the Ring of Solomon, and the Holy Lamen. You will also need to establish the same kind of sacred space as for Heptarchic rituals. You will not have to create your own prayers or talismans for this work. If you wish to use an incense, I suggest frankincense, church incense, or Abramelin incense. As before, a plain white robe would be appropriate attire—and it must be perfectly clean.

You will also need to make a "perfected copy" of the *Book of Loagaeth.*[143] All items used in its creation (pen and ink, paper, the silk covering, etc.) must be ritually purified beforehand, and you must purify yourself through washing, fasting, and prayer before working on the book. You are also required to be alone when you do the work.

The creation of the book is a monumental task that requires much dedication and devotion; many consider it an important part of the Gebofal process. Dee and Kelley left us the tables of *Loagaeth* written in English letters. Before you can use the book in your magick, you will need to convert all the letters into Angelical characters and write the text so that it reads from right to left—just as you would see in a Hebrew or Arabic book.

Once you have copied the forty-nine tables—in proper Angelical—into a bound book, you must cover the book with light blue–colored silk. On the front, paint the following title in Angelical characters (see figure 2; note that the seven wax seals in that figure are not required here) in letters of gold: *Amzes Naghezes Hardeh*.[144]

As you might imagine, with forty-nine huge tables filled with letters on the front and back, this leaves a lot of room for errors. The work must be done slowly and carefully, checking and double-checking for mistakes along the way. The angels gave Dee forty days to complete the task, and even he failed to accomplish the feat in that time. Fortunately, we are not given the same time limit to create our own copies—we need only to work when inspired to do so.

Besides the perfected copy of *Loagaeth*, you will also need to have the forty-eight Angelical Callings and the Prayer of Enoch on hand, as you will be reciting them every day. At the end of this book I will append a copy of my Angelical psalter—including all of the Angelical Callings, their translations, and an easy-to-understand pronunciation guide.

Ritual Preparation

Dee was instructed to purify himself for nine days before attempting Gebofal,[145] which is possibly based upon the nine-day purification outlined in the *Key of Solomon the King*. You must isolate yourself as much as possible for the entire period, eat a fasting diet that includes no meat, and engage in prayer (especially confession) and washing.[146] During this period, you may also prepare the magickal tools and sacred space.

There are no magickal days or times associated with this work; you are to undertake the ritual only when God calls you to do so—that is when you feel inspired. (And then it will be only for important "big picture" purposes, rather than day-to-day magickal uses.) However, once begun, you must commit to the entire process (nine days of purification followed by forty-nine days of invocations) without interruption. This is a lengthy and intensive ritual that will occupy your attentions—morning, noon, and night—for over two months.

The angels began the *Loagaeth* revelations on Good Friday and continued for forty-eight days. It would be traditional to begin the Gebofal working on the morning after Good Friday. Whatever day you choose, make sure your nine days of purification end on the night before your chosen start date.

The Gebofal Ritual

Day 1

Just before dawn, wash yourself thoroughly and don a clean white robe. Enter your sacred space and put on the Ring of Solomon and the Holy Lamen of Dignification. Sit at the Holy Table—facing east—and lay the *Book of Loagaeth* in front of you. Open it to the second table (as the first table is not accessible via Gebofal) and recite the Prayer of Enoch:

The Prayer of Enoch[147]

Lord God, the fountain of true wisdom, thou that openest the secrets of thy own self unto man, thou knowest mine imperfection and my inward darkness. How can I (therefore) speak unto them that speak not after the voice of man, or worthily call on thy name, considering that my imagination is variable and fruitless and unknown to myself? Shall the sands seem to invite the mountains or can the small rivers entertain the wonderful and unknown waves?

Can the vessel of fear, fragility, or that which is of a determined proportion lift up himself, heave up his hands, or gather the sun into his bosom? Lord, it cannot be. Lord, my imperfection is great. Lord, I am less than sand. Lord, thy good angels and creatures excel me far—our proportion is not alike, our sense agreeth not. Notwithstanding, I am comforted, for that we have all one God, all one beginning from thee, that we respect thee as creator. Therefore will I call upon thy name, and in thee I will become mighty. Thou shalt light me, and I will become a seer. I will see thy creatures and will magnify thee amongst them. Those that come unto thee have the same gate, and through the same gate descend such as thou sendest.

Behold, I offer my house, my labor, my heart and soul, if it will please thy angels to dwell with me, and I with them. To rejoice with me that I may rejoice with them. To minister unto me, that I may magnify thy name. Then, lo, the tables (which I have provided and, according to thy will, prepared) I offer unto thee, and unto thy holy angels, desiring them, in and through thy holy names. That as thou art their light and comfortest them, so they, in thee, will be my light and comfort. Lord, they prescribe not laws unto thee, so it is not meet that I prescribe laws unto them. What it pleaseth thee to offer, they receive. So what it pleaseth them to offer unto me, will I also receive.

Behold, I say (O Lord), if I shall call upon them in thy name, be it unto me in mercy, as unto the servant of the Highest. Let them also manifest unto me, how by what words and at what time I shall call them. O Lord, is there any that measure the heavens that is mortal? How, therefore, can the heavens enter into mans' imagination? Thy creatures are the glory of thy countenance. Hereby thou glorifiest all things, which glory excelleth and (O Lord) is far above my understanding. It is great wisdom to speak and talk according to understanding with kings. But to command kings by a subjected commandment is not wisdom unless it come from thee.

Behold, Lord, how shall I therefore ascend into the heavens? The air will not carry me, but resisteth my folly. I fall down, for I am of the earth. Therefore, O thou very light and true comfort that canst and mayest and dost command the heavens: behold, I offer these tables unto thee. Command them as it pleaseth thee.

And O you ministers and true lights of understanding, governing this earthly frame and the elements wherein we live, do for me as for the servant of the Lord; and unto whom it hath pleased the Lord to talk of you.

Behold, Lord, thou hast appointed me forty-nine times. Thrice forty-nine times will I lift my hands unto Thee.[148] *Be it unto me as it pleaseth thee and thy holy ministers. I require nothing but thee, and through thee and thy honor and glory. But I hope I shall be satisfied and shall not die (as thou hast promised) until thou gather the clouds together and judge all things; when in a moment I shall be changed and dwell with thee forever.*

Then recite the first Angelical Calling, which is the key of the second table of *Loagaeth*. Afterward, sit back and meditate, pray, and/or begin to skry, allowing the angels to converse with you about the mysteries contained in their table. Record any insights or visions you gain; however, do not become discouraged if you do not experience much at this early point. If you do nothing more than spend a while in silent meditation, it will be enough.

Repeat this entire process again at noon, and then once again at dusk so the angels of the second table are invoked three times over the course of the day.

Days 2 through 48

At dawn of the next day, repeat the same process as before. Wash thoroughly, then sit at the Holy Table wearing the ring and lamen. This time, open the book to the third table. Recite the Prayer of Enoch followed by the second Angelical Calling, the key of the third table of *Loagaeth*. Once again, sit and meditate, pray, and/or skry for what the angels may have to teach you—if anything—about their table and its key. Again, do not be disappointed if you do not see or hear the angels yet. Just know they are there and that you have invoked their influence in your life. Repeat the invocation process again at noon and once more at dusk.

For the next forty-six days, repeat the same process three times each day—morning, noon, and dusk. On the third day, you must open *Loagaeth* to the fourth table and use the third calling. On the fourth day, open it to the fifth table and use the fourth calling, and so on. Each time, open the book to the proper table, then recite the Prayer of Enoch and finally the table's key to call down its angels. Meditate, pray, or skry, and record any insights or visions you are granted.

Day 49 (Completion)

Once again, just before dawn, wash thoroughly. As the sun rises, don the clean robe along with the ring and lamen and sit at the Holy Table. This time, however, open the *Book of Loagaeth* to the first table—the gate that has no Angelical key to open it. Recite the Prayer of Enoch, then meditate or pray as before. Repeat at noon and again at dusk. That will complete the operation of Gebofal.

The forty-eight gates that you have opened are called the Gates of Wisdom or the Gates of Understanding by the angels. Opening them all is how we attain the forty-ninth gate. While we may not be able to pass through that gate, we can receive divine inspiration and blessings through it. That is the ultimate goal of Gebofal, and you will see its results manifest over the days, weeks, months, or even years that follow.

Chapter Ten

The Parts of the Earth System

"And (the Holy City) had a wall great and high, and had twelve gates, and at the gates twelve angels, and names written thereon, which are the names of the twelve tribes of the children of Israel." (Revelation 21:12)

The Thirty Aethyrs

"And the likeness of the firmament upon the heads of the living creatures was as the colour of the terrible crystal, stretched forth over their heads above." (Ezekiel 1:22)

The final thirty tables of the *Book of Loagaeth* represent what Dee called the "thirty Aethyrs" or "Aires." These are thirty heavens (also called firmaments) that extend from earth all the way to God's throne. The angels who live in these heavens are in charge of the stars (as in astrology) and therefore influence the destinies of all created things. These angels are governed primarily by the twelve archangels (or kings) of the zodiac—who are, in turn, under the authority of the seven arch-angels of the planets.

The Parts of the Earth

"Ask of me, and I shall give thee...the uttermost Parts of the Earth for thy possession." (Psalms 2:8)

Meanwhile, the earth is divided into ninety-one (really ninety-two) regions or provinces called the Parts of the Earth. The angelic governments of the primary ninety-one parts are distributed among the thirty Aethyrs: three parts assigned to each heaven, except for the lowest and most earthly heaven, which governs four. (The hidden "ninety-second part" does not fall into the thirty Aethyrs. I will return to this part later in this section.) These regions are governed by the twelve zodiacal kings, who command large numbers of servient angels. In this way, each region of the world is associated with a sign of the zodiac, along with the planet that rules the sign.[149] If we know which angels govern a given region of the world, then we can contact those angels for information about the people and nations that reside there or even influence them directly.

Here are the names of the twelve kings of the zodiac, along with the sign, ruling planet, and associated tribe of Israel:

Table 14: *The Twelve Archangelic Kings of the Zodiac*

	ZODIACAL KING	SIGN	PLANET	TRIBE[150]
1	Olpaged	Aries	Mars	Dan
2	Ziracah	Taurus	Venus	Ruben
3	Hononol	Gemini	Mercury	Judah
4	Zarnaah	Cancer	Luna	Manasseh
5	Gebabal	Leo	Sol	Asher
6	Zurchol	Virgo	Mercury	Simeon
7	Alpudus	Libra	Venus	Issachar
8	Cadaamp	Scorpio	Mars	Benjamin

9	Zarzilg	Sagittarius	Jupiter	Naphtali
10	Lavavoth	Capricorn	Saturn	Gad
11	Zinggen	Aquarius	Saturn	Zebulun
12	Arfaolg	Pisces	Jupiter	Ephraim

Following is a chart of the thirty Aethyrs including which tables of *Loagaeth* represent them, which Parts of the Earth they contain, the names of the earthly nations that reside there, which zodiacal kings govern them, and how many servient angels answer to those kings.

Table 15: ***The Ninety-One Parts of the Earth***

	LOAGAETH	PARTS OF THE EARTH	NATIONS OF MAN[151]	ZODIACAL KINGS	SERVIENT ANGELS (= TOTAL)
1. Lil	Table 20	1. Occodon 2. Pascomb 3. Valgars	Egyptus Syria Mesopotamia[152]	Zarzilg Zinggen Alpudus	7209 2360 5362 (=14931)
2. Arn	Table 21	4. Doagnis 5. Pacasna 6. Dialioa	Cappadocia Tuscia Asia Minor	Zarnaah Ziracah Ziracah	3636 2362 8962 (=15960)
3. Zom	Table 22	7. Samapha 8. Virooli 9. Andispi	Hyrcaina Thracia Gosmam	Zarzilg Alpudus Lavavoth	4400 3660 9236 (=17296)
4. Paz	Table 23	10. Thotanp 11. Axziarg 12. Pothnir	Thebaidi Parsadal India	Lavavoth Lavavoth Arfaolg	2360 3000 6300 (=11660)
5. Lit	Table 24	13. Lazdixi 14. Nocamal 15. Tiarpax	Bactriane Cilicia Oxiana	Olpaged Alpudus Zinggen	8630 2306 5802 (=16738)
6. Maz	Table 25	16. Saxtomp 17. Vavaamp 18. Zirzird	Numidia Cyprus Parthia	Gebabal Arfaolg Gebebal	3620 9200 7220 (=20040)

	LOAGAETH	PARTS OF THE EARTH	NATIONS OF MAN[151]	ZODIACAL KINGS	SERVIENT ANGELS (= TOTAL)
7. Deo	Table 26	19. Opmacas 20. Genadol 21. Aspiaon	Getulia Arabia Phalagon	Zarnaah Hononol Zinggen	6363 7706 6320 (=20389)
8. Zid	Table 27	22. Zamfres 23. Todnaon 24. Pristac	Mantiana Soxia Gallia	Gebabal Olpaged Zarzilg	4362 7236 2302 (=13900)
9. Zip	Table 28	25. Oddiorg 26. Cralpir 27. Doanzin	Assyria Sogdiana Lydia	Hononol Lavavoth Zarzilg	9996 3620 4230 (=17846)
10. Zax	Table 29	28. Lexarph 29. Comanan 30. Tabitom	Caspis Germania Trenam	Zinggen Alpudus Zarzilg	8880 1230 1617 (=11727)
11. Ich	Table 30	31. Molpand 32. Usnarda 33. Ponodol	Bithynia Gracia Lacia	Lavavoth Zurchol Hononol	3472 7236 5234 (=15942)
12. Loe	Table 31	34. Tapamal 35. Gedoons 36. Ambriol	Onigap India Major Orchenij	Zurchol Cadaamp Ziracah	2658 7772 3391 (=13821)
13. Zim	Table 32	37. Gecaond 38. Laparin 39. Docepax	Achaia Armenia Nemro-diana	Lavavoth Olpaged Alpudus	8111 3360 4233 (=15684)
14. Uta	Table 33	40. Tedoond 41. Vivipos 42. Ooanamb	Paphlo-gonia Phasiana Chaldei	Gebabal Alpudus Arfaolg	2673 9236 8230 (=20139)
15. Oxo	Table 34	43. Tahamdo 44. Nociabi 45. Tastoxo	Itergi Macedonia Garaman-nia	Zarzilg Lavavoth Arfaolg	1367 1367 1886 (=4620)
16. Lea	Table 35	46. Cucarpt 47. Lauacon 48. Sochial	Sauroma-tica Ethiopia Fiacim	Ziracah Hononol Arfaolg	9920 9230 9240 (=28390)

	LOAGAETH	PARTS OF THE EARTH	NATIONS OF MAN[151]	ZODIACAL KINGS	SERVIENT ANGELS (= TOTAL)
17. Tan	Table 36	49. Sigmorf 50. Avdropt 51. Tocarzi	Colchia Cireniaca Nasamoma	Ziracah Olpaged Zarzilg	7623 7132 2634 (=17389)
18. Zen	Table 37	52. Nabaomi 53. Zafasai 54. Yalpamb	Carthago Coxlant Adumea	Gebabal Alpudus Arfaolg	2346 7689 9276 (=19311)
19. Pop	Table 38	55. Torzoxi 56. Abriond 57. Omagrap	Parstavia Celtica Vinsan	Arfaolg Cadaamp Zinggen	6236 6732 2388 (=15356)
20. Chr	Table 39	58. Zildron 59. Parziba 60. Totocan	Tolpam Carcedoma Italia	Gebabal Hononol Alpudus	3626 7629 3634 (=14889)
21. Asp	Table 40	61. Chirzpa 62. Toantom 63. Vixpalg	Brytania Phenices Comaginen	Arfaolg Cadaamp Zurchol	5536 5635 5658 (=16829)
22. Lin	Table 41	64. Ozidaia 65. Paraoan[153] 66. Calzirg	Apulia Marmarica Concava Syria	Arfaolg Olpaged Arfaolg	2232 2326 2367 (=6925)
23. Tor	Table 42	67. Ronoomb 68. Onizimp 69. Zaxanin	Gebal Elam Adunia	Zarnaah Lavavoth Zinggen	7320 7262 7333 (=21915)
24. Nia	Table 43	70. Orcanir 71. Chialps 72. Soageel	Media Arriana Chaldea	Zarnaah Lavavoth Zinggen	8200 8360 8216 (=24796)
25. Uti	Table 44	73. Mirzind 74. Obvaors 75. Ranglam	Sercia Populi Persia Gongatha	Zarnaah Ziracah Arfaolg	5632 6333 6236 (=18201)
26. Des	Table 45	76. Pophand 77. Nigrana 78. Bazchim	Gorsin Hispania Pamphilia	Arfaolg Cadaamp Arfaolg	9232 3620 5637 (=18489)

	LOAGAETH	PARTS OF THE EARTH	NATIONS OF MAN[151]	ZODIACAL KINGS	SERVIENT ANGELS (= TOTAL)
27. Zaa	Table 46	79. Saziami 80. Mathula 81. Orpanib	Oacidi Babylon Median	Ziracah Zarnaah Gebabal	7230 7560 7263 (=22043)
28. Bag	Table 47	82. Labnixp 83. Pocisni 84. Oxlopar	Adumian Felix Arabia Metagoni-tidim	Lavavoth Zarzilg Zurchol	2630 7236 8200 (=18066)
29. Rii	Table 48	85. Vastrim 86. Odraxti 87. Gomziam	Assyria Affrica Bactriani	Hononol Zarnaah Arfaolg	9632 4236 7635 (=21503)
30. Tex	Table 49	88. Taoagla 89. Gemnimb 90. Advorpt 91. Doxinal	Asnan Phrygia Creta Mauritania	Arafolg Zarnaah Hononol Zurchol	4632 9636 7632 5632 (=27532)

The "Hidden" Part of the Earth: Laxdizi or Paraoan

As mentioned in chapter 2's section on the Parts of the Earth, there are actually ninety-two Parts of the Earth in Dee's system. However, only ninety-one of them are mentioned in the journals. Plus, of the listed ninety-one parts, one of them stands apart from the others in a manner that is not fully understood. I think there may be some overlap or even confusion between these two unique parts, and I will briefly cover them here.

Let us first consider Paraoan, the sixty-fifth Part of the Earth in the list recorded by Dee. In the next section we will see how the Great Table of the Earth was formed by compiling the names of the ninety-two parts into a large grid divided into four quadrants, or Watchtowers. There are letters from twenty-two parts contained in each quadrant, and three parts' letters are used to form a large cross in the center of the diagram, making a total of ninety-one parts. Finally, one further name is separated between all four quadrants, written with backward letters—forming a somewhat hidden ninety-second Part of the Earth. These backward letters form the name Paraoan.

In order to explain the backward letters and the separation of those letters between the Watchtowers, the angels told Dee that any nation touched by the *N* in Paraoan would "be consumed with fire and swallowed into hell, as Sodom was for wickedness. The end of all things is even at hand. And the earth must be purified and delivered to another." A few pages later, he was told, "Every letter in Paraoan is a living fire, but all of one quality and one creation. But unto *N* is delivered a viol of destruction..."[154] Apparently, Paraoan has something to do with the End Times and the Tribulation, but the angels were never specific about the subject in the journals. Therefore, for the purpose of this introductory book, I will save my theories for a later publication.

Meanwhile, you will note that Paraoan *is* included in Dee's list of the ninety-one parts. This means that one of the other parts—one of the twenty-two found in each quadrant of the Great Table—is missing from Dee's list for some unknown reason. A careful analysis of the twenty-two names in each Watchtower reveals that the name Laxdizi is missing from Dee's list (not to be confused with part number 13, Lazdixi). That means it was never associated with a specific place on the planet, nor with any nation or people, nor with one of the thirty Aethyrs.

My suspicion is that Paraoan and Laxdizi had somehow become confused with one another. Dee listed Paraoan as the sixty-fifth Part of the Earth, covering the nation of Marmarica (which existed in northern Africa, between modern Libya and Egypt)[155]—but why should Marmarica, in particular, be consumed with fire? Furthermore, the angels said that *any* nation falling within Paraoan would be subject to such catastrophe, suggesting that perhaps that part is not a fixed location at all. Therefore, could it be that Laxdizi was supposed to be the sixty-fifth Part of the Earth (Marmarica) all along, and Paraoan was supposed to be the part without a specific location or nation?

Unfortunately, this question is never answered by Dee. Therefore, I have opted to leave Paraoan in the above table as the sixty-fifth Part of the Earth, as it appears that way in Dee's journals. However, personally, I would replace Paraoan with Laxdizi in that table and reserve Paraoan itself as the true "hidden" Part of the Earth.[156]

The Parts of the Earth and the Great Table

The ninety-two names of the Parts of the Earth—with a few mysterious spelling changes[157]—can be arranged upon a large 25 × 27 grid called the Great Table of the Earth.[158] The Great Table is divided into four quarters, each containing the names of twenty-two parts. Three further parts (Lexarph, Comanan, and Tabitom, found in the tenth Aethyr) are arranged upon a central cross where the four quadrants join together. Finally, the letters of the "averse" part (Paraoan) are found dispersed in pairs throughout the four quadrants.[159]

Following is Dee's diagram of the parts arranged upon the Great Table. Each character, or sigil, below represents one seven-lettered Part of the Earth, each one beginning with a capital letter. Each quarter of the Great Table also includes a short dash, which represents the two letters of Paraoan found in that quarter:

Figure 51: *The Parts of the Earth Sigils on the Great Table. These "sigils" indicate how to arrange the names of the Parts of the Earth into the Great Table. It illustrates the thirty Aethyrs stretched out like a firmament (sky) above the face of the earth. I have made corrections to these sigils based upon Dee's personal grimoire.*

Skrying the Parts of the Earth

Dee failed to record instructions for the Parts of the Earth system, or perhaps the records have not survived. We only know that the parts are opened by reciting one of the final thirty Angelical Calls, inserting the name of the Aethyr that contains the Part(s) of the Earth you wish to view.[160] We also know that the Holy Lamen included a special skrying stone, through which Dee was to "behold (privately to thyself), the state of God's people through the whole earth."[161] Therefore, we can also assume it was intended for use with the Parts of the Earth system.

Another aspect of the system that we lack is an updated and modernized list of the nations covered by the Parts of the Earth. Dee's angels assured him this list would change over time (nations rise and fall, new lands are discovered, etc.). Because this current book is concerned with the Enochian system as Dee recorded it, I will save my work on updating the list of nations in the parts for the later advanced publication.

Fortunately, more than enough information has survived to allow us to construct what the ritual might have looked like:

What You Will Need

- Holy Table (with its seals, ensigns, and silks)
- Ring of Solomon
- Holy Lamen (along with the skrying stone that you intend to use with the lamen)
- *Book of Loagaeth*
- White robe
- For incense, use a scent sacred to the planet that rules the governing sign of the zodiac
- You will need to write a prayer to the Highest and to the zodiacal king you wish to invoke
- No talismans are associated with this system

Ritual Preparation

Again I suggest a nine-day purification including isolation, prayer, and a fasting or vegetarian diet. (If the matter is urgent, a shorter time of purification may be acceptable, even as little as twelve hours.) Prepare the ritual space with the Holy Table and implements. Recite the prayer to the Highest and to the zodiacal king at least three times each day (at morning, noon, and dusk).

I would perform the skrying on the day sacred to the planet that rules the sign of the zodiacal king (for example, the kings of Gemini or Virgo would be invoked on Wednesday), so make sure the nine days of purification end on the night before your chosen day. The next day, you may perform the ritual at any convenient time or you might perform it during the proper planetary hour. (The hour beginning at sunrise always belongs to the planet that governs the entire day. Thus, for example, Wednesday at dawn is always the day and hour of Mercury.)

The Skrying Ritual

1) On the day you have chosen to perform the ritual, and just before the chosen hour, wash thoroughly. Enter your sacred space and don your clean white robe. Put on the Ring of Solomon and place the Holy Lamen around your neck. Place the *Book of Loagaeth* on the Holy Table and open it to the leaf that represents the Aethyr containing your target Part of the Earth. Sit, or have your skryer sit, at the Holy Table while you perform the invocations.

2) Open the ritual with psalms and/or prayers that relate to your goal. Especially recite the invocations you composed to the Highest and to the zodiacal king you wish to summon.

3) Now take off the lamen and place it *face down* directly atop the Seal of the True God upon the Holy Table. Set the skrying stone upon the lamen so it rests in the circle made from the five angels' names.

4) Finally, recite the Angelical Call of the Aethyr that contains the Part(s) of the Earth you wish to view. The zodiacal king who governs the Aethyr should appear. (It is not clear if he will arrive with his servient angels.) Welcome him, then ask him questions or make your requests. Record any information, insights, or visions you obtain.

   The king should be able to grant you visions of the Part(s) of the Earth—or the people who live there—that you desire to see. You can also converse with him about the nations that reside in those parts and even make requests that involve those nations.

5) When you are finished, thank the angel. Close with psalms and prayers of thanksgiving.

Chapter Eleven

The Great Table of the Earth (Watchtowers)

"Also out of the midst (of the whirlwind) came the likeness of four living creatures...And every one had four faces, and every one had four wings... As for the likeness of their faces, they four had the face of a man, and the face of a lion, on the right side: and they four had the face of an ox on the left side; they four also had the face of an eagle." (Ezekiel 1:5–6, 10)

"The four houses are the four Angels of the Earth, which are the four Overseers, and Watch-towers, that the eternal God in His providence hath placed against the usurping blasphemy, misuse and stealth of the wicked and great enemy, the Devil." (the angel Ave, June 20, 1584)

On the following page is the Great Table of the Earth, a diagram showing the names of the angels who govern the four quarters of the world. The Great Table is divided into four quadrants called Watchtowers, each one representing one of the four world civilizations: Eastern, Western, Northern, and Southern. Thus, if one wishes to affect the Western nations (Europe, America, etc.), one must call upon the angels from the Western Watchtower. If one wishes to affect the Eastern

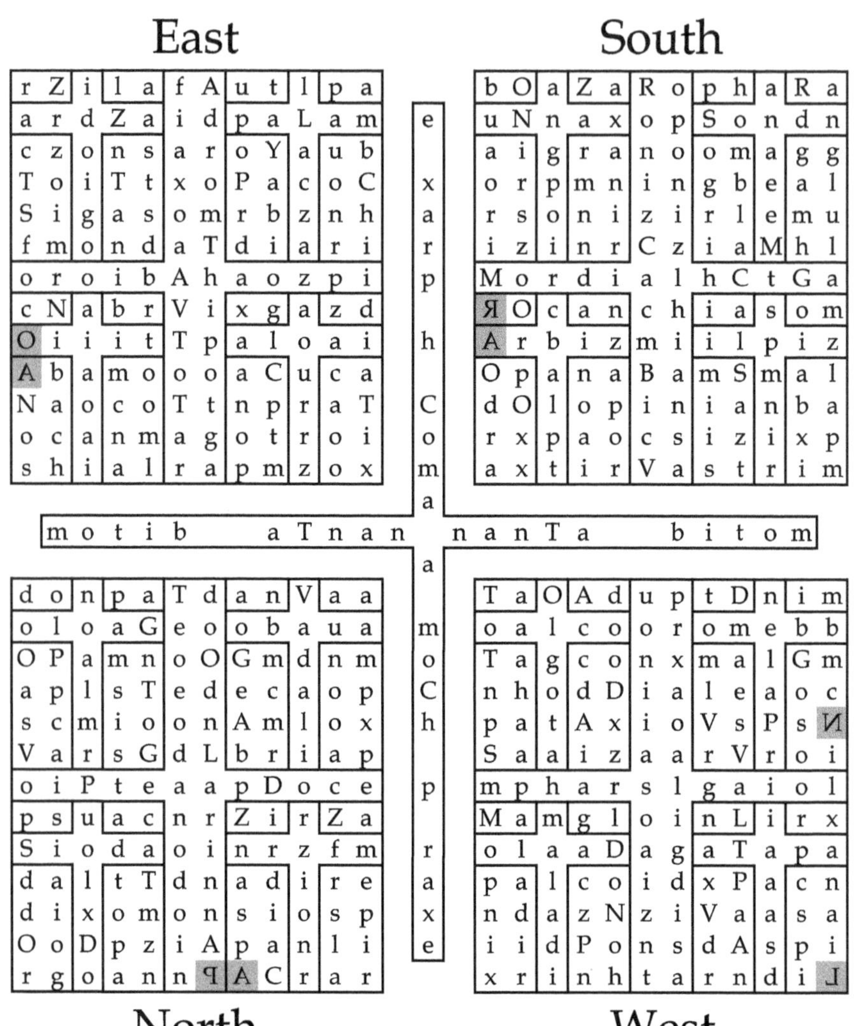

Figure 52: *The Great Table of the Earth with the Four Watchtowers Separated*

nations (East Asia, Japan, etc.), one must call upon the angels from the Eastern Watchtower, and so on.[162]

The four Watchtowers are bound together in the Great Table by a large cross, which Dee named the Black Cross or Cross of Union. Most of the letters that fall upon the Black Cross are used to generate the names of demons. However, a few of the letters are used to generate names of God that govern certain Watchtower angels.

The Four Alchemical Colors of the Watchtowers

There are also colors associated with each Watchtower. These colors were revealed to Kelley during the very first vision of the Watchtowers.[163] In that vision, the Watchtowers were not large grids filled with letters; they were actual fortified watchtowers placed in the four quarters of the world. The massive doors of the towers opened, carpets were rolled out, and the hierarchies of angels emerged in royal procession. Each carpet was given a specific color:

East: Red

South: White

West: Green

North: Black

These four colors appear in many places in esoteric literature. Three such instances may have had the most influence on Dee. One, found in the book of Revelation, is the colors of the horses of the four Horsemen of the Apocalypse.[164] Second are the colors given to the four Almadels in the *Almadel of Solomon* found in the *Lemegeton*. The third, and perhaps most important source, is alchemy—where each color represents a stage of the alchemical process.[165] As we shall soon see, the Watchtowers—and the angels that reside within them—do indeed appear to have an alchemical focus.

The Four Seals of the Watchtowers

Later, Kelley would be shown several seals, or symbols, that appeared to represent each individual Watchtower.[166] They were shown upon a clay table divided into four quadrants, representing the Great Table of the Earth itself.

Upon the upper-left corner—or the Watchtower of the East—was a capital *T* with four beams of light issuing from its top. The angel Ave explained this was one and the same with the first character in the circumference of the Seal of the True God—a capital *T* with the number 4 above it. This, it was explained, was a symbol of the cross of the Crucifixion with the INRI plaque nailed above the sacrificed Christ.[167] As it happens, INRI was later adopted as an alchemical formula: *Igne Natura Renovatur Integra,* "Through fire, nature is reborn whole." Ave referred to the four beams of light issuing from the *T* as the "four powers of God principle in earth."

Figure 53: *Seal of the Eastern Watchtower*

Upon the upper-right corner—the Watchtower of the South—was a plain cross with arms of equal length. Ave explained that this was the same cross found upon the Seal of the True God in the last place of the "table of the seven angels who stand in the presence of God." This also corresponds to the cross found in the very center of the seal, where it represents the earth. As Ave said, "The earth is the last, which is with the angels but not as the angels."

Figure 54: *Seal of the Southern Watchtower*

Next, upon the lower-right corner—representing the Watchtower of the West—appeared another equal-armed cross. This one was surrounded by letters and numbers: b, 4, b, and 6. Ave explained that this cross could be found upon the 4×8 Ensign of Creation, which happens to be the Ensign of Mercury / Wednesday.[168]

Figure 55: *Seal of the Western Watchtower*

You may have noticed that all of these symbols are crosses, fittingly representing the fact that each Watchtower is divided into four smaller quadrants, much as the Great Table itself is divided into four Watchtowers.

However, when Kelley attempted to view the final seal in the lower-left corner of the clay table—representing the Watchtower of the North—he only saw a small pinpoint of smoke, and Ave had nothing to say in explanation. Almost immediately, the entire scene was obscured by a mist and the vision was over.

It seems apparent that the seal of the Northern Watchtower was withheld from Dee and Kelley, though Dee makes no mention of the fact in his journal entry. He does appear to hint at it much later in the journals, where he mentions "4 Characters... and one of them closed" in relation to the Great Table.[169]

When he recorded the seals in his personal grimoire, he held the place of the missing fourth seal with a diagram of a little puff of smoke, leading many Enochian scholars to assume the puff of smoke was itself the fourth seal. I find that to be very unlikely. Because each of the other three seals were crosses, and each already existed somewhere else in the Enochian system (specifically upon the Seal of the True God and the Ensigns of Creation), I find it quite probable that the fourth seal should follow the same pattern. It is likely a cross, and it may very well be one of the many crosses found within the ensigns—perhaps even one of several found upon the Ensign of Mercury.

The Names and Offices of the Watchtower Angels

The offices of the angels in each Watchtower are the same as those in the other three. The only difference between them is the location on earth that each group of angels governs. (Choose the Watchtower that governs the world civilization you wish to influence.) Therefore, the following angelic offices apply to all four Watchtowers:

1. Human Knowledge and Counsel on any Matter.
2. Medicine.
3. Mixture of Substances.
4. Metals and Stones.
5. Transportation.
6. The Four Elements.
7. Discovery of Secrets.
8. Transformation.
9. Mechanical Crafts.

Figure 56: *The Offices of the Watchtower Angels*

Note: In Early Modern English, Dee's native language, some letters were considered interchangeable, such as U and V or X and Z. On the Great Table, I have left the letters exactly as Dee recorded them. However, in the following lists, I have modernized the use of such letters for ease of pronunciation. So you will find some cases where I have written a Z while an X appears on the Great Table, or where I have written a U in place of a V, etc.

The Twelve Names of God

> *"Behold," sayeth your God, "I am a circle on whose hands stand 12 Kingdoms."* (The Third Angelical Call)

The Great Table of the Earth is governed overall by twelve names of God, just as the physical earth is governed by the twelve signs of the zodiac.[170] You can find three of these names written upon the horizontal arm of the Great Cross in each Watchtower. Dee created a diagram of all the names written upon twelve banners, divided into four groups, with three names at each point of the compass (see figure 10).[171] The twelve names are as follows:

Table 16: *The Twelve Names of God*

	EAST	SOUTH	WEST	NORTH
1	Oro	Mor	Mph	Oip
2	Ibah	Dial	Arsl	Teaa
3	Aozpi	Hctga	Gaiol	Pdoce

Dee never recorded specific associations between these names and the signs of the zodiac. However, there is reason to suspect the names, taken in groups of three, represent the four zodiacal triplicities, which Dee illustrated in his diagram of the Holy City: Fire signs in the east, Earth signs in the south, Air signs in the west, and Water signs in the north (see figure 8).[172]

The only use for these twelve names mentioned in Dee's journals is during the lengthy Great Table rite of initiation, where all twelve names are invoked together as the ruling authority of the four Watchtowers. (The rite will be outlined later in this chapter.) However, it is reasonable to assume they should be used when working with the Watchtower angels at any time.

The Twenty-Four Elders

"And round about the throne were four and twenty seats: and upon the seats I saw four and twenty elders sitting, clothed in white raiment; and they had on their heads crowns of gold." (Revelation 4:4)

Figure 57: *The Four Great Crosses*

Notice that each Watchtower is divided into four subquadrants joined together by a large central cross. There are six names upon the arms of this large cross, for a total of twenty-four such names in the entire Great Table. These are the twenty-four elders described in the book of Revelation, as quoted above.

The office of the elders is to give knowledge and judgment in all human affairs. They will give council and advice on important situations. It seems most likely they are intended to be called in groups of six. Their names are as follows:

Table 17: The Twenty-Four Elders

	EAST	SOUTH	WEST	NORTH
1	Abioro (or Habioro)	Aidrom (or Laidrom)	Srahpm (or Lsrahpm)	Aetpio (or Aaetpio)
2	Aaoxaif	Aczinor	Saiinou	Adoeoet
3	Htmorda	Lzinopo	Laoaxrp	Alndvod [173]
4	Haozpi (or Ahaozpi)	Lhctga (or Alhctga)	Lgaiol (or Slgaiol)	Apdoce (or Aapdoce)
5	Hipotga	Lhiansa	Ligdisa	Arinnap[174]
6	Autotar	Acmbicu	Soaiznt	Anodoin

Note that two of the elders in each Watchtower have names of only six letters (such as Abioro). However, those two can be expanded to seven letters when "the wrath of God is to be increased" (such as Habioro).[175]

Call upon the elders in one of the names of God that governs their point of the compass. Each direction has two God names: one for calling peaceful elders and one for their wrathful aspect:

Table 18: *The Peaceful and Wrathful Names of God*

	EAST	SOUTH	WEST	NORTH
Peaceful:	Bataiva	Iczhhca	Raagios	Edlprna
Wrathful:	Bataivh	Iczhhcl	Raagiol	Edlprna

You will find these names of God in the center of the Great Crosses that bear the elders' names, written in the form of a spiral (or *galgal* in Hebrew). The first version of each of these names invokes the elders in their peaceful and friendly aspect, while the second version invokes their wrathful (even tyrannical) aspect.[176] These wrathful names of God would, of course, be used with the wrathful names of the elders.

Dee never associated the elders with astrological forces; however, Qabalistic tradition has long associated them with the zodiac—two elders to each of the twelve signs.[177] Therefore, it is possible that the three pairs of elders found in each Watchtower, along with the divine name that governs them, are associated with the zodiacal triplicity of their point of the compass.[178]

The Angels (and Demons) of the Subquadrants

The large cross in the center of each Watchtower binds together four subquadrants. Each subquadrant contains the names of eight angels (and four demons) who are active in their quarter of the world and those names of God that command them. It is interesting to note that most of the angels have offices related to the practice of alchemy, such as medicine, transforming and combining natural substances, and working with metals, precious stones, and the four classical elements.

Figure 58: *Subquadrant with Calvary Cross*

You will note that each subquadrant in the Watchtowers is marked by a traditional Christian-style crucifix called a Calvary Cross.[179] Each Calvary Cross in the Great Table contains two names of God: one written downward and one written across. Beneath the arms of the cross we find the names of four angels who answer directly to the two names of God written upon it. The first divine name (written downward) will summon the angels, while the second name (written across) is used to command them.

The names of four further angels can be found above the arms of the Calvary Cross, where you can see there are four letters (not including the letter inside the cross). All four of these angels share the same four letters in their names; only the order of the letters is different in each. The first angel's name is written directly in the subquadrant. The other angels' names are found by taking the first letter of the name and moving it to the back of the name, done three times to reveal the other three angels. (It follows this pattern: ABCD, BCDA, CDAB, and DABC.) These angels are governed by a name of God formed by prefixing the corresponding letter from the Black Cross to the name of the first angel in the group (as in EABCD).

As I mentioned previously, the subquadrants also contain the names of demons, or "wicked angels." They are found with the names of the four angels beneath the arms of each Calvary Cross. Simply remove the final two letters of an angel's name, then prefix the corresponding letter from the Black Cross to form a name of three letters. Most of these demons have powers that directly oppose the angels' powers.

Dee listed the specific powers of the demons along with the (reversed) names of God that will command them, implying that they do have a role to play in the overall system. However, when Dee asked if the demons should be called during the Great Table initiation ritual, the angels replied that they were "at no time to be called." Instead, Dee was urged to use the power of the angels to banish such demons when they arise.

The Upper-Left Subquadrants

r	Z	i	l	a
a	r	d	Z	a
c	z	o	n	s
T	o	i	T	t
S	i	g	a	s
f	m	o	n	d

East

b	O	a	Z	a
u	N	n	a	x
a	i	g	r	a
o	r	p	m	n
r	s	o	n	i
i	z	i	n	r

South

d	o	n	p	a
o	l	o	a	G
O	P	a	m	n
a	p	l	s	T
s	c	m	i	o
V	a	r	s	G

North

T	a	O	A	d
o	a	l	c	o
T	a	g	c	o
n	h	o	d	D
p	a	t	A	x
S	a	a	i	z

West

Figure 59: *The Four Upper-Left Subquadrants*

The Angels of Healing and Medicine

The angels in charge of healing and the making of medicines are found beneath the Calvary Cross in each upper-left subquadrant of the Great Table. For most healing purposes, these angels will each have four-lettered names. However, if the disease is thought to be incurable, a fifth letter—taken from the Calvary Cross itself—may be included in the center of the angels' names for added power.

Their names are as follows:

Table 19: *The Angels of Healing and Medicine*

	EAST	SOUTH	WEST	NORTH
1	Czns (Czons)	Aira (Aigra)	Taco (Tagco)	Opmn (Opamn)
2	Tott (Toitt)	Ormn (Orpmn)	Nhdd (Nhodd)	Apst (Aplst)
3	Sias (Sigas)	Rsni (Rsoni)	Paax (Patax)	Scio (Scmio)
4	Fmnd (Fmond)	Iznr (Izinr)	Saiz (Saaiz)	Vasg (Varsg)

The divine names from the Calvary Crosses that govern these angels are:

	EAST	SOUTH	WEST	NORTH
Summon:	Idoigo	Angpoi	Olgota	Noalmr
Command:	Ardza	Unnax	Oalco	Oloag

Summon the angels by the first (longer) name. Command them by the second (shorter) name.

The Demons of Sickness and Disease

The demons in this subquadrant inflict disease and injury upon their victims.

Their names are as follows:

Table 20: *The Demons of Sickness and Disease*

	EAST	SOUTH	WEST	NORTH
1	Xcz	Xai	Mta	Mop
2	Ato	Aor	Onh	Oap
3	Rsi	Rrs	Cpa[180]	Csc
4	Pfm	Piz	Hsa	Hua

To summon and command these demons, you must invoke the Calvary Cross names backward:

	EAST	SOUTH	WEST	NORTH
Summon:	Ogiodi	Iopgna	Atoglo	Rmlaon
Command:	Azdra	Xannu	Oclao	Gaolo

The Angels of Conjoining Natural Substances

The mixing together of natural substances is an important part of medicine, alchemy, and science in general. The creation of medicinal elixers, perfume tinctures, witch's brews, mixed incenses, oils, etc., are all governed by these angels. Their names are found above the Calvary Cross in the upper-left subquadrant of each Watchtower.

These angels can teach you the mysteries of mixing natural substances together to create new substances. They can tell you the effects of each ingredient as well as the combined effect when they are mixed.

Their names are as follows:

Table 21: *The Angels of Conjoining Natural Substances*

	EAST	SOUTH	WEST	NORTH
1	Rzla	Boza	Taad	Dopa
2	Zlar	Ozab	Aadt	Opad
3	Larz	Zabo	Adta	Pado
4	Arzl	Aboz	Dtaa	Adop

These angels are under the command of the following names of God:

EAST	SOUTH	WEST	NORTH
Erzla	Eboza	Ataad	Adopa

There are no demons associated with the angels of natural substances.

The Upper-Right Subquadrants

u	t	l	p	a
p	a	L	a	m
o	Y	a	u	b
p	a	c	o	C
r	b	z	n	h
d	i	a	r	i

East

p	h	a	R	a
S	o	n	d	n
o	m	a	g	g
g	b	e	a	l
r	l	e	m	u
i	a	M	h	l

South

a	n	V	a	a
o	b	a	u	a
G	m	d	n	m
e	c	a	o	p
A	m	l	o	x
b	r	i	a	p

North

t	D	n	i	m
o	m	e	b	b
m	a	l	G	m
l	e	a	o	c
V	s	P	s	И
r	V	r	o	i

West

Figure 60: *The Four Upper-Right Subquadrants*

The Angels of Metals and Precious Stones

The angels in charge of metals and precious stones are found in the upper-right subquadrant of each Watchtower, just below the arms of the Calvary Cross. They can teach you the virtues of the seven alchemical metals (lead, tin, iron, gold, copper, mercury, and silver) as well as how to find and use them. They also teach the finding, virtues, and uses of jewels. These angels have names of four letters, though a fifth letter can be added from the Calvary Cross when the matter is urgent.

Their names are as follows:

Table 22: *The Angels of Metals and Precious Stones*

	EAST	SOUTH	WEST	NORTH
1	Oyub (Oyaub)	Omgg (Omagg)	Magm (Malgm)	Gmnm (Gmdnm)
2	Paoc (Pacoc)	Gbal (Gbeal)	Leoc (Leaoc)	Ecop (Ecaop)
3	Rbnh (Rbznh)	Rlmu (Rlemu)	Vssn (Vspsn)	Amox (Amlox)
4	Diri (Diari)	Iahl (Iamhl)	Rvoi (Rvroi)	Brap (Briap)

The divine names from the Calvary Crosses that govern these angels are:

	EAST	SOUTH	WEST	NORTH
Summon:	Llacza	Anaeem	Nelapr	Vadali
Command:	Palam	Sondn	Omebb	Obava

Summon the angels by the first (longer) name. Command them by the second (shorter) name.

The Demons of Money and Greed

The demons in this subquadrant are the princes of the greedy upon the earth. They have the power to bring coined money. (Their opposing angels bring raw metals, but not coined.)

The demons' names are as follows:

Table 23: *The Demons of Money and Greed*

	EAST	SOUTH	WEST	NORTH
1	Xoy	Xom	Mma	Mgm
2	Apa	Agb	Ole	Oec
3	Rrb	Rrl	Cvs	Cam
4	Pdi	Pia	Hru	Hbr

To summon and command these demons, you must invoke the Calvary Cross names backward:

	EAST	SOUTH	WEST	NORTH
Summon:	Azcall	Meeana	Rpalen	Iladav
Command:	Malap	Ndnos	Bbemo	Avabo

The Angels of Transportation

These angels can cause anyone or anything to be moved from one location to another. This likely means they can protect travelers as well. Their names are found above the Calvary Cross in the upper-right sub-quadrant of each Watchtower.

Their names are as follows:

Table 24: *The Angels of Transportation*

	EAST	SOUTH	WEST	NORTH
1	Utpa	Phra	Tdim	Anaa
2	Tpav	Hrap	Dimt	Naaa
3	Paut	Raph	Imtd	Aaan
4	Autp	Aphr	Mtdi	Aana

These angels are under the command of the following names of God:

EAST	SOUTH	WEST	NORTH
Eutpa	Ephra	Atdim	Aanaa

There are no demons associated with the angels of transportation.

The Lower-Right Subquadrants

x	g	a	z	d
a	l	o	a	i
a	C	u	c	a
n	p	r	a	T
o	t	r	o	i
p	m	z	o	x

East

i	a	s	o	m
i	l	p	i	z
m	S	m	a	l
i	a	n	b	a
i	z	i	x	p
s	t	r	i	m

South

Z	i	r	Z	a
n	r	z	f	m
a	d	i	r	e
s	i	o	s	p
p	a	n	l	i
A	C	r	a	r

North

n	L	i	r	x
a	T	a	p	a
x	P	a	c	n
V	a	a	s	a
d	A	s	p	i
r	n	d	i	J

West

Figure 61: *The Four Lower-Right Subquadrants*

The Angels of the Four Elements (Air, Water, Earth, Fire)

These angels' names appear beneath the arms of the Calvary Crosses in the lower-right subquadrants of the Watchtowers. They are the angels of the four philosophical elements of alchemy: Air (or heat and moisture), Water (or cold and moisture), Earth (or cold and dryness), and Fire (or heat and dryness). They know the qualities and uses of the four elements in alchemy or magick. Note that these are the only elemental angels found in the entire Great Table.

Their names usually have four letters each, but if the matter is urgent a letter may be taken from the Calvary Cross and placed into the center of the name for added power. Their names are as follows:

Table 25: *The Angels of the Four Elements*

	EAST	SOUTH	WEST	NORTH
Air:	Acca (Acuca)	Msal (Msmal)	Xpcn (Xpacn)[181]	Adre (Adire)
Water:	Npat (Nprat)	Iaba (Ianba)	Vasa (Vaasa)	Sisp (Siosp)
Earth:	Otoi (Otroi)	Izxp (Izixp)	Dapi (Daspi)	Pali (Panli)
Fire:	Pmox (Pmzox)	Stim (Strim)	Rnil (Rndil)	Acar (Acrar)

The divine names from the Calvary Cross that govern these angels are:

	EAST	SOUTH	WEST	NORTH
Summon:	Aourrz	Spmnir	Iaaasd	Rzionr
Command:	Aloai	Ilpiz	Atapa	Nrzfm

Summon the angels by the first (longer) name. Command them by the second (shorter) name.

The Demons of the Four Elements

The demons in this subquadrant were never directly mentioned in Dee's journals. However, they should represent the destructive aspects of the elements. House fires, floods, storms, and earthquakes are just some of the negative forces embodied by these demons.

Their names are as follows:

Table 26: *The Demons of the Four Elements*

	EAST	SOUTH	WEST	NORTH
Air:	Cac	Cms	Rxp	Rad
Water:	Onp	Oia	Ava	Asi
Earth:	Mot	Miz	Xda	Xpa
Fire:	Apm	Ast	Ern	Eac

To summon and command these demons, you must invoke the Calvary Cross names backward:

	EAST	SOUTH	WEST	NORTH
Summon:	Zrruoa	Rinmps	Dsaaai	Rnoizr
Command:	Iaola	Zipli	Apata	Mfzrn

The Angels of Secrets

These angels appear above the arms of the Calvary Crosses in the lower-right subquadrants of the Watchtowers. They are skilled in the discovery of the secrets of any person whatsoever. They usually have names of four letters each; however, if the matter is urgent, an extra letter can be taken from the Calvary Cross and inserted into the middle of the angel's name for added power.

Their names are as follows:

Table 27: *The Angels of Secrets*

	EAST	SOUTH	WEST	NORTH
1	Xgzd	Iaom	Nlrx	Ziza
2	Gzdx	Aomi	Lrxn	Izaz
3	Zdxg	Omia	Rxnl	Zazi
4	Dxgz	Miao	Xnlr	Aziz

These angels are under the command of the following names of God:

EAST	SOUTH	WEST	NORTH
Hxgzd	Hiaom	Pnlrx	Pziza

There are no demons associated with the angels of secrets.

The Lower-Left Subquadrants

c	N	a	b	r
O	i	i	i	t
A	b	a	m	o
N	a	o	c	o
o	c	a	n	m
s	h	i	a	l

East

Я	O	c	a	n
A	r	b	i	z
O	p	a	n	a
d	O	l	o	p
r	x	p	a	o
a	x	t	i	r

South

p	s	u	a	c
S	i	o	d	a
d	a	l	t	T
d	i	x	o	m
O	o	D	p	z
r	g	o	a	n

North

M	a	m	g	l
o	l	a	a	D
p	a	l	c	o
n	d	a	z	N
i	i	d	P	o
x	r	i	n	h

West

Figure 62: *The Four Lower-Left Subquadrants*

The Angels of Transformation (of Form but Not Essence)

These angels' names appear beneath the arms of the Calvary Crosses in the lower-left subquadrants of the Watchtowers. Their exact powers are not made clear in Dee's journals. They may be in charge of the alchemical transformation of substances: changing matter from one state to another (such as solid to liquid or liquid to gas), the chemical transformation of poisonous substances into medicines, and even the transmutation of lead into gold.

On the other hand, they are said to be able to transform the form of something but not its true essence. This brings to mind shapeshifting spells found in many grimoires that often promise an illusory transformation only. These spells often involve the mage taking on the form of an animal or of another person. It could very well be that these angels are in charge of all of these things.

For most purposes, these angels each have four-lettered names. However, if the desired transformation is massive or complex, a fifth letter can be taken from the Calvary Cross and included in the center of the angel's name for added power. Their names are as follows:

Table 28: *The Angels of Transformation*

	EAST	SOUTH	WEST	NORTH
1	Abmo (Abamo)	Opna (Opana)	Paco (Palco)	Datt (Daltt)[182]
2	Naco (Naoco)	Doop (Dolop)	Ndzn (Ndazn)	Diom (Dixom)
3	Ocnm (Ocanm)	Rxao (Rxpao)	Iipo (Iidpo)	Oopz (Oodpz)
4	Shal (Shial)	Axir (Axtir)	Xrnh (Xrinh)	Rgan (Rgoan)

The divine names from the Calvary Cross that govern these angels are:

	EAST	SOUTH	WEST	NORTH
Summon:	Aiaoai	Cbalpt	Maladi	Volxdo
Command:	Oiiit	Arbiz	Olaad	Sioda

Summon the angels by the first or longer name. Command them by the second or shorter name.

The Demons of Transformation (?)

The demons in this subquadrant were never directly mentioned in Dee's journals, and it is unclear what forces they embody. Many grimoires associate shapeshifting spells directly with the powers of demons, so the same may be the case here. However, it is not clear exactly how their powers of transformation differ from those of their opposing angels.

Their names are as follows:

Table 29: *The Demons of Transformation (?)*

	EAST	SOUTH	WEST	NORTH
1	Cab	Cop	Rpa	Rda
2	Ona	Odo	And	Adi
3	Moc	Mrx	Xii	Xoo
4	Ash	Aax	Exr	Erg

To summon and command these demons, you must invoke the Calvary Cross names backward:

	EAST	SOUTH	WEST	NORTH
Summon:	Iaoaia	Tplabc	Idalam	Odxlov
Command:	Tiiio	Zibra	Daalo	Adois

The Angels of Mechanical Arts

These angels appear above the arms of the Calvary Crosses in the lower-left subquadrants of the Watchtowers. They are said to be skilled and powerful in the "mechanical arts." In Dee's time, the term "mechanical" was not a reference to machinery but to work done with the hands. Painting, sketching, sculpting, writing, construction, and even the building and repair of machines are all examples of mechanical arts.

Their names are as follows:

Table 30: *The Angels of Mechanical Arts*

	EAST	SOUTH	WEST	NORTH
1	Cnbr	Roan	Magl	Psac
2	Nbrc	Oanr	Aglm	Sacp
3	Brcn	Anro	Glma	Acps
4	Rcnb	Nroa	Lmag	Cpsa

These angels are under the command of the following names of God:

EAST	SOUTH	WEST	NORTH
Hcnbr	Hroan	Pmagl	Ppsac

There are no demons associated with the angels of the mechanical arts.

The Great Table Rite of Initiation[183]

"One book of perfect paper. One labor of a few days. The calling of them together, and the yielding of their promise, the repetition of the names of God, are sufficient." (the angel Ave)

Before you can work with any of the entities listed upon the Great Table, it is first necessary to undertake a nineteen-day ritual of initiation. This consists of calling each day upon all the names of God and the angels found in the Watchtowers and asking them to guide, teach, and protect you throughout your life. Once this is accomplished, you should have ready access to any of the angels without need of complex evocation ceremonies.

The Book of Supplication[184]

The primary tool of the Great Table initiation is the Book of Supplication. This is a book of prayer that first calls upon the twelve names of God (Oro, Ibah, Aozpi, etc.) and then upon each of the thirty-six groups of angels from the Watchtowers by the divine names that govern them. When Dee asked what form the book and its prayers should take, he was told to follow his own inspiration (for the angel Ave told him that "invocation proceedeth of the good will of man"). It was only necessary that the names of God should be invoked and the angels invited and asked for a promise to minister unto the aspirant. The prayers should come from the heart of the aspirant, rather than using prayers created by others. Nothing was said about consecrating the paper and ink used to construct the book, though it would not be harmful to do so.

Fortunately, Dee left us his own Book of Supplication contained in his personal grimoire,[185] so we can at least get an idea of what it should look like. It begins with a diagram of the Great Table, followed by the diagram of the Twelve Banners. These are followed by the invocation of the twelve names of God and invitations to the thirty-six groups of Watchtower angels.

I would like to quote one of Dee's angelic invitations here for you to see, in order to get an idea of how the prayers should be written. However, this should not be used as a "form letter" to call all of the Watchtower angels. As Dee was instructed, you must create your own versions of these invitations.

The Invitation of the Four Good Angels of Medicine in the East:

You angels of light Czns or Czons, Tott or Toitt, Sias or Sigas, Fmnd or Fmond, dwelling in the eastern part of the universe, powerful in the administering of the strong and healthy medicine of God and in the dispensing of cures. In the Name of the omnipotent, living, and true God, I, John Dee, by the grace of God of the Celestial City of Jerusalem, and through the reverence and obedience which you owe to the same, our God, and through these His divine and mystical names IDOIGO and ARDZA, I vehemently and faithfully require of you, one and all, to come before me, I beseech you, at whatever moment of time I wish for the duration of my natural life. I summon you by the names of God, IDOIGO and ARDZA, to perform, to accomplish, and to complete all my requests, abundantly, excellently, thoroughly, pleasantly, plentifully, and perfectly, in any and all things, through every possible medicine and through the peculiar strength and power of your office and ministry. Through the Sacrosanct Names of God IDOIGO and ARDZA. Amen.+

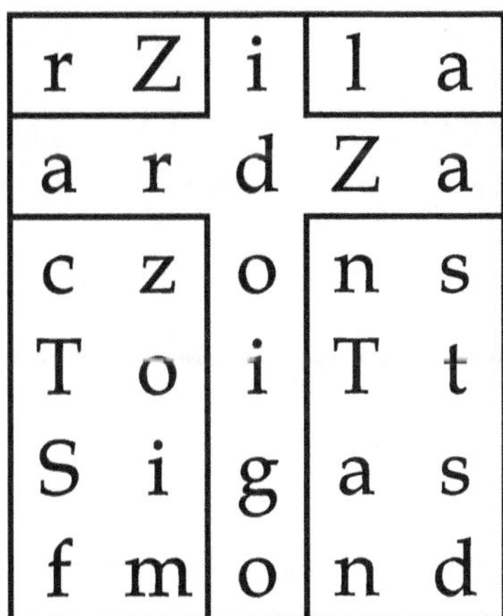

Figure 63: *Eastern Subquadrant of Medicine*

Notice that Dee covered some specific ground in his prayer, which you will also want to cover in your own. First, he called upon the angels by their regular names and their alternates. He described their office. He used both names of God in this case (though after the initiation is complete, only the first name would be used to call; the second would be used to command them). He asked that they appear to him and complete his requests at any time he calls them throughout his entire life. (He made no mention of the demons or the reversed names of God.)

When creating your own invitations, make sure to cover these points along with anything else you are inspired to mention. Also avoid making them too long or elaborate, as you will be reciting all thirty-six of these invocations nearly every day of the rite. (Dee's angels told him each prayer need only be "a short and brief speech.") You will need to write prayers for the following into your own Book of Supplication:

0) **The Fundamental Obeisance to God:** Invoking the twelve divine names that govern the Great Table: Oro, Ibah, Aozpi, Mor, Dial, Hctga, Oip, Teaa, Pdoce, Mph, Arsl, Gaiol. Ask that the angels who are listed in your book be sent to you over the coming days, and that they faithfully and obediently serve you for the rest of your life. Otherwise it should cover much of the same ground as described above.

1) The Invitation of the Six Elders of the East (peaceful *and* **wrathful names)**

2) **The Invitation of the Six Elders of the South (peaceful *and* wrathful names)**

3) **The Invitation of the Six Elders of the West (peaceful *and* wrathful names)**

4) **The Invitation of the Six Elders of the North (peaceful *and* wrathful names)**

5) **The Invitation of the Four Angels of Medicine in the East**

6) The Invitation of the Four Angels of Medicine in the South

7) The Invitation of the Four Angels of Medicine in the West

8) The Invitation of the Four Angels of Medicine in the North

9) The Invitation of the Four Angels of Metals and Jewels in the East

10) The Invitation of the Four Angels of Metals and Jewels in the South

11) The Invitation of the Four Angels of Metals and Jewels in the West

12) The Invitation of the Four Angels of Metals and Jewels in the North

13) The Invitation of the Four Angels of Transformation in the East

14) The Invitation of the Four Angels of Transformation in the South

15) The Invitation of the Four Angels of Transformation in the West

16) The Invitation of the Four Angels of Transformation in the North

17) The Invitation of the Four Angels of the Four Elements in the East

18) The Invitation of the Four Angels of the Four Elements in the South

19) The Invitation of the Four Angels of the Four Elements in the West

20) The Invitation of the Four Angels of the Four Elements in the North

21) The Invitation of the Four Angels of Natural Substances in the East

22) The Invitation of the Four Angels of Natural Substances in the South

23) The Invitation of the Four Angels of Natural Substances in the West

24) The Invitation of the Four Angels of Natural Substances in the North

25) The Invitation of the Four Angels of Transformation in the East

26) The Invitation of the Four Angels of Transformation in the South

27) The Invitation of the Four Angels of Transformation in the West

28) The Invitation of the Four Angels of Transformation in the North

29) The Invitation of the Four Angels of Mechanical Arts in the East

30) The Invitation of the Four Angels of Mechanical Arts in the South

31) The Invitation of the Four Angels of Mechanical Arts in the West

32) The Invitation of the Four Angels of Mechanical Arts in the North

33) The Invitation of the Four Angels of Transformation in the East

34) The Invitation of the Four Angels of Transformation in the South

35) The Invitation of the Four Angels of Transformation in the West

36) The Invitation of the Four Angels of Transformation in the North

What You Will Need

Along with the Book of Supplication, you will need:

- the Holy Table with its ensigns, seals, and silks
- the Ring of Solomon
- the Holy Lamen

I suggest having your skrying receptacle in place upon the Holy Table, though it should not be necessary to use it until the final day of the rite.

You will also need a clean white linen robe that also only will be used on the final day of the ritual. (The robe and Book of Supplication will never be used again after the rite is complete.)

And while incense is not mentioned in Dee's journals, I would suggest using "church" incense or incense of Abramelin.

The Nineteen-Day Watchtower Initiation Ritual

Prepare the Book of Supplication as described above, then establish your sacred space as usual, along with the Enochian magickal tools and furniture. No magickal timing is suggested for this work, though dawn is always a good choice for summoning these kinds of angels.

Days 1–4:

Wash yourself thoroughly and don clean garments. (Do not wear the white linen robe yet! You can use a black robe if you wish.) Enter your sacred space and put on the ring and lamen. Face eastward, recite the Fundamental Obeisance to God you have written in your Book of Supplication, then leave the sacred space and do not disturb it again for the rest of the day.

Days 5–18:

Over the next fourteen days, repeat the procedure from the first four days: wash yourself, then don clean garments along with the ring and lamen. Facing eastward, recite the Fundamental Obeisance to God.

Then recite all thirty-six invitations to the good angels of the Watchtowers from your Book of Supplication. I suggest reading the invitations in groups of four. Begin by reading the first invitation toward the east. Then move to face the south for the second invitation, then the west for the third, and finally read the fourth invitation toward the north. This would be traditional in Renaissance angel magick but is not mentioned in Dee's journals. In practice, it will result in your making nine complete rounds of your sacred space.

Day 19:

On the final day, wash yourself and don the white linen robe. Enter your sacred space and put on the ring and lamen. Sit—or have your skryer sit—at the Holy Table before the skrying receptacle. Recite the Fundamental Obeisance to God, then call the Watchtower angels (in general) to appear and make themselves known. Spend as long as you feel necessary with the angels, and record any visions, inspiration, or instructions you receive.

After the initiation ritual is completed, put away the white linen robe and the Book of Supplication. They no longer have a part to play in the magick and are not to be used again. Dee's journals include no instructions for disposing of these items. I would not recycle them for other uses; perhaps they should be buried or burned. It may be worthwhile to ask the angels what should be done with them.

Working with the Watchtower Angels

Dee never recorded a procedure for summoning the Watchtower angels after the initiation ritual. In theory, it would not be very different from the Heptarchia evocations, except the Watchtower angels are given no seals or talismans. If any talisman were to be made and used, I suspect it would be a simple word-square made from the portion of the Watchtower in which the angel(s) are found.[186] Otherwise, one could simply lay the diagram of the complete Great Table of the Earth upon the Holy Table.

In any case, you will want to set up the Holy Table with its seals, ensigns, silks, and skrying receptacle. You will need a clean robe or garment (but not the white linen robe you used during the initiation). And, of course, you will need the Ring of Solomon and the Holy Lamen.

You will also need to write two prayers, or invocations. The first should be a prayer to the Highest, calling upon Him by several specific names: first, if you are working with the entire Great Table, you will want to invoke all twelve divine names (Oro, Ibah, Aozpi, etc.). However, if you are working with a single Watchtower, invoke only the three names that govern that Watchtower. Secondly, the prayer should also invoke the name of God that governs the angel(s) you wish to summon. (Remember, the angels found beneath the arms of the Calvary Crosses are governed by two names of God. Invoke both of those names in this prayer to the Highest.) Finally, ask that God—in those names—will send the angel(s) to you, to appear before you and accomplish your desire.

The second prayer should be an invitation to the angel(s) you wish to summon. Invoke them by the name of God that directly governs them, and state your desire clearly. (For the angels beneath the Calvary Crosses, use the longer name of God to compel them to appear, then ask that your desire be fulfilled by the shorter divine name.)

Though Dee's records make no mention of ritual preparation for this work, I suggest undertaking some period of purification before attempting to call these angels. The same nine-day preparation suggested for Gebofal would work here, or you might choose a number more appropriate for the Great Table, such as twelve days or four days. In any case, I wouldn't do less than twelve hours of purification beforehand.

Whatever you are inspired to do, make sure to include a recitation of your prayer to the Highest each day. I suggest reading while kneeling and facing east: once at dawn, twice at noon, three times in the afternoon, and four times at dusk.

At your chosen time of working, wash thoroughly and enter your sacred space. Put on the ring and lamen. If you wish, place the Great Table (or a word-square made from the proper portion of the Great Table) upon the Holy Table, just in front of the skrying receptacle. Sit—or have your skryer sit—at the Holy Table and begin to gaze into the skrying receptacle.

Begin by reciting the prayer to the Highest again. Then recite the invitation to the angel(s) you wish to summon. I would repeat this invitation up to four times or until the angel(s) appear. Once they make themselves known, you may converse with them, state your desire, and record any visions, instructions, or inspiration you receive.

Once complete, thank the angels for coming and close the ceremony with prayers of thanks.

Chapter Twelve

Neo-Enochiana

Everything up to this point has been Dee-purist Enochiana, taken directly from Dee's journals and presented in a form in which Dee himself might have practiced. Everything from this point will focus upon the neo-Enochian system, drawing from *Book H* and the *Concourse of the Forces*.

To begin with, neo-Enochian makes use of the Reformed Great Table of Raphael. This version of the Great Table does appear in Dee's journals, but it was not directly related to the rest of his magickal system. Instead, it was used to decipher an encrypted message from God (transmitted through Kelley to Dee). Because of this, various changes were made in the ordering of the Watchtowers as well as some changes to their lettering. You can see the Reformed Great Table of Raphael in figure 5. This version of the Great Table is the one found on the frontispiece of *Book H*.

It is also noteworthy that the Reformed Great Table of *Book H* does not include the mysterious Black Cross that binds together Dee's original Watchtowers in the Great Table. Instead, the three Parts of the Earth that are written upon it (Lexarph, Comanan, and Tabitom, excluding the initial *L*) are broken down into four sets of five letters:[187]

e	x	a	r	p
h	C	o	m	a
n	a	n	T	a
b	i	t	o	m

This little table does appear in Dee's journals[188] but not as part of the Great Table. Its purpose was merely to illustrate to Dee how to separate the letters of the three Parts of the Earth so they would fit properly into the Black Cross. It is never hinted that EXARP, HCOMA, NANTA, and BITOM are words in their own right. Still, the author of *Book H* decided to eliminate the Black Cross from his Great Table and replace it with the little table above, which he called the Table of Union. The methods he gave for forming names from the Watchtowers with letters from the Table of Union are largely similar to Dee's original instructions, except they have been altered or expanded. (This is why the *Book H* version of the system includes a somewhat different set of angel names than we find in Dee's personal grimoire.)

The combination of the Reformed Great Table of Raphael with the Table of Union is the very hallmark of the neo-Enochian tradition.

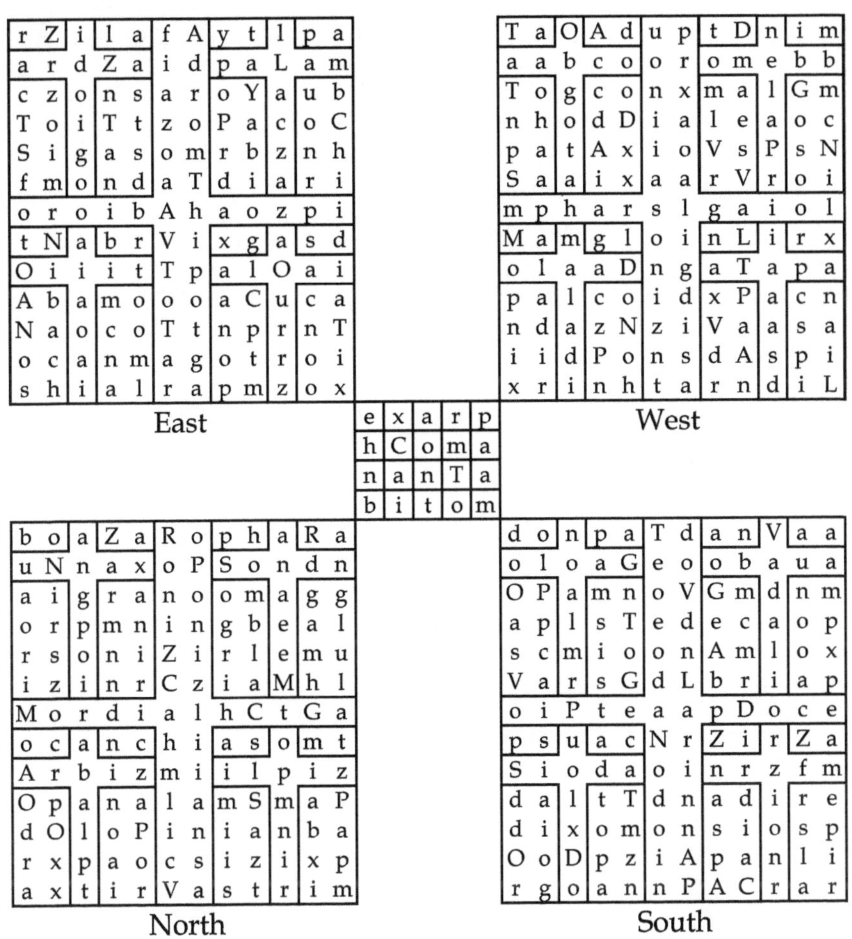

Figure 64: *The Reformed Great Table of Raphael with the Table of Union (Book H)*[189]

The Colors of the Watchtowers

The Watchtowers and Table of Union are colored according to their Golden Dawn–based elemental associations:

Table 31: *Colors of the Elements*

Spirit = white (The supplemental, or "flashing," color to white is black.)[190]
Air = yellow (The flashing color is violet.)
Water = blue (The flashing color is orange.)
Earth = black (The flashing color is white.)
Fire = red (The flashing color is green.)

The Table of Union, representing Spirit, is drawn upon a white background.

- The letters EXARP, representing Spirit of Air, are drawn in yellow.
- The letters HCOMA, representing Spirit of Water, are drawn in blue.
- The letters NANTA, representing Spirit of Earth, are drawn in black.
- The letters BITOM, representing Spirit of Fire, are drawn in red.

Spirit is also represented in each Watchtower via the five crosses (the Great Cross in the center and the four Calvary Crosses in each subquadrant). All of these have a white background, and the lettering upon them is the flashing color black.

The four subquadrants of each Watchtower are colored according to the subquadrant's element:

Figure 65: *The Four Elements in a Watchtower*

The Watchtower of the East, representing the element of Air, is drawn upon a yellow background.

- The upper-left subquadrant represents Air of Air. Because yellow letters on a yellow background would be invisible, the letters are instead drawn in the flashing color violet.
- The upper-right subquadrant represents Water of Air. Its letters are drawn in blue.
- The lower-right subquadrant represents Fire of Air. Its letters are drawn in red.
- The lower-left subquadrant represents Earth of Air. Its letters are drawn in black.

The Watchtower of the South, representing the element of Fire, is drawn upon a red background.

- The upper-left subquadrant represents Air of Fire. Its letters are drawn in yellow.
- The upper-right subquadrant represents Water of Fire. Its letters are drawn in blue.
- The lower-right subquadrant represents Fire of Fire. Its letters are drawn in the flashing color green.
- The lower-left subquadrant represents Earth of Fire. Its letters are drawn in black.

The Watchtower of the West, representing the element of Water, is drawn upon a blue background.

- The upper-left subquadrant represents Air of Water. Its letters are drawn in yellow.
- The upper-right subquadrant represents Water of Water. Its letters are drawn in the flashing color orange.
- The lower-right subquadrant represents Fire of Water. Its letters are drawn in red.
- The lower-left subquadrant represents Earth of Water. Its letters are drawn in black.

The Watchtower of the North, representing the element of Earth, is drawn upon a black background.

- The upper-left subquadrant represents Air of Earth. Its letters are drawn in yellow.
- The upper-right subquadrant represents Water of Earth. Its letters are drawn in blue.
- The lower-right subquadrant represents Fire of Earth. Its letters are drawn in red.
- The lower-left subquadrant represents Earth of Earth. Its letters are drawn in the flashing color white.

These Watchtower tablets, along with the Table of Union, can be painted and hung in their respective quarters in your temple. The Table of Union should be placed in the center of the room, upon the altar.

The Angelic Hierarchies of the Watchtowers

The Highest Spiritual Names

The highest, most divine names upon the Watchtowers are those found in the five crosses of each Watchtower—that is, the Great Cross and the Calvary Crosses found in each subquadrant.

The three names of God that govern the entire Watchtower are found upon the horizontal arm of the Great Cross in the center of each tablet:

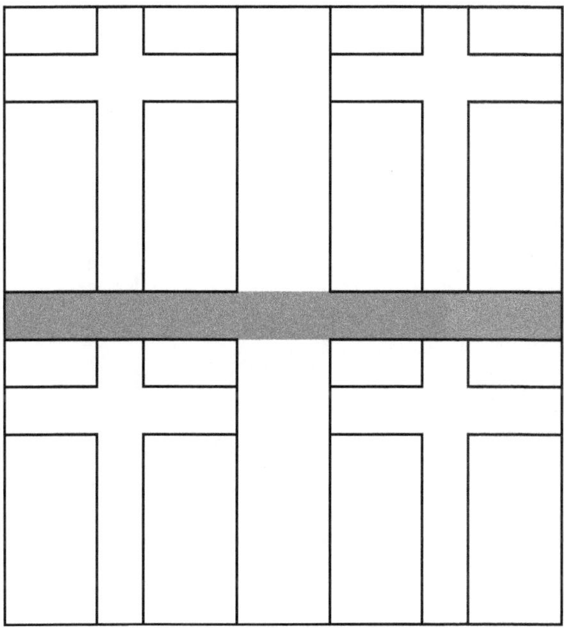

Figure 66: *The Horizontal Arm of the Great Cross (Three Names of God)*

Table 32: *The Twelve Elemental Names of God*

Eastern (Air)	Oro, Ibah, and Aozpi
Southern (Fire)	Oip, Teaa, and Pdoce
Western (Water)	Mph, Arsl, and Gaiol
Northern (Earth)	Mor, Dial, and Hctga

These names are often used to designate an entire Watchtower. For example, the Watchtower of the East might be called the "Oro Tablet" and the Watchtower of the South might be called the "Oip Tablet."

The name of the Great King of each Watchtower, representing the sun operating in its element, is found in a spiral pattern in the center of the tablet's Great Cross.

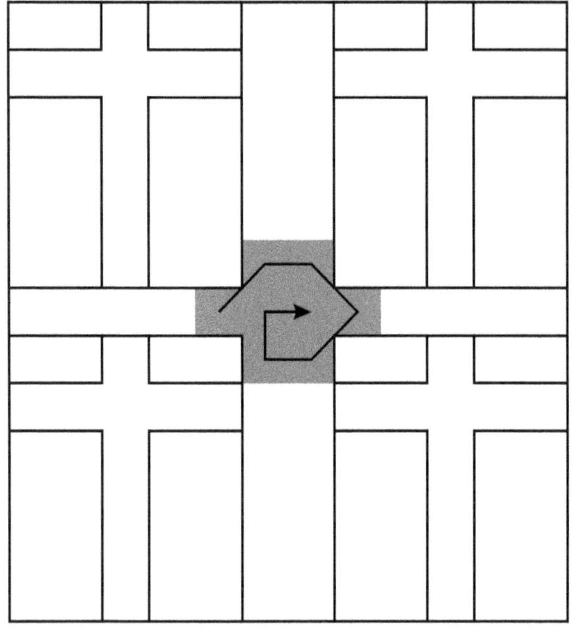

Figure 67: *The Spiral Center (Great King) of a Great Cross*

In the neo-Enochian system, this Great King is considered a solar archangel rather than a name of God.

Table 33: *The Four Solar Kings of the Elements*

Eastern	Bataivah, Sol in Air
Southern	Edlprnaa, Sol in Fire
Western	Raagiosl, Sol in Water
Northern	Iczhihal, Sol in Earth

The remaining six planets operating in each element are represented by the six seniors (or elders) of the apocalypse. Their names are found upon the four arms of the Great Cross in each tablet:

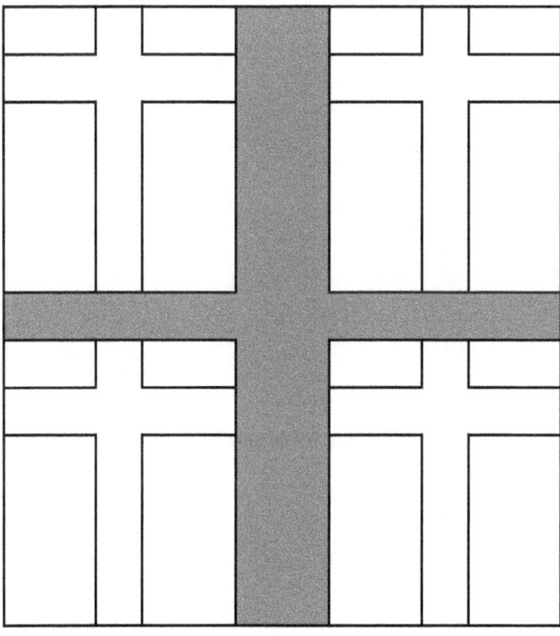

Figure 68: *The Great Cross (the Twenty-Four Elders)*

Table 34: *The Twenty-Four Planetary Elders of the Elements*

	EASTERN (AIR)	SOUTHERN (FIRE)	WESTERN (WATER)	NORTHERN (EARTH)
Mars:	Habioro	Aaetpio	Lsrahpm	Laidrom
Jupiter:	Aaozaif	Adoeoet	Saiinov	Aczinor
Luna:	Htmorda	Alndvod	Laoaxrp	Lzinopo
Venus:	Ahaozpi	Aapdoce	Slgaiol	Alhctga
Saturn:	Hipotga	Arinnap	Ligdisa	Liiansa
Mercury:	Autotar	Anodoin	Soniznt	Ahmlicu

Finally, there are two names of God found in each subquadrant of the Watchtowers. One name is used to summon of the angels of its subquadrant; the other is used when commanding those angels:

Figure 69: *The Four Calvary Crosses (Divine Names of Summoning and Command)*

Table 35: ***The Elemental Divine Names of Summoning and Command***

		EASTERN	SOUTHERN	WESTERN	NORTHERN
Air Subquads	**Summon:**	Idoigo	Noalmr	Obgota	Angpoi
	Command:	Ardza	Oloag	Aabco	Unnax
Water Subquads	**Summon:**	Llacza	Vadali	Nelapr	Anaeem
	Command:	Palam	Obaua	Omebb	Sondn
Earth Subquads	**Summon:**	Aiaoai	Uolxdo	Maladi	Abalpt
	Command:	Oiiit	Sioda	Olaad	Arbiz
Fire Subquads	**Summon:**	Aourrz	Rzionr	Iaaasd	Opmnir
	Command:	Aloai	Nrzfm	Atapa	Ilpiz

An example: if one wishes to work magick concerning storms, it would be best to call upon the angels in the watery subquadrant of the Eastern Watchtower—the angels of Water of Air. Thus, you would summon those angels in the name of God Llacza and command them in the name Palam.

On the other hand, if you wished to work magick concerning the passions of love or war, you might choose the angels of the fiery subquadrant of the Western Watchtower—the angels of Fire (passion) of Water (emotions). Summon them in the name of God Iaaasd and command them in the name Atapa.

The Angels and Spirits of the Subquadrants

The keys to the Golden Dawn's method of drawing names from the Watchtowers' subquadrants are the letters of the Table of Union and the five elements attributed to them:

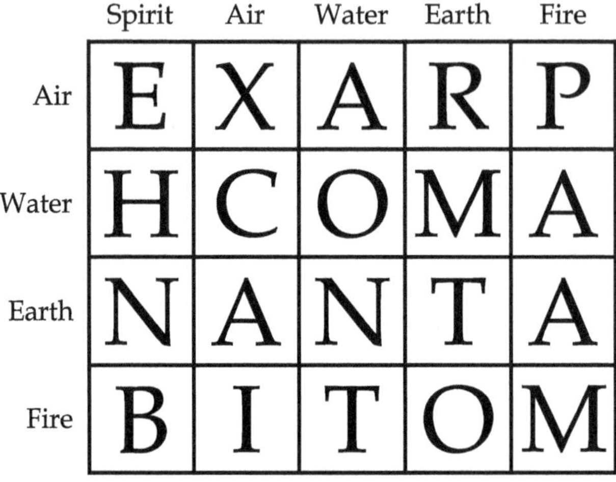

	Spirit	Air	Water	Earth	Fire
Air	E	X	A	R	P
Water	H	C	O	M	A
Earth	N	A	N	T	A
Fire	B	I	T	O	M

Figure 70: *The Elements on the Table of Union*

There are four letters above the arms of the Calvary Cross in each subquadrant of each Watchtower. These letters form the names of four kherubic angels who govern the subquadrant. The same four letters are used in the name of each kherub, simply anagramming the letters to form the different names.

Each kherub answers to an archangel whose name is the same as the kherub's, with one letter from the Table of Union prefixed to it. This letter from the Table of Union will always be the first of the letters associated with the Watchtower, which represents the Spirit of the Watchtower's element; thus, E (from EXARP) for all kherubic archangels in the Eastern Watchtower, H (from HCOMA) for the kherubic archangels of the Western Watchtower, N (from NANTA) for the kherubic archangels of the Northern Watchtower, and B (from BITOM) for the kherubic archangels of the Southern Watchtower:

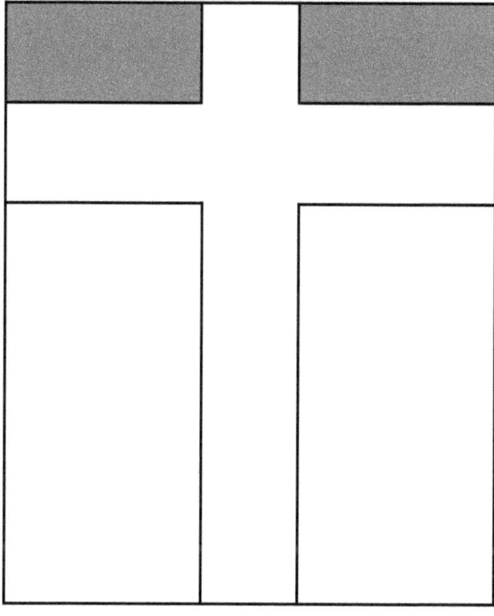

Figure 71: *Subquadrant Kherubic Squares*

Table 36: *Air Subquadrant Kherubs*

	E. (AIR OF AIR) ARCHANGEL/ KHERUB	S. (AIR OF FIRE) ARCHANGEL/ KHERUB	W. (AIR OF WATER) ARCHANGEL/ KHERUB	N. (AIR OF EARTH) ARCHANGEL/ KHERUB
1	Erzla/Rzla	Bdopa/Dopa	Htaad/Taad	Nboza/Boza
2	Ezlar/Zlar	Bopad/Opad	Haadt/Aadt	Nozab/Ozab
3	Elarz/Larz	Bpado/Pado	Hadta/Adta	Nzabo/Zabo
4	Earzl/Arzl	Badop/Adop	Hdtaa/Dtaa	Naboz/Aboz

Table 37: *Water Subquadrant Kherubs*

	E. (WATER OF AIR) ARCHANGEL/ KHERUB	S. (WATER OF FIRE) ARCHANGEL/ KHERUB	W. (WATER OF WATER) ARCHANGEL/ KHERUB	N. (WATER OF EARTH) ARCHANGEL/ KHERUB
1	Eytpa/Ytpa	Banaa/Anaa	Htdim/Tdim	Nphra/Phra
2	Etpay/Tpay	Bnaaa/Naaa	Hdimt/Dimt	Nhrap/Hrap
3	Epayt/Payt	Baaan/Aaan	Himtd/Imtd	Nraph/Raph
4	Eaytp/Aytp	Baana/Aana	Hmtdi/Mtdi	Naphr/Aphr

Table 38: *Earth Subquadrant Kherubs*

	E. (EARTH OF AIR) ARCHANGEL/ KHERUB	S. (EARTH OF FIRE) ARCHANGEL/ KHERUB	W. (EARTH OF WATER) ARCHANGEL/ KHERUB	N. (EARTH OF EARTH) ARCHANGEL/ KHERUB
1	Etnbr/Tnbr	Bpsac/Psac	Hmagl/Magl	Nocnc/Ocnc
2	Enbrt/Nbrt	Bsacp/Sacp	Haglm/Aglm	Ncnco/Cnco
3	Ebrtn/Brtn	Bacps/Acps	Hglma/Glma	Nncoc/Ncoc
4	Ertnb/Rtnb	Bcpsa/Cpsa	Hlmag/Lmag	Ncocn/Cocn

Table 39: *Fire Subquadrant Kherubs*

	E. (FIRE OF AIR) ARCHANGEL/ KHERUB	S. (FIRE OF FIRE) ARCHANGEL/ KHERUB	W. (FIRE OF WATER) ARCHANGEL/ KHERUB	N. (FIRE OF EARTH) ARCHANGEL/ KHERUB
1	Exgsd/Xgsd	Bziza/Ziza	Hnlrx/Nlrx	Nasmt/Asmt
2	Egsdx/Gsdx	Bizaz/Izaz	Hlrxn/Lrxn	Nsmta/Smta
3	Esdxg/Sdxg	Bzazi/Zazi	Hrxnl/Rxnl	Nmtas/Mtas
4	Edxgs/Dxgs	Baziz/Aziz	Hxnlr/Xnlr	Ntasm/Tasm

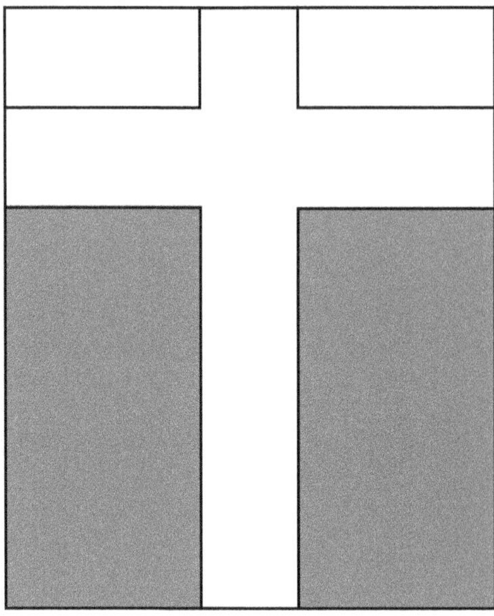

Figure 72: *Subquadrant Servient Squares*

Beneath the arms of every Calvary Cross are four groups of letters. By anagramming the four letters in each group, as we did for the kherubs above, we find the names of sixteen angels in each subquadrant. These are servient angels of the elements, who work closest to the physical world.

Every servient angel answers to an archangel, just as the kherubs did above. To form the names of these archangels, you must use the letters from the Table of Union that are associated with the entire Watchtower. Prefix the specific letter that represents the subquadrant's element to the name of the servient angel.

For example, the letters associated with the Eastern Watchtower are EXARP. The four letters associated with the subquadrants are X (Air), A (Water), R (Earth), and P (Fire). The same pattern follows for the other three groups of Table of Union letters: C, O, M, and A for the Western Watchtower; A, N, T, and A for the Northern Watchtower; and I, T, O, and M for the Southern Watchtower. The angels' names are as follows:

Table 40: *Air Subquadrant Servient Angels*

	E. (AIR OF AIR) ARCHANGEL/ ANGEL	S. (AIR OF FIRE) ARCHANGEL/ ANGEL	W. (AIR OF WATER) ARCHANGEL/ ANGEL	N. (AIR OF EARTH) ARCHANGEL/ ANGEL
1	Xczns/Czns	Iopmn/Opmn	Ctoco/Toco	Aaira/Aira
2	Xznsc/Znsc	Ipmno/Pmno	Cocot/Ocot	Airaa/Iraa
3	Xnscz/Nscz	Imnop/Mnop	Ccoto/Coto	Araai/Raai
4	Xsczn/Sczn	Inopm/Nopm	Cotoc/Otoc	Aaair/Aair
5	Xtott/Tott	Iapst/Apst	Cnhdd/Ngdd	Aormn/Ormn
6	Xottt/Ottt	Ipsta/Psta	Chddn/Hddn	Armno/Rmno
7	Xttto/Ttto	Istap/Stap	Cddnh/Ddnh	Amnor/Mnor
8	Xttot/Ttot	Itaps/Taps	Cdnhd/Dnhd	Anorm/Norm
9	Xsias/Sias	Iscio/Scio	Cpaax/Paax	Arsni/Rsni
10	Xiass/Iass	Icios/Cios	Caaxp/Aaxp	Asnir/Snir
11	Xassi/Assi	Iiosc/Iosc	Caxpa/Axpa	Anirs/Nirs
12	Xssia/Ssia	Iosci/Osci	Cxpaa/Xpaa	Airsn/Irsn
13	Xfmnd/Fmnd	Ivasg/Vasg	Csaix/Saix	Aiznr/Iznr
14	Xmndf/Mndf	Iasgv/Asgv	Xaixs/Aixs	Aznri/Znri
15	Xndfm/Ndfm	Isgva/Sgva	Cixsa/Ixsa	Anriz/Nriz
16	Xdfmn/Dfmn	Igvas/Gvas	Cxsai/Xsai	Arizn/Rizn

Table 41: *Water Subquadrant Servient Angels*

	E. (WATER OF AIR) ARCHANGEL/ ANGEL	S. (WATER OF FIRE) ARCHANGEL/ ANGEL	W. (WATER OF WATER) ARCHANGEL/ ANGEL	N. (WATER OF EARTH) ARCHANGEL/ ANGEL
1	**Aoyub/Oyub**	**Tgmnm/Gmnm**	**Omagm/Magm**	**Nomgg/Omgg**
2	Ayubo/Yubo	Tmnmg/Mnmg	Oagmm/Agmm	Nmggo/Mggo
3	Auboy/Uboy	Tnmgm/Nmgm	Ogmma/Gmma	Nggom/Ggom
4	Aboyu/Boyu	Tmgmn/Mgmn	Ommag/Mmag	Ngomg/Gomg
5	**Apaoc/Paoc**	**Tecop/Ecop**	**Oleoc/Leoc**	**Ngbal/Gbal**
6	Aaocp/Aocp	Tcope/Cope	Oeocl/Eocl	Nbalg/Balg
7	Aocpa/Ocpa	Topec/Opec	Oocle/Ocle	Nalgb/Algb
8	Acpao/Cpao	Tpeco/Peco	Ocleo/Cleo	Nlgba/Lgba
9	**Arbnh/Rbnh**	**Tamox/Amox**	**Ovssn/Vssn**	**Nrlmv/Rlmu**
10	Abnhr/Bnhr	Tmoxa/Moxa	Ossnv/Ssnv	Nlmvr/Lmur
11	Anhrb/Nhrb	Toxam/Oxam	Osnvs/Snvs	Nmvrl/Murl
12	Ahrbn/Hrbn	Txamo/Xamo	Onvss/Nvss	Nvrlm/Urlm
13	**Adiri/Diri**	**Tbrap/Brap**	**Orvoi/Rvoi**	**Niahl/Iahl**
14	Airid/Irid	Trapb/Rapb	Ovoir/Voir	Nahli/Ahli
15	Aridi/Ridi	Tapbr/Apbr	Ooirv/Oirv	Nhlia/Hlia
16	Aidir/Idir	Tpbra/Pbra	Oirvo/Irvo	Nliah/Liah

Table 42: *Earth Subquadrant Servient Angels*

	E. (EARTH OF AIR) ARCHANGEL/ ANGEL	S. (EARTH OF FIRE) ARCHANGEL/ ANGEL	W. (EARTH OF WATER) ARCHANGEL/ ANGEL	N. (EARTH OF EARTH) ARCHANGEL/ ANGEL
1	**Rabmo/Abmo**	**Odatt/Datt**	**Mpaco/Paco**	**Topna/Opna**
2	Rbmoa/Bmoa	Oattd/Attd	Macop/Acop	Tpnao/Pnao
3	Rmoab/Moab	Ottda/Ttda	Mcopa/Copa	Tnaop/Naop
4	Roabm/Oabm	Otdat/Tdat	Mopac/Opac	Taopn/Aopn
5	**Rnaco/Naco**	**Odiom/Diom**	**Mndzn/Ndzn**	**Tdoop/Doop**
6	Racon/Acon	Oiomd/Iomd	Mdznn/Dznn	Toopd/Oopd
7	Rcona/Cona	Oomdi/Omdi	Mznnd/Znnd	Topdo/Opdo
8	Ronac/Onac	Omdio/Mdio	Mnndz/Nndz	Tpdoo/Pdoo
9	**Rocnm/Ocnm**	**Ooopz/Oopz**	**Miipo/Iipo**	**Trxao/Rxao**
10	Rcnmo/Cnmo	Oopzo/Opzo	Mipol/Ipol	Txaor/Xaor
11	Rnmoc/Nmoc	Opzoo/Pzoo	Mpoli/Poli	Taorx/Aorx
12	Rmocn/Mocn	Ozoop/Zoop	Molip/Olip	Torxa/Orxa
13	**Rshal/Shal**	**Organ/Rgan**	**Mxrnh/Rnhx**	**Taxir/Axir**
14	Rhals/Hals	Oganr/Ganr	Mrnhx/Rnhx	Txira/Xira
15	Ralsh/Alsh	Oanrg/Anrg	Mnhxr/Nhxr	Tirax/Irax
16	Rlsha/Lsha	Onrga/Nrga	Mhxrn/Hxrn	Traxi/Raxi

Table 43: *Fire Subquadrant Servient Angels*

	E. (FIRE OF AIR) ARCHANGEL/ ANGEL	S. (FIRE OF FIRE) ARCHANGEL/ ANGEL	W. (FIRE OF WATER) ARCHANGEL/ ANGEL	N. (FIRE OF EARTH) ARCHANGEL/ ANGEL
1	**Pacca/Acca**	**Madre/Adre**	**Axpcn/Xpcn**	**Amsap/Msap**
2	Pccaa/Ccaa	Mdrea/Drea	Apcnx/Pcnx	Asapm/Sapm
3	Pcaac/Caac	Mread/Read	Acnxp/Cnxp	Aapms/Apms
4	Paacc/Aacc	Meadr/Eadr	Anxpc/Nxpc	Apmsa/Pmsa
5	**Pnpnt/Npnt**	**Msisp/Sisp**	**Avasa/Vasa**	**Alaba/Iaba**
6	Ppntn/Pntn	Misps/Isps	Aasav/Asav	Aabal/Abai
7	Pntnp/Ntnp	Mspsi/Spsi	Asava/Sava	Abala/Baia
8	Ptnpn/Tnpn	Mpsis/Psis	Aavas/Avas	Aalab/Aiab
9	**Potoi/Otoi**	**Mpali/Pali**	**Adapi/Dapi**	**Aizxp/Izxp**
10	Ptoio/Toio	Malip/Alip	Aapid/Apid	Azxpi/Zxpi
11	Poiot/Oiot	Mlipa/Lipa	Apida/Pida	Axpiz/Xpiz
12	Pioto/Ioto	Mipal/Ipal	Aidap/Idap	Apizx/Pizx
13	**Ppmox/Pmox**	**Macar/Acar**	**Arnix/Rnil**	**Astim/Stim**
14	Pmoxp/Moxp	Mcara/Cara	Anixr/Nilr	Atims/Tims
15	Poxpm/Oxpm	Marac/Arac	Aixrn/Ilrn	Aimst/Imst
16	Pxpmo/Xpmo	Mraca/Raca	Axrni/Lrni	Amsti/Msti

The Evil Spirits of the Watchtowers

Though they are not mentioned in the *Concourse of the Forces*, the Golden Dawn also recognized the evil spirits of the Watchtowers. However, like the rest of the Watchtower hierarchies, the Order had their own method of generating these entities' names, and they also recognized a greater number of such spirits than we see in Dee's original system.

Each spirit is formed of one-half of the name of a servient angel with the appropriate letter from the Table of Union prefixed onto it. The rule is the same as for the servient-square archangels: X, A, R, and P are used for the four subquadrants of the Eastern Watchtower; C, O, M, and A are used in the Western Watchtower; A, N, T, and A are used in the Northern Watchtower; and I, T, O, and M are used in the Southern Watchtower.

It is unclear if the spirit names were then intended to be anagrammed to form new names. If not, then there are only eight spirits in each subquadrant. If anagramming is intended, then there are sixteen evil spirits in each. To save space, I will only offer eight names for each subquadrant here; the student can easily form the remaining names by following the rules already given.

These evil spirits will each represent a force counter to the nature of the related servient angel. Thus, for example, the servient angel Adre resides in the Fire subquadrant of the Southern Watchtower, representing Fire of Fire (or pure elemental Fire). He represents all things related to passion, energy, fire, and heat. The two spirits formed from his name are Mad and Mre, both of whom represent such things as lethargy, indifference, and the dying embers of fires. As always in the neo-Enochian system, the natures of the elements and sub-elements determine the natures of the entities involved.

Table 44: *Evil Spirits of the Air Subquadrants*

	E. (AIR OF AIR)	S. (AIR OF FIRE)	W. (AIR OF WATER)	N. (AIR OF EARTH)
1/2)	Xcz/Xns	Iop/Imn	Cto/Cco	Aai/Ara
3/4)	Xto/Xtt	Iap/Ist	Cnh/Cdd	Aor/Amn
5/6)	Xsi/Xas	Isc/Iio	Cpa/Cax	Ars/Ani
7/8)	Xfm/Xnd	Iva/Isg	Csa/Cix	Aiz/Anr

Table 45: *Evil Spirits of the Water Subquadrants*

	E. (WATER OF AIR)	S. (WATER OF FIRE)	W. (WATER OF WATER)	N. (WATER OF EARTH)
1/2)	Aoy/Aub	Tgm/Tnm	Oma/Ogm	Nom/Ngg
3/4)	Apa/Aoc	Tec/Top	Ole/Ooc	Ngb/Nal
5/6)	Arb/Anh	Tam/Tox	Ovs/Osn	Nrl/Nmu
7/8)	Adi/Ari	Tbr/Tap	Orv/Ooi	Nia/Nhl

Table 46: *Evil Spirits of the Earth Subquadrants*

	E. (EARTH OF AIR)	S. (EARTH OF FIRE)	W. (EARTH OF WATER)	N. (EARTH OF EARTH)
1/2)	Rab/Rmo	Oda/Ott	Mpa/Mco	Top/Tna
3/4)	Rna/Rco	Odi/Oom	Mnd/Mzn	Tdo/Top
5/6)	Roc/Rnm	Ooo/Opz	Mii/Mpo	Trx/Tao
7/8)	Rsh/Ral	Org/Oan	Mxr/Mnh	Tax/Tir

Table 47: ***Evil Spirits of the Fire Subquadrants***

	E. (FIRE OF AIR)	S. (FIRE OF FIRE)	W. (FIRE OF WATER)	N. (FIRE OF EARTH)
1/2)	Pac/Pca	Mad/Mre	Axp/Acn	Ams/Aap
3/4)	Pnp/Pnt	Msi/Msp	Ava/Asa	Aia/Aba
5/6)	Pot/Poi	Mpa/Mli	Ada/Api	Aiz/Axp
7/8)	Ppm/Pox	Mac/Mar	Arn/Ail	Ast/Aim

In order to work with the neo-Enochian angels, it is necessary to construct a truncated pyramid for the Watchtower cell in which your chosen angel resides. (I will give instructions for this later.) However, you will notice that the name of every angel (or spirit) covers more than one cell. Therefore, you will need to remember that the entity's home location is the cell that holds the first letter of his name.

For example, if you wish to work with the Fire of Earth sub-element (volcanoes, forest fires, etc.), you might choose to summon the servient angel Msap. His name is found beneath the arms of the Calvary Cross in the Fire subquadrant (lower right) of the Northern Watchtower. Though his name covers four cells, his home cell is the one containing the letter M.

Meanwhile, Msap has three brothers—Sapm, Apms, and Pmsa—whose names all cover the same four cells. The angel Sapm finds his home in the cell containing the letter S. His brother Apms is located in the cell containing the letter A. The fourth angel in this group, Pmsa, is found in the next cell holding the letter P. This rule applies to every angel or spirit in the Watchtowers.

The Tetragrammaton and the Watchtowers

In order to create any angel's pyramid, you will need to know the element of the Watchtower and the sub-element of the subquadrant, both of which are covered in the previous section. However, in order to figure out the correspondences—tarot, astrological, geomantic, and Hebrew—for a given pyramid, you will also need to know exactly how the name of God—Tetragrammaton (YHVH)—is applied to the Watchtower cells.

The Golden Dawn adepts created a complex system for assigning the four letters of the Tetragrammaton to the cells of the Watchtowers. In some cases, the letters run forward in a row and sometimes backward. Sometimes they are written downward in a column and sometimes upward. In many cases, the reasons are obvious—such as when the letter associated with the Watchtower's element is written first, followed by the rest of the letters in order. Yet, in many cases, it is unclear why they chose to write the name upward or downward, or why they chose to start each name from one corner of a subquadrant or another.

While the system itself has been outlined in detail in the *Concourse of the Forces*, the exact reasoning behind it has, to my knowledge, never been published. Therefore, rather than attempting to explain or apologize for the system, here I will simply provide an easy reference guide to finding the letter or letters of the Tetragrammaton that are applied to every cell of the Watchtowers. In the following section, I will explain how to use the elements and the letters of the Tetragrammaton to create any truncated pyramid square you might need in your magick.

The Tetragrammaton and the Elements

First, you must understand that the Golden Dawn associated the four letters of the Tetragrammaton (יהוה) to the classical elements in the following order:

Table 48: ***The Tetragrammaton and the Four Elements***

י (Y)	=	Fire (△)
ה (H)	=	Water (▽)
(V)	=	Air (🜁)
ה[191] (H)	=	Earth (♄)[192]

Naturally, these four letters are each assigned to an entire Watchtower based upon their elemental associations. Likewise, each subquadrant is assigned a letter based upon its element:

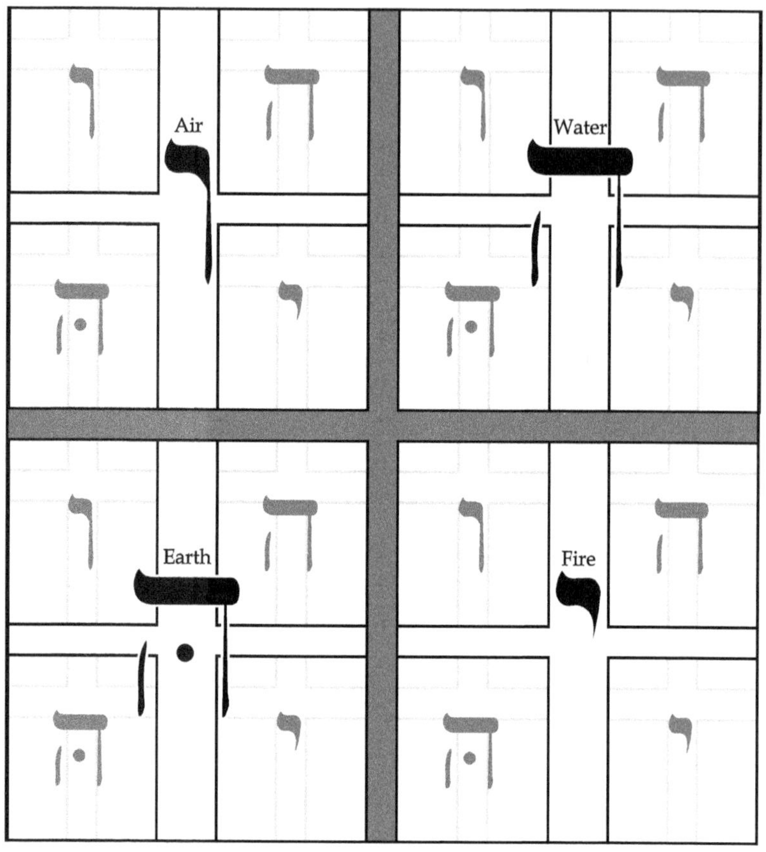

Figure 73: *The Tetragrammaton on the Great Table*

The Table of Union, as well, is given a couple layers of symbolism. The four "words"[193] EXARP, HCOMA, NANTA, and BITOM are each assigned a letter of the Tetragrammaton:

EXARP = Air/

HCOMA = Water/ה

NANTA = Earth/ה

BITOM = Fire/י

Then, each letter in each "word" is assigned to Spirit and the four elements, giving each individual letter a sub-elemental association. For example, EXARP alone represents Spirit of Air, Air of Air, Water of Air, Earth of Air, and Fire of Air, in order. This allows each "word" in the Table of Union to associate directly with the various sub-elements found in the subquadrants of the Watchtowers.

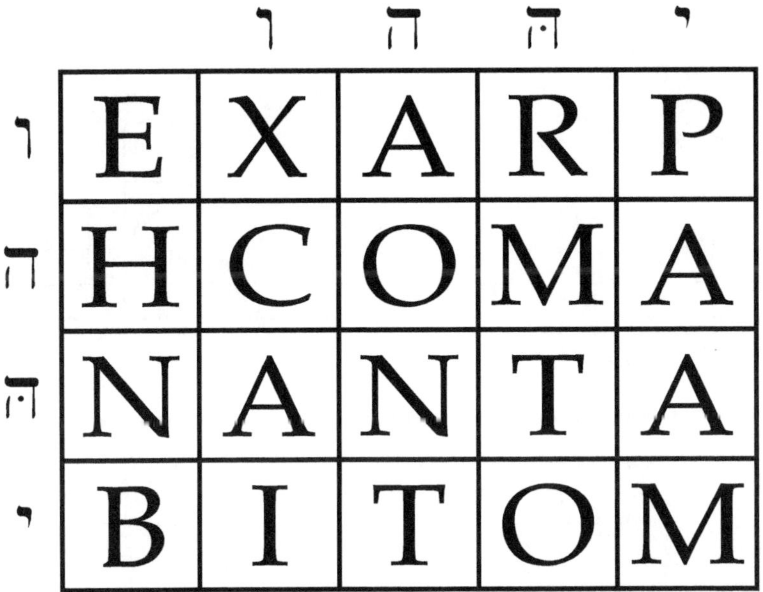

Figure 74: *The Tetragrammaton on the Table of Union*

The Tetragrammaton and the Watchtower Cells

Next, the four letters are assigned to the cells of the Great Crosses. Each letter covers three cells each. The Hebrew letter at the top and at the extreme left of each Great Cross is always the letter that rules the entire Watchtower:

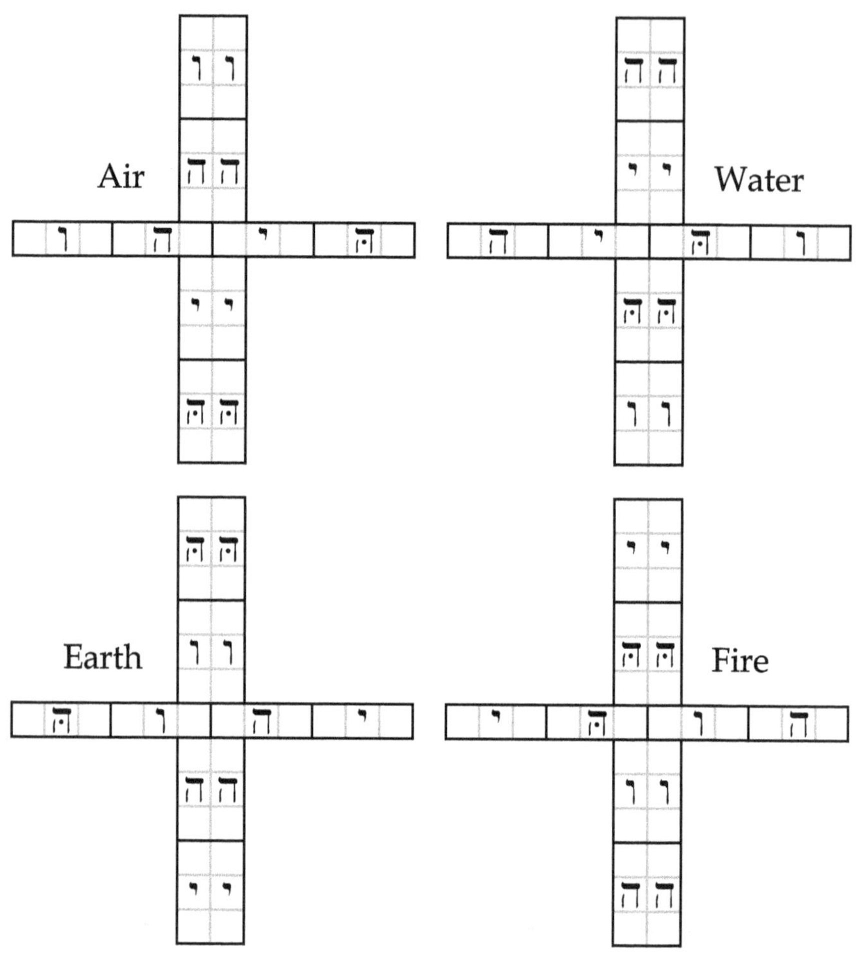

Figure 75: *The Tetragrammaton on the Great Crosses*

Then, the Tetragrammaton is assigned to the cells of the subquadrants. It begins with the four "kherubic" cells found above the arms of each Calvary Cross. The Tetragrammaton is written leftward or rightward depending on the subquadrant. (See figure 76—the horizontal arrows indicate which direction the Tetragrammaton runs in each case.)

For the servient cells beneath the arms of each Calvary Cross, the Tetragrammaton is written in the same order used for the kherubic squares above it—but written downward instead. (See figure 76—the vertical arrows indicate which direction the Tetragrammaton runs in each case.)

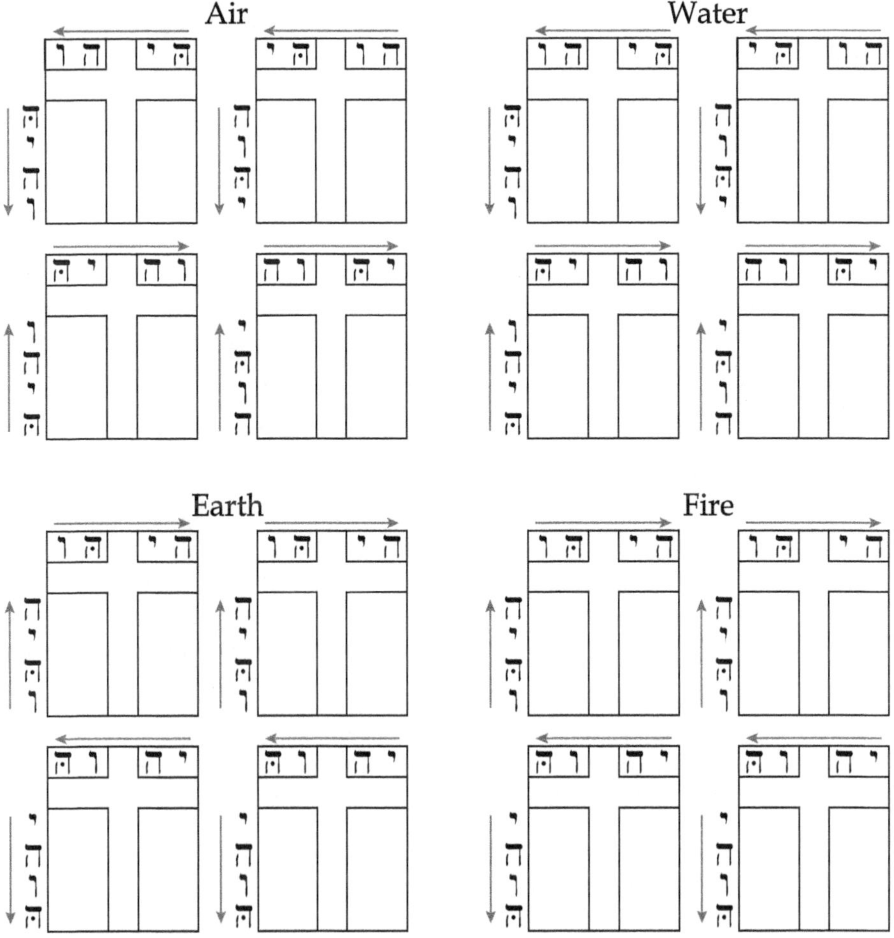

Figure 76: ***The Tetragrammaton in the Subquadrants***

The servient squares are special because they are each assigned two letters of the Tetragrammaton. The first letter is always the same as the kherubic square directly above it (at the top of the same column). The second is always from the Tetragrammaton written alongside the sub-quadrant, taking the letter from the same row, or rank. The column and rank letters assigned to each servient cell both will be used to construct that cell's pyramid.

The Tetragrammaton and Astrology in the Watchtowers

Before we can go further, you will need to understand astrological triplicities and qualities.

If you have studied astrology at all, you are likely already familiar with the triplicities. Basically, each sign of the zodiac is assigned one of the four elements. Since there are twelve signs, that means the four elements are assigned to three signs each, called the elemental triplicities. They are as follows:

Table 49: *The Four Zodiacal Triplicities*

Fire Triplicity	Aries ♈ Leo ♌ Sagittarius ♐
Water Triplicity	Cancer ♋ Scorpio ♏ Pisces ♓
Air Triplicity	Libra ♎ Aquarius ♒ Gemini ♊
Earth Triplicity	Capricorn ♑ Taurus ♉ Virgo ♍

Meanwhile, each sign of the zodiac is also assigned a quality: cardinal, fixed, or mutable. Each triplicity includes one sign of each quality. Since there are four triplicities, that give us four signs of each quality in the zodiac.

Table 50: *The Three Zodiacal Qualities*

QUALITY	FIRE	WATER	AIR	EARTH
Cardinal	Aries	Cancer	Libra	Capricorn
Fixed	Leo	Scorpio	Aquarius	Taurus
Mutable	Sagittarius	Pisces	Gemini	Virgo

Finally, the Golden Dawn also assigned the letters of the Tetragrammaton to these qualities. This should not be confused with the elemental attributions above.

י = cardinal signs

ה = fixed signs

= mutable signs

You'll notice this does not leave any signs for the final H, so that letter is simply given the four elements:

ה = Fire, Water, Air, and Earth

In the construction of the Golden Dawn's Enochian truncated pyramids, it is necessary to know the elemental attributions of the Tetragrammaton and the zodiacal triplicities as well as the Order's attribution of the Tetragrammaton to the cardinal, fixed, and mutable qualities. Plus, of course, you will need to know which letter or letters of the Tetragrammaton are assigned to each cell in the Watchtower subquadrants. Taking all of these together, we can figure out exactly which astrological force is working in any given cell.

The Astrological Forces of the Kherubic Squares

First, let's start with the four cells above the arms of each Calvary Cross, known as the kherubic squares. These squares are always assigned the four symbols of the Holy Living Beasts (also known as the kherubim) described in the first chapter of Ezekiel and the fourth chapter of the book of Revelation: the lion, the eagle, the man, and the bull. These four are given symbols taken from astrology but should not be confused with the actual signs of the zodiac:

Table 51: *The Four Kherubs of the Elements*

	BEAST	ELEMENT
י	Lion ♌	Fire
ה	Eagle	Water
	Man ♒	Air
ח	Bull ♉	Earth

If you refer to the charts I gave in the section on the Tetragrammaton and the Watchtower cells, you can easily find which letter of YHVH is assigned to any kherubic square. That letter will tell you which of the kherubic symbols should be assigned to that square. It's that easy.

The Astrological Forces of the Servient Squares

As you have seen, the four groups of cells beneath the arms of the Calvary Crosses—called the servient squares—are each assigned two letters of the Tetragrammaton. The first is assigned to the column and is taken from the kherubic square above it. The second is assigned to the row (or rank) and is taken from the letters written off to the side of the subquadrant. These two letters help us determine which sign of the zodiac will be assigned to each square.

The triplicity element attributed to each servient square is taken from the kherubic square at the top of its column. Thus, if the sign of the kherubic square is the bull, then the zodiacal signs in the entire column will be from the Earth triplicity. On the other hand, if the kherubic square were the lion, the triplicity of the column would be Fire. The same goes for eagle/Water and man/Air.

Meanwhile, the Tetragrammaton letters assigned to each rank of servient squares determine the quality of the zodiac signs. For example, if a given rank of letters is assigned to V (), to which the Golden Dawn assigned all mutable signs, then we know the four mutable signs will appear in that row. On the other hand, if the letter assigned to a rank is H (ה), to which the Golden Dawn attributed all fixed signs, we know that row of servient squares will contain the fixed signs. If the letter of the row is Y (י), to which the Golden Dawn assigned all cardinal signs, then the zodiac signs in that row will be cardinal.

Note: If the letter assigned to the row is the H-final (ה), which has no zodiacal quality, the sigils of the four elements will be placed in that row instead.

In this way, the two letters of the Tetragrammaton assigned to each servient square will tell you the triplicity and quality of the zodiac sign associated with it. If, for example, a square is assigned the fixed Fire sign, we know it is Leo, or if it is assigned the mutable Earth sign, we know it is Virgo, etc.

Putting It All Together: Working Out a Subquadrant

To illustrate this process, let us work out the zodiac for one of the subquadrants. By doing this, you will see how simple the process really is in practice. We will use the Fire subquadrant of the Eastern Watchtower as our example.

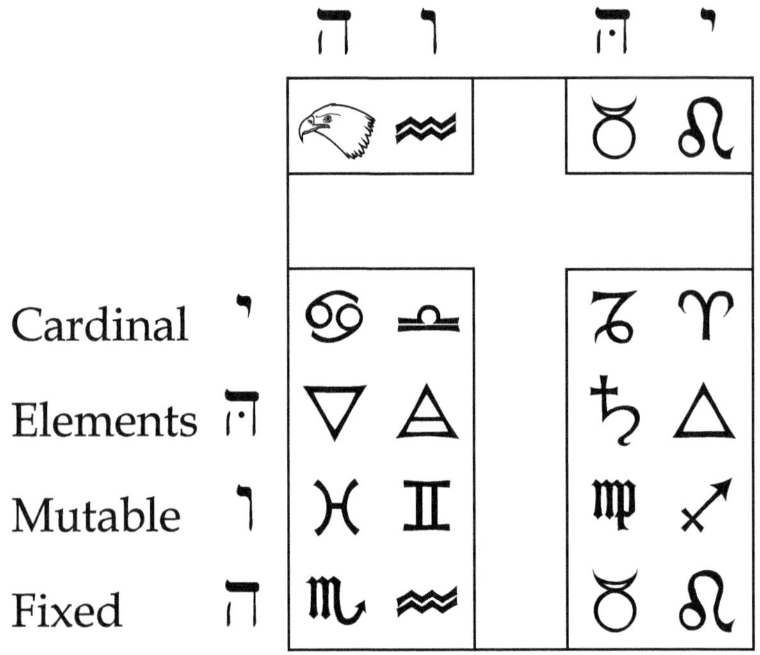

Figure 77: *The Fire of Air Subquadrant*

1) First, refer to the previously given charts for the letters of the Tetragrammaton assigned to the kherubic squares of this subquadrant. Then place the four kherubic symbols in these four cells. Going from left to right:
   - The Eagle (Water) is placed in the cell assigned to ה.
   - Aquarius the Man (Air) is placed in the cell assigned to .

- Taurus the Bull (Earth) is placed in the cell assigned to ה.
- Finally, the Lion of Leo (Fire) is placed in the cell assigned to י.

2) Now look at the first row of servient squares beneath the Calvary Cross and refer to the chart showing which letter of the Tetragrammaton is assigned to it. This row is assigned to י in this case, which means all the signs in this rank will be cardinal. From left to right:
   - The kherubic symbol at the top of the first column is the Eagle (Water), so the zodiacal sign in this cell will be cardinal Water: Cancer.
   - The kherubic symbol at the top of the second column is the Aquarian symbol of Man (Air), so the sign in this cell will be cardinal Air: Libra.
   - The kherubic symbol at the top of the third column is the Bull (Earth), so the sign of this cell is cardinal Earth: Capricorn.
   - Finally, the kherubic symbol atop the fourth column is the Lion (Fire), so the sign of this cell is cardinal Fire: Aries.

3) Moving on to the second rank of servient squares, our charts show that the letter ה is assigned to this row. There are no zodiac signs associated with this letter of the Tetragrammaton, so we simply place the symbols of the elements there instead. From left to right:
   - This first column is still the Water column, so this cell will have the symbol for Water.
   - The second column is the Air column, so this cell will have the symbol for Air.
   - The third column is the Earth column, so this cell will be Earth—for which the Golden Dawn used the symbol of Saturn.
   - The fourth column is the Fire column, so this cell will have the symbol for Fire.

4) Moving on to the third rank of servient squares, our charts show that the letter is assigned to this row, so all the signs in this row will be mutable. From left to right:
    - This first column is the Water column, so this cell will be mutable Water: Pisces.
    - The second column is the Air column, so this cell will be mutable Air: Gemini.
    - The third column is the Earth column, so this cell will be mutable Earth: Virgo.
    - The fourth column is the Fire column, so this cell will be mutable Fire: Sagittarius.

5) At last we reach the fourth and final rank of servient squares. The charts show that the letter ה is assigned to this row, so all the signs in this row will be fixed. From left to right:
    - This first column is the Water column, so this cell will be fixed Water: Scorpio.
    - The second column is the Air column, so this cell will be fixed Air: Aquarius.
    - The third column is the Earth column, so this cell will be fixed Earth: Taurus.
    - The fourth column is the Fire column, so this cell will be fixed Fire: Leo.

Now you have both the elemental and the astrological associations for every cell surrounding the Calvary Cross in the Fire subquadrant of the Eastern Watchtower. By following the instructions above and referring to the charts of the Tetragrammaton applied to the Watchtowers, you can discover these associations for any of the 320 kherubic and servient squares throughout the entire Great Table of the Earth.

One can also work out the astrological and qabalistic associations for all of the cells of the Great Crosses and the Calvary Crosses in the Watchtowers. However, they follow a different set of rules that represent an advanced practice somewhat beyond this beginner's introduction. I have chosen to focus entirely upon the kherubic and servient squares of the subquadrants, as those are the ones you will most likely employ for any practical magickal purpose. If you wish to study the advanced Watchtower mysteries, I refer you either to the *Concourse of the Forces* itself or to the more recent *Book of the Concourse of the Watchtowers* by Tabatha Cicero.

Geomancy and the Watchtowers

Geomancy means "divination by earth," and it was one of the favored methods of divination employed by the Golden Dawn. To briefly explain, it involved using a consecrated stick to poke a random number of holes in the ground (or a box of dirt) while concentrating on a question. This was called "squilling." The resulting number of dots would then be used to calculate one of sixteen geomantic figures.

In a simple reading this would be done just once, and the resulting geomantic figure would be the answer to the question. Each figure had a meaning of its own, plus it was associated with an astrological sign and element that would further illuminate the answer.

In a more complex practice the diviner would repeat the squilling process several times, and the resulting group of geomantic figures would be placed upon a zodiacal chart (according to their astrological associations). This would then be interpreted like any zodiacal chart in order to find a detailed answer to the question.[194]

When it comes to Golden Dawn neo-Enochiana, it is the astrological associations of the sixteen geomantic figures that are important. Once you know the zodiacal and elemental forces assigned to any given cell of a Watchtower, you can easily look up the associated geomantic figure[195]—which will be written upon one of the sides of that cell's truncated pyramid. Following is a chart showing the geomantic figures along with their names, meanings, and astrological associations:

Table 52: *The Geomantic Figures*

FIGURE	NAME (DEFINITION)	ASTROLOGY
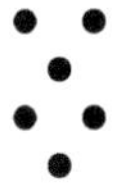 ● ● ● ● ● ●	Acquisitio (Acquisition)	Sagittarius/Jupiter
 ● ● ● ● ● ●	Amissio (Loss)	Taurus/Venus
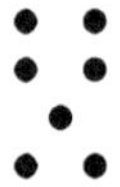 ● ● ● ● ● ● ●	Albus (White)	Gemini/Mercury
 ● ● ● ● ● ● ●	Rubeus (Red)	Scorpius/Mars
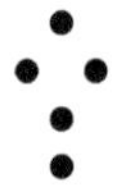 ● ● ● ● ●	Puella (Girl)	Libra/Venus
 ● ● ● ● ●	Puer (Boy)	Aries/MarsMars
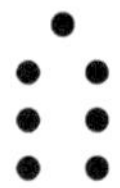 ● ● ● ● ● ● ●	Laetitia (Happiness)	Pisces/Jupiter
 ● ● ● ● ● ● ●	Tristitia (Sorrow)	Aquarius/Saturn

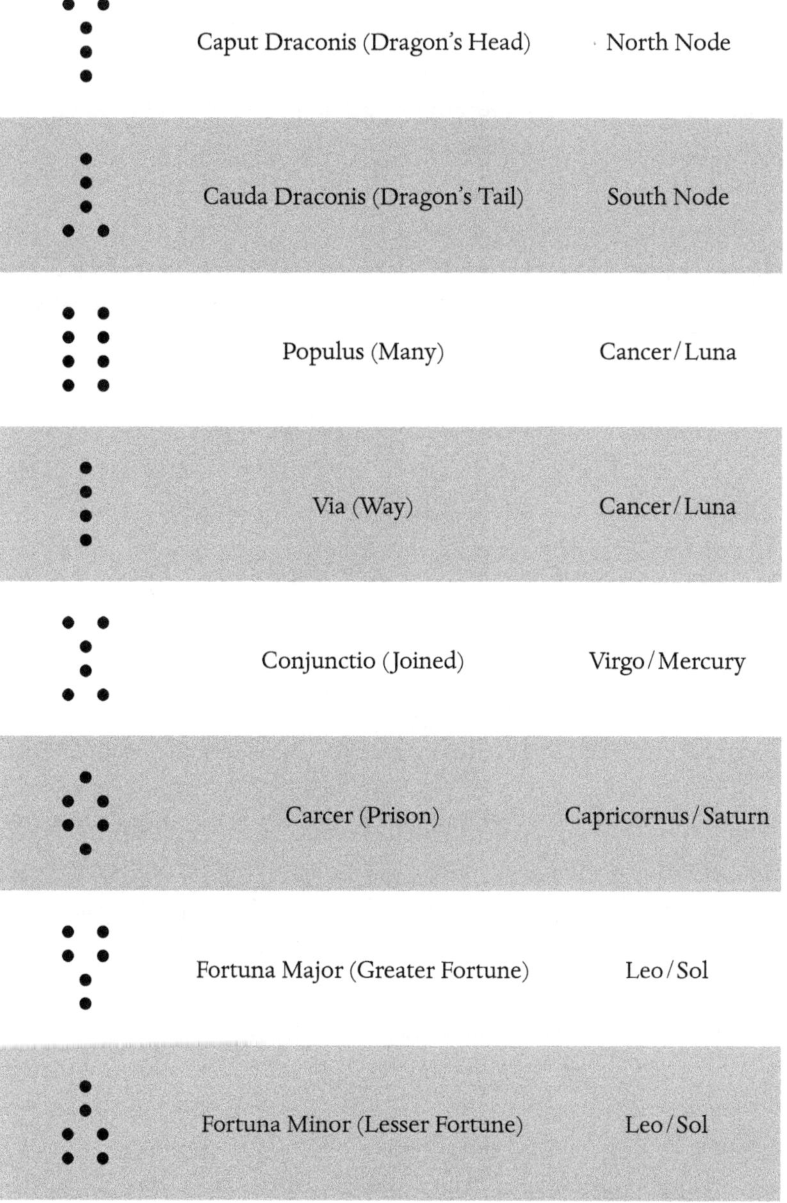

Caput Draconis (Dragon's Head)	North Node
Cauda Draconis (Dragon's Tail)	South Node
Populus (Many)	Cancer / Luna
Via (Way)	Cancer / Luna
Conjunctio (Joined)	Virgo / Mercury
Carcer (Prison)	Capricornus / Saturn
Fortuna Major (Greater Fortune)	Leo / Sol
Fortuna Minor (Lesser Fortune)	Leo / Sol

The Tarot and the Watchtowers

The Golden Dawn also assigned astrological and elemental attributes to all the cards of the tarot, a system of divination they held in even higher regard than geomancy. For example, the four suits of the Lesser Arcana were assigned to Fire (Wands), Water (Cups), Air (Swords), and Earth (Pentacles).

The cards in these suits, numbered from two to ten, were each assigned a zodiacal sign from its elemental triplicity. For example, the numbered cards of the suit of Wands represented Aries, Leo, and Sagittarius. The suit of Cups represented Cancer, Scorpio, and Pisces. The suit of Swords represented Libra, Aquarius, and Gemini. Finally, the suit of Pentacles represented Capricorn, Taurus, and Virgo.

The Major Arcana, too, was associated with the astrological forces. There are twenty-two cards in the Major Arcana, and they were assigned to the twelve signs of the zodiac, the seven planets, and three of the four elements. (Earth was excluded, but the card of Saturn doubled as the Major Arcana's Earth card.[196]) The twenty-two letters of the Hebrew alphabet were also assigned to these same cards, being assigned the same astrological forces as the tarot.

Finally, even the Lesser Arcana's court cards (King, Queen, Knight, and Knave) were assigned to the sub-elements. Thus, for example, the king of the suit of Wands represented Fire of Fire. His queen represented Water of Fire; their knight (or prince) represented Air of Fire; and the knave (or page) stood for Earth of Fire. These four royals represented the same four sub-elements in each suit.

Because of this, it is possible to assign a tarot card to almost any cell of the Watchtowers and even to the Table of Union. These, too, would be used in the formation of a truncated pyramid. Therefore, I will here provide a list of the tarot cards and which astrological force each represents. I will restrict this list, for now, to the Major Arcana and the court cards of the Lesser Arcana. The numbered cards of the Lesser Arcana, standing for the triplicities, are reserved for advanced Enochian work.

Table 53: *Hebrew Letter Correspondences*

	HEBREW LETTER	TAROT TRUMP	ASTROLOGICAL SYMBOL
1)	א	Fool	🜁
2)	ב	Magician	☿
3)	ג	High Priestess	☽
4)	ד	Empress	♀
5)	ה	Emperor	♈
6)		Hierophant	♉
7)	ז	Lovers	♊
8)	צ	Chariot	♋
9)	ת	Strength	♌
10)	י	Hermit	♍
11)	כ	Wheel of Fortune	♃
12)	ל	Justice	♎
13)	מ	Hanged Man	🜄
14)	נ	Death	♏
15)	שׁ	Temperance	♐
16)	ע	Devil	♑
17)	פ	Tower	♂
18)	ס	Star	♒
19)	ק	Moon	♓

20)	ר	Sun	☉
21)	ו	Judgment	△
22)	ת	Universe	♄

I have already explained how the Golden Dawn assigned the elements and sub-elements to the Table of Union. In the following chart, I have illustrated how the sixteen court cards (and the four aces) of the Lesser Arcana are applied to it:

Table 54: ***The Tarot and the Table of Union***

	SPIRIT	AIR	WATER	EARTH	FIRE
AIR	Ace Swords	Prince Swords	Queen Swords	Page Swords	King Swords
WATER	Ace Cups	Prince Cups	Queen Cups	Page Cups	King Cups
EARTH	Ace Pents	Prince Pents	Queen Pents	Page Pents	King Pents
FIRE	Ace Wands	Prince Wands	Queen Wands	Page Wands	King Wands

In the next chapter I will describe how to use the astrological associations for the Watchtower squares, along with the above lists and charts, to construct the truncated pyramids. I will also explain how to create some associated talismanic figures, and then I will outline how to use them together in a magickal ceremony.

The Forty-Eight Angelical Callings and the Watchtowers

In the first part of this book I explained the origin and original use for the forty-eight Angelical Callings. They were invocations intended to open the gates of, and summon angels from, the forty-eight tables of the *Book of Loagaeth*. The system given for this was called Gebofal by the angels in Dee's records.

However, the early adepts of the Golden Dawn did not know about Gebofal and made the assumption that the Callings were intended to summon angels from the four Watchtowers instead. Therefore, they created their own unique system in which the calls are associated with the Watchtowers and their subquadrants, as well as with the Table of Union. This is one of those key points of disagreement between Dee-purist and neo-Enochian practitioners, though there are those who feel the Golden Dawn's system has its merits in spite of the older association of the calls to *Loagaeth*. (The argument is that the Watchtowers are ultimately connected to *Loagaeth*, which is true, and therefore it might not be outright incorrect to use the calls in conjunction with them.)

In any case, the Golden Dawn system has been using the calls to summon its unique hierarchy of Watchtower angels for over one hundred years, and thus it has a long tradition to support it. If you choose to use neo-Enochian techniques, you will need to know which calls are used to open the various portions of the Great Table. The associations are as follows:

Call 1: Used to invoke the forces of the Table of Union as a whole. This call is always used in neo-Enochian invocations.

Call 2: Used to invoke the pure spiritual forces of the Table of Union, represented in the tablet by the first letter of each line: E, H, N, B.

Call 3: Used to invoke elemental Air. It relates to the line EXARP from the Table of Union, the Eastern Watchtower as a whole, and the Air of Air subquadrant.

Call 4: Used to invoke elemental Water. It relates to the line HCOMA from the Table of Union, the Western Watchtower as a whole, and the Water of Water subquadrant.

Call 5: Used to invoke elemental Earth. It relates to the line NANTA from the Table of Union, the Northern Watchtower as a whole, and the Earth of Earth subquadrant.

Call 6: Used to invoke elemental Fire. It relates to the line BITOM from the Table of Union, the Southern Watchtower as a whole, and the Fire of Fire subquadrant.

Call 7: Used to invoke the Water of Air subquadrant in the Eastern Watchtower.

Call 8: Used to invoke the Earth of Air subquadrant in the Eastern Watchtower.

Call 9: Used to invoke the Fire of Air subquadrant in the Eastern Watchtower.

Call 10: Used to invoke the Air of Water subquadrant in the Western Watchtower.

Call 11: Used to invoke the Earth of Water subquadrant in the Western Watchtower.

Call 12: Used to invoke the Fire of Water subquadrant in the Western Watchtower.

Call 13: Used to invoke the Air of Earth subquadrant in the Northern Watchtower.

Call 14: Used to invoke the Water of Earth subquadrant in the Northern Watchtower.

Call 15: Used to invoke the Fire of Earth subquadrant in the Northern Watchtower.

Call 16: Used to invoke the Air of Fire subquadrant in the Southern Watchtower.

Call 17: Used to invoke the Water of Fire subquadrant in the Southern Watchtower.

Call 18: Used to invoke the Earth of Fire subquadrant in the Southern Watchtower.

Calls 19–48: Used exactly as they were intended in Dee's original system: to skry the Parts of the Earth and the thirty Aethyrs. Since this aspect of the system is explained in detail in the Dee-purist section of this grimoire, I will refer the reader there for more information. The only difference is that Golden Dawn–style invocations would be used for the skrying rituals rather than for Dee's Renaissance angel magick–style of ritual. For more on the Golden Dawn's ritual methods, see chapter 13.

Chapter Thirteen

Creating a Neo-Enochian Truncated Pyramid

Choosing a Square: Define Your Magickal Goal

To use the Golden Dawn's system of neo-Enochiana for practical magickal purposes, you will first need to choose a cell from the Great Table. And to do that, you will need to define your magickal goal. Once you know what you need, determine which Watchtower and subquadrant holds the name(s) of the angel or angels you should summon. I touched on this in chapter 12. You must first decide which of the four elements governs the goal of your magick. Many books have been written about the four elements and the various aspects of life they govern, so I will be rather brief here:

Fire will govern anything involving energy, passion, dominance, victory, etc. Water governs emotions, creativity, happiness, etc. Air governs the intellect, sciences, business, travel, etc. And Earth governs the physical world, the home, family, money, etc.

You then need to refine your magickal goal according to the subelements. For instance, if you decide your magickal goal involves the

Fire of passion, you can then determine if that passion is about love (Water of Fire), science or business (Air of Fire), your home or money (Earth of Fire), etc. If no sub-element seems to quite fit, you can simply choose the pure element by using, for example, Fire of Fire.

Make sure you pick the correct sub-element. For instance, Water of Air could be invoked to bring happiness into your business or area of academic study. In nature it would represent rain, hail, clouds, and fog. On the other hand, Air of Water would be invoked to bring the power of your intellect into areas of life generally overruled by emotion; thus, it can help you make good decisions in your emotional relationships. In nature it would represent the waves that oxygenate the waters of the sea. As you can see, this is vastly different than Water of Air, so choose your sub-element carefully.

Once you have made this decision, you will know which subquadrant in which Watchtower serves your purposes. For higher spiritual purposes, you should summon one or more of the kherubs above the arms of the Calvary Cross in that subquadrant. For more practical purposes, you will want to summon one or more of the servient angels. The Watchtower cell you will choose will be the one holding the first letter of the angel's name.

In most cases, you will likely call just one of the four primary angels whose names appear beneath the arms of the Calvary Cross. It is possible to call more than one angel at a time. However, since you will likely be making just one truncated pyramid per ritual, you may want to call only the angel whose name begins with the letter on the top of that pyramid.

Constructing the Truncated Pyramid

Now let us put together your pyramid. Here is what the figure looks like when drawn in two dimensions on paper:

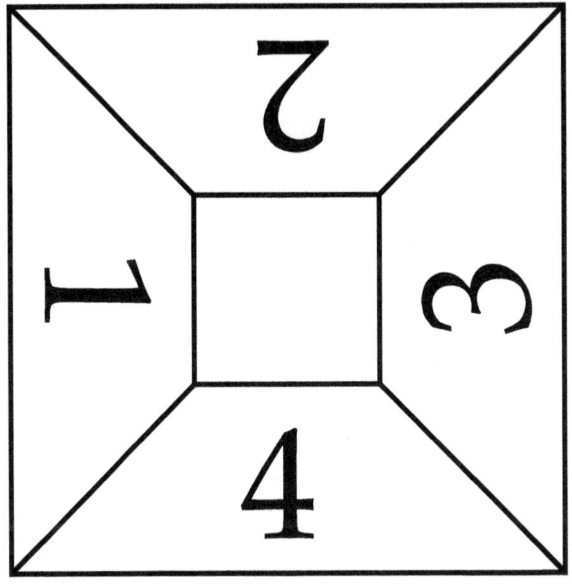

Figure 78: *A Truncated Pyramid*

This is what a truncated pyramid would look like if you were above it looking straight down onto it. The central square is the top of the pyramid, and the numbered portions are the sides. All the figures you draw or paint on the sides should be oriented with their tops pointing toward the center square. It is acceptable to create your own pyramid as such a two-dimensional figure—especially if you intend to draw it upon a talisman. However, the Golden Dawn recommended using cardboard to fashion a three-dimensional pyramid shape and painting it with the appropriate figures and colors.

Golden Dawn Enochan pyramids are very colorful objects. The colors I have already explained for each Watchtower are taken into consideration, but any individual pyramid will have more colors based on the sub-elements, tarot, astrology, and other occult forces contained in the

Watchtower cell. Note that the Golden Dawn makes use of different "color scales" in their pyramids, but I will stick to just one scale (called the Queen Scale) for this primer, which is the same one I have used throughout the book.

Here is an outline of what should appear on each portion of the pyramid:

Top

Contains the letter of the Watchtower cell, which is the first letter of the angel's name. Traditionally, the Angelical character for this letter was used rather than the English equivalent. (I am including the Angelical characters in appendix I.) The background of the top of every pyramid is white because it represents the spiritual force that governs the elemental forces of the four sides. The letter itself will be black (the flashing color to white).

The figures painted on the four sides of the pyramid will differ depending on whether it represents a kherubic angel or a servient angel:

Kherubic Pyramids

As an example, I have chosen the Fire of Air sub-element. Therefore, I will focus upon the Eastern (Air) Watchtower, Fire subquadrant (lower right). And since I wish to work with Fire of Air, I might as well choose the kherub of Fire within that subquadrant. If you look at the Eastern Watchtower in figure 76, you will find the Fire kherub in the Fire subquadrant is on the far right of its line (assigned to the letter Yod י). The letter of that cell on the Great Table is D, the first letter of the name Dxgs (see figure 64).

We already know the top of the pyramid will be white with a black letter upon it, as this is true of all pyramid squares. Now let us decorate and color the sides:

Side 1

Here you will represent a tarot court card. Its suit is determined by the subquadrant's element, and the court figure is determined by the kherub of the square.

In the case of our example, this would be the King of Wands. The subquadrant's element is Fire, which is related to the suit of Wands in the tarot. The kherub is the Fire (or Yod י) kherub, so the figure will be a king; thus we have the King of Wands. If you need a guide to this, see table 54 about the tarot and the Table of Union. Find your subquadrant's element on the left-hand side of the chart—that's the suit. Then scan across the chart to the column of your kherub's element. That will show you the proper court card to use.

The background color of this pyramid side will always be the element of the subquadrant (or tarot suit), and the lettering upon it will be in the flashing color. In our example, the background will be fire red and the symbol of the court card will be green.

Fire is always red (flashing green), Water is blue (flashing orange), Air is yellow (flashing violet), and Earth is black (flashing white).

Side 2

Here you will inscribe the symbol of the entire Watchtower's element. The background color is the color of the element, and the symbol is in the flashing color.

In our example, the Watchtower is of the East (Air), so the background will be yellow and the elemental symbol will be purple.

The Southern Watchtower is red (flashing green), the Western Watchtower is blue (flashing orange), the Eastern Watchtower is yellow (flashing violet), and the Northern Watchtower is black (flashing white).

Side 3

Here inscribe the symbol of the square's kherub. The Fire kherub takes the symbol of the lion (or Leo), the Water kherub takes the symbol of the eagle's head, the Air kherub takes the symbol of Aquarius, and the Earth kherub takes the symbol of the ox (or Taurus).

The colors of this side are always the same as the colors of side #1. The background is the color of the subquadrant, and the symbol is drawn in the flashing color.

In our example, the kherub's symbol is that of Leo, its background is red, and the symbol is green. (Note these colors would be the same even if we had focused upon one of the other kherubs. The colors here are based upon the subquadrant.)

Side 4

Finally, inscribe the elemental symbol of the subquadrant on this side. The background is the color of the element of the subquadrant, and the symbol is drawn in the flashing color.

In our example, this is the symbol of Fire and is once again a red background with a green symbol.

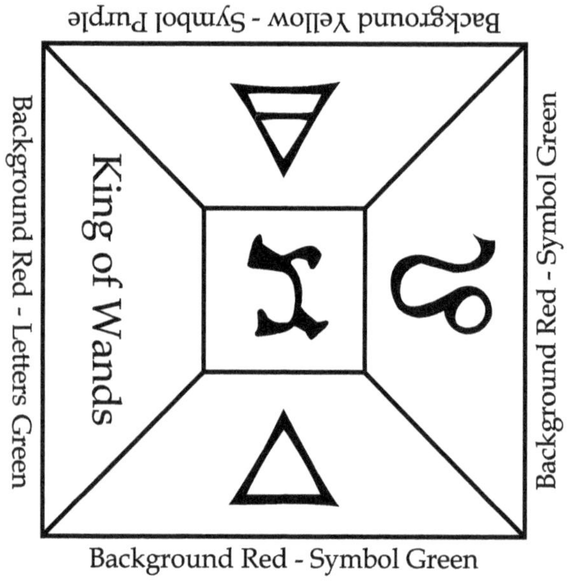

Figure 79: *Example Kherubic Pyramid (Fire of Air)*

Servient Pyramids

For an example of a servient square pyramid, we will stay in the Fire of Air subquadrant (Eastern Watchtower, lower-right subquadrant). We will move to the square of the first servient angel found beneath the arms of the Calvary Cross. Its letter is A, and it begins the name of the angel Alai.

As always, the top of the pyramid will contain the letter of the square in Angelical, which in our example is an A. Its background color is white and the letter is black.

All four sides of a servient pyramid have two symbols because each servient square of the Watchtowers is assigned two letters of the Tetragrammaton. One comes from the row the angel is found in, and the other is from the kherubic column it falls under. Refer to the Tetragrammaton in the Subquadrants chart in figure 76 to determine which two Hebrew letters govern your chosen square.

In our example, the letter of the row is Yod (י), representing cardinal zodiac signs, and the letter of the kherub at the top of the column is Heh (ה), representing the element of Water. Now let's examine the four sides.

Side 1

Here inscribe the elemental symbol of the Watchtower and the astrological symbol of the square. (Refer to chapter 12's section on the astrological forces of the servient squares.) The background color is the color of the Watchtower's element, and the symbols are in the flashing color.

In our example, we draw in the symbol of Air, as this is the Eastern (Air) Watchtower. This particular square represents cardinal Water and therefore is ruled by the zodical sign of Cancer, so we also include that symbol. The background is yellow (for Air), and the symbols are drawn in purple.

Side 2

Here inscribe the symbol of the column's kherubic element and the Major Arcana tarot card assigned to the square's astrological sign. (See chapter 12's section on tarot and the Watchtowers.) The background color is the color of the element of the kherub, and the symbols are in the flashing color.

In our example, this side would include the symbol of Water (as it is ruled by the Water kherub of this subquadrant). It would also include the Chariot, as that is the tarot trump associated with Cancer. The background of this side would be blue, and the symbols would be orange.

Side 3

Here inscribe the elemental symbol of the subquadrant and the geomantic figure assigned to the astrological sign of the square. (See chapter 12's section on geomancy and the Watchtowers.) The background color is the color of the element of the subquadrant, and the symbols are in the flashing color.

In our example, this side would contain the symbols of Fire (we are in the Fire subquadrant of the Watchtower) and at least one of the geomantic figures assigned to Cancer. The background would be red and the symbols drawn in green.

Side 4

Finally, on this side put the elemental symbol of the letter of Tetragrammaton that rules the rank (row) of the square. If the rank is ruled by Yod (י), the symbol of Fire is used. If the rank is ruled by Heh (ה), the symbol of Water will be used. If the rank is ruled by Vav (), the symbol of Air will be used. And if the rank is ruled by Heh-final (ה), the symbol of Earth will appear here.

Also on this side, include the Hebrew letter assigned to the Major Arcana tarot card of this square. (See chapter 12's section on tarot and the Watchtowers.) The background color is the color of the element of the Tetragrammaton letter, and the symbols are in the flashing color.

In our example, the elemental symbol of fire would appear here, as this row of the subquadrant is assigned to Yod (י). The Hebrew letter assigned to both Cancer and the Chariot card is Cheth (צ). The background would be red (for Fire), and the symbols would be green.

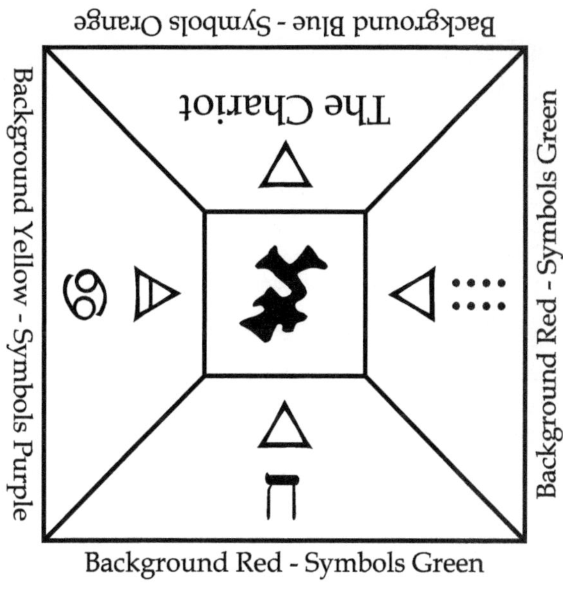

Figure 80: *Example Servient Pyramid (Fire of Air, Letter A, Cancer)*

Every Pyramid Has Its Sphinx

As I mentioned in the neo-Enochian history chapter, the *Concourse of the Forces* explains that every pyramid fashioned from the Watchtower squares also has a sphinx. This sphinx is a composite animal/human figure that represents the elemental forces of the pyramid itself. The Golden Dawn referred to this as a "talismanic image"—a visual representation of occult forces suitable for skrying or inscribing upon talismans.

An Enochian sphinx is composed of portions of the four biblical kherubim (as described in the first chapter of Ezekiel and the fourth chapter of the Revelation of St. John) who represent the four elements (see table 51).

Referring back to figure 78, where each side of a truncated pyramid was given a number:

- the side labeled 2 represents the head of the sphinx
- the sides labeled 1 and 3 represent the upper body and arms of the sphinx, as well as whether or not the sphinx will have wings
- the final side, labeled 4, will represent the lower body and legs of the sphinx

This sphinx, then, embodies the combined elemental force of its particular cell in the Watchtower.

As an example, let us continue using the same square as before (the Fire of Air square of the angel Alai). The upper side of the pyramid (side 2) is associated with elemental Water; thus the sphinx will have the head of an eagle. The two outer sides (1 and 3) are associated with Air and Fire; thus the sphinx's upper body will be a mixture of a man and a lion. (Since neither side 1 nor side 3 was Water, and thus did not include the eagle, this figure will have no wings.) Finally, side 4 was associated with Fire, so our sphinx will have the lower body and legs of a lion.

As you can imagine, there are many possible combinations, depending on where in the Watchtowers the square is found; thus, there are many different kinds of sphinxes.

The Coptic-Egyptian Gods of the Pyramids[197]

In the history section of this book, I mentioned that the symbol of the truncated pyramid is older than the Golden Dawn. You can see a version of it on the back of the American dollar bill, where it appears with the ancient Egyptian symbol of the all-seeing eye of God at its summit. This symbol—an eye in a triangle—suggests that the capstone of the world pyramid is divinity itself, not something made by human hands. The flat surface at the top of the structure is a holy place where man and God meet, and ancient civilizations often built temples upon such high places (take, for example, the ziggurats of Babylon).

The neo-Enochian truncated pyramids are no exception to this philosophy. The flat surface at the top of the pyramid is a holy place where the Angelical letter of the Watchtower square is inscribed. Furthermore, the Golden Dawn associated a Coptic-Egyptian deity with this space. As the sphinx embodies the elemental forces of the four sides of the pyramid, the deity represents the divine force that resides at its summit. In this way, the pyramid becomes a literal throne for a god of the world.

Like the sphinx, the deity of the pyramid is a talismanic image. It can be drawn or painted on paper in the proper colors and placed upon the altar during the invocation ceremony, or it can be painted upon cardboard and given a base so that it can stand directly upon the altar pyramid. Even better, it can be sculpted so that it becomes a three-dimensional statue of the god.

Following is a list of the fifteen Coptic-Egyptian deities used in the Golden Dawn's Enochian system. The god assigned to any given pyramid is determined by the combination of elements on the four sides. After you have fashioned your truncated pyramid, refer to this list to see which god it belongs to.

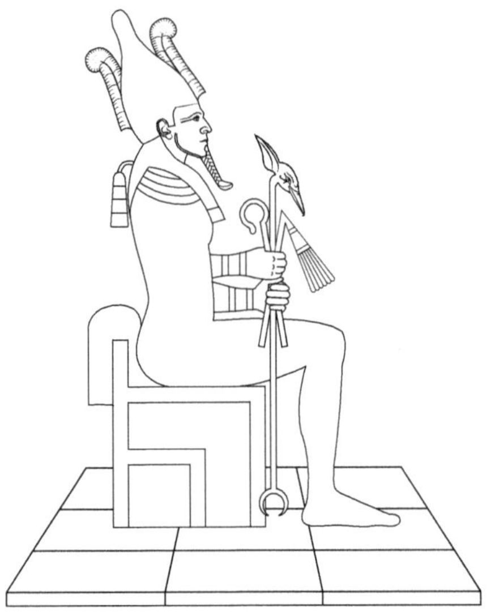

Figure 81: *Osiris*

1. **Osiris:** The first pharaoh of Egypt. After his death, he became the king of the underworld. In later Egyptian and Coptic religion he became a dying and rising solar god.

   Spirit: Each side of his pyramid has a different element—Fire, Water, Air, and Earth—showing the four elements in perfect balance under the presidency of Spirit. His image is a man mummified in white cloth sitting upon a white and yellow throne. His crown is white with yellow and white feathers, and his pectoral collar is striped white, red, blue, yellow, and black. He carries three scepters colored red, blue, and yellow. His throne is set upon a white base.

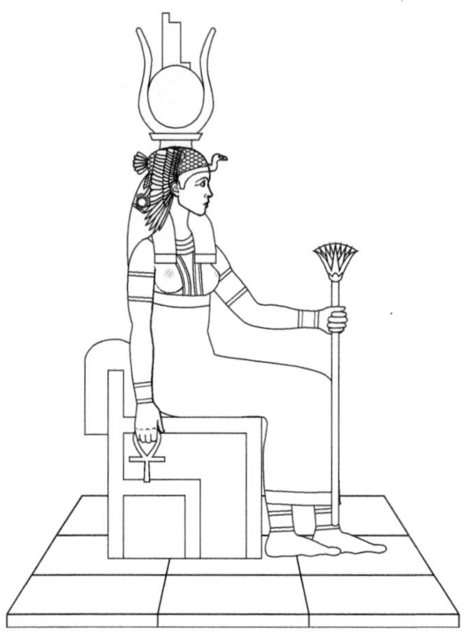

Figure 82: *Isis*

2. **Isis:** Wife of Osiris and the great Mother Goddess of Egypt. She and Osiris were the parents of Horus, the god of the living pharaoh of Egypt.

   Water: At least three out of four sides of her pyramid are Water. (The fourth side does not matter in this case.) Her image is of a woman sitting upon a blue throne and wearing a blue dress. Her pectoral collar and headdress are striped blue and orange. She carries a blue ankh and a lotus scepter. Her throne is set upon a blue and orange base.

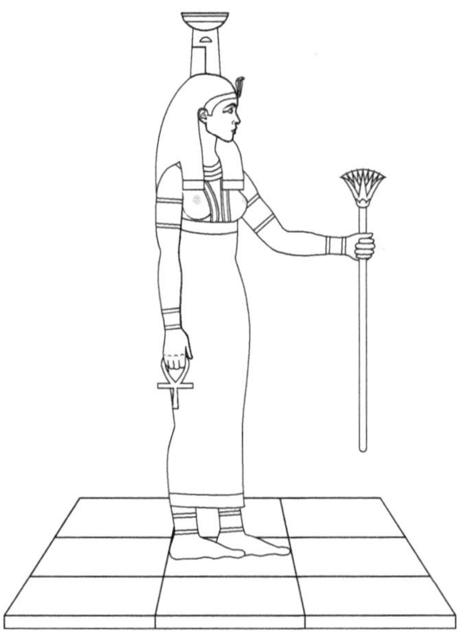

Figure 83: *Nephthys*

3. **Nephthys:** Sister of Isis and wife of Osiris's brother Set. When Osiris was murdered by Set, Nephthys aided her sister in recovering Osiris's body.

   Earth: At least three out of four sides of her pyramid are Earth. (The fourth side does not matter in this case.) Her image is of a woman wearing a black dress and headdress. She wears a pectoral collar striped black and white. She carries a black ankh and a lotus scepter, and her headdress includes a black serpent on its brow. She stands on a black and white base.

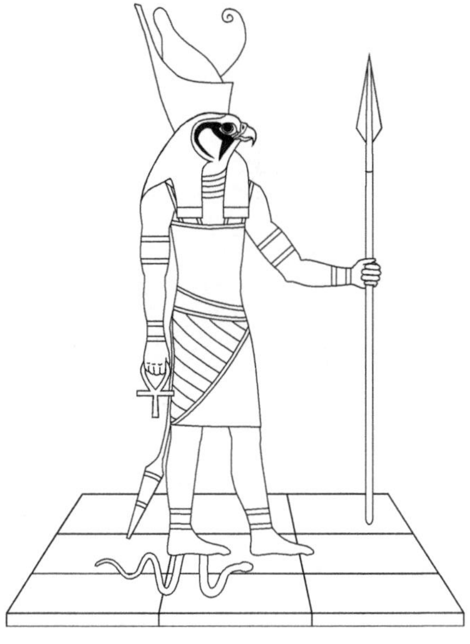

Figure 84: *Horus*

4. **Horus:** Son of Isis and Osiris, and god of the living pharaoh of Egypt. He was conceived just before Osiris entered the underworld to become king of the dead, and he eventually grew up to overthrow his uncle Set and reclaim his father's throne.

   Fire: At least three out of four sides of his pyramid are Fire. (The fourth side does not matter in this case.) His image is of a man with the head of a falcon. He wears a red and green tunic, a green pectoral collar, and a red headdress topped with the white and red double-crown of Egypt. He carries a red ankh and a scepter, and he stands upon a red and green base.

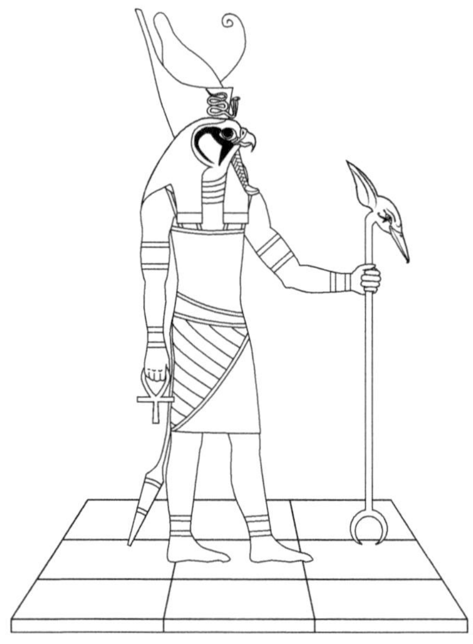

Figure 85: *Aroueris*

5. **Aroueris (Horus the Elder):** A brother of Osiris, husband of Hathor, and powerful celestial god. His right eye is the sun, and his left eye is the moon.

   Air: At least three out of four sides of his pyramid are Air. (The fourth side does not matter in this case.) His image is of a man with the head of a falcon. He wears a yellow and violet tunic, a yellow pectoral collar, and a violet headdress. He also wears the double-crown of Egypt, though his is colored yellow and violet. He carries a yellow ankh and a scepter, and he stands upon a yellow and violet base.

Figure 86: *Hathor*

6. **Athor (Hathor):** Daughter of the sun god Ra. She is the goddess of love, passion, joy, and—as the Eye of Ra—vengeance and destruction. An archetypal mother goddess, Hathor was one of the most popular deities in ancient Egypt.

   Balanced Water/Earth: Two sides of her pyramid are Water and two are Earth. Her image is of a woman wearing a blue and black dress, a blue pectoral collar, and a black horned headdress. The headdress is surmounted by a blue disk and blue feathers. She carries a black ankh and a blue lotus scepter, and she stands upon a black and blue base.

Figure 87: *Sothis*

7. **Sothis:** She is an incarnation of Isis, representing the star Sirius that appeared in the sky when the Nile rose each year.

   Balanced Fire/Water: Two sides of her pyramid are Fire and two are Water. Her image is of a woman wearing a red and blue dress, blue pectoral collar, and a red horned headdress. The headdress is surmounted by a blue disk and blue feathers. She carries a red ankh and a blue lotus scepter, and she stands upon a blue and red base.

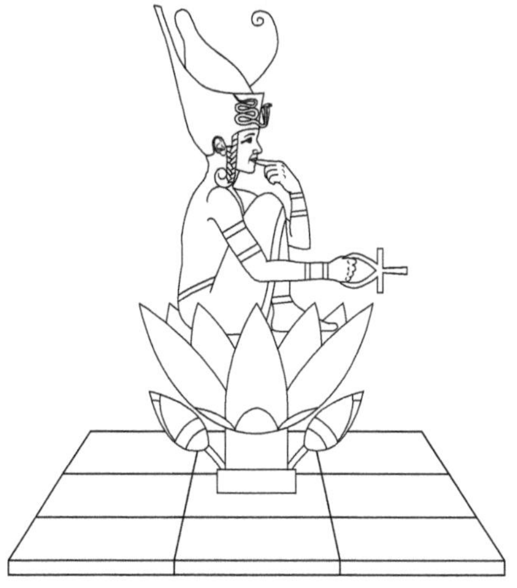

Figure 88: *Harpocrates*

8. **Harpocrates (Horus the Younger):** The newborn or child form of Horus, son of Isis and Osiris. As a young god and the rightful heir to the throne of Egypt, Horus had to be hidden from his uncle Set until he came of age; otherwise, Set would have killed him to protect his claim on the throne. Thus, Harpocrates is known as a god of silence.

   Balanced Air/Water: Two sides of his pyramid are Air and two are Water. His image is a youth wearing a yellow and blue tunic, a yellow pectoral collar, and a blue headdress. He also wears the double-crown of Egypt, colored yellow and blue. He holds a blue ankh and stands in the "sign of silence"—meaning his left fingertip is pressed against his lips. Sometimes he is depicted kneeling upon a lotus blossom. He rests upon a yellow and blue base.

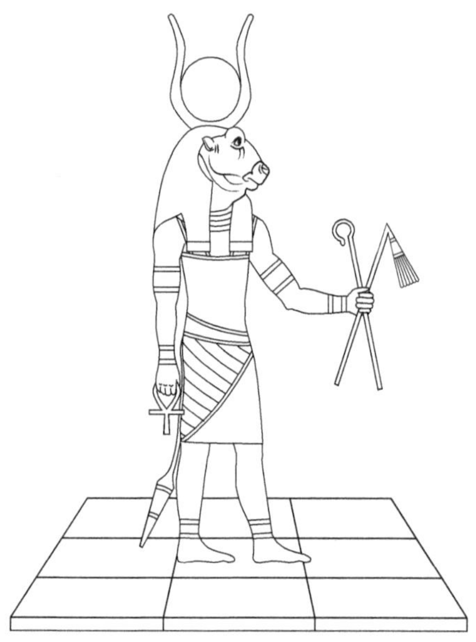

Figure 89: *Apis/Hapis*

9. **Apis (or Hapis):** A bull god who was identified with Osiris in later Egypt. Whereas Osiris was the king of the dead, Apis represented the renewal of life. It is suggested the horned crowns worn by many Egyptian deities are, in fact, the horns of the Apis bull.

   Balanced Fire/Earth: Two sides of his pyramid are Fire and two are Earth. His image is that of a man with the black head of a bull. He wears a black and red tunic, a black pectoral collar, and a red headdress. Atop the headdress are his black horns and a red disk. He carries two scepters, one red and one black. (He may also carry a red and black ankh.) He stands upon a black and red base.

Figure 90: *Anubis*

10. **Anubis:** The jackal-headed god of the tomb and guide to the underworld, Anubis officiates the weighing of the heart in the scales of Ma'at to determine the fate of a departed soul.

    Balanced Air/Earth: Two sides of his pyramid are Air and two are Earth. His image is that of a man with the black head of a jackal. He wears a yellow tunic, a black pectoral collar, and a yellow headdress. He carries a black ankh and a yellow scepter or sword. He stands upon a base of yellow and black.

Figure 91: *Pasht/Bast*

11. **Pasht (Pakhet—a form of Bast/Bastet):** A lion goddess in early Egypt and the goddess of domestic cats in later Egypt, Bast was known as a household protector. It is unlikely her name was ever Pasht, though there is likely an association with the name Pakhet.

    Balanced Fire/Air: Two sides of her pyramid are Fire and two are Air. Her image is that of a woman with the head of a cat. She wears a red dress and pectoral collar and a yellow headdress. She carries a yellow ankh and a red lotus scepter. She stands upon a red and yellow base.

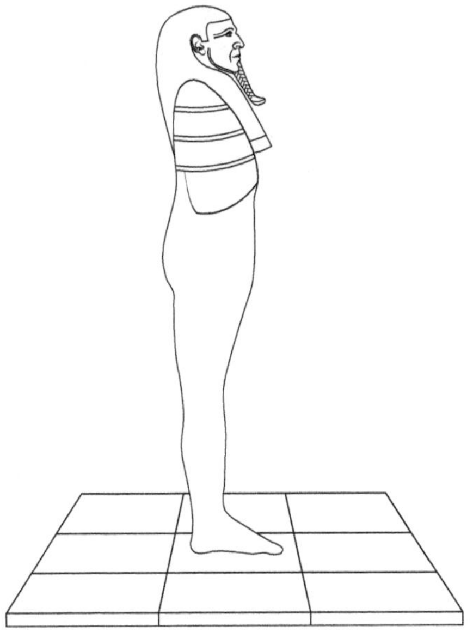

Figure 92: *Ameshet*

12. **Ameshet (or Amset, Amseti, Imseti):** One of the sons of Horus who guarded the body and organs of the deceased in the tomb. Ameshet especially guarded the liver. In the neo-Enochian system, he is the servant of Nephthys.

    Fire/Water/Earth: His pyramid has one side each of Fire, Water, and Earth. (The fourth side does not matter in this case.) His image is that of a man mummified in white cloth. He wears a black headdress and a pectoral collar striped red, blue, and black. He stands upon a base of red, blue, and black.

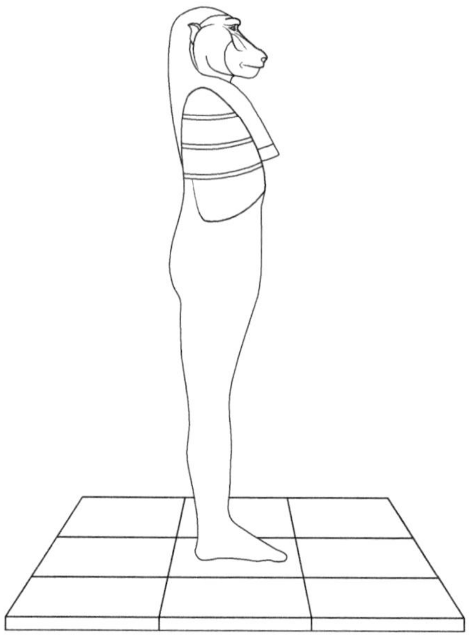

Figure 93: *Ahepi/Hapi*

13. **Ahepi (or Hapi):** One of the sons of Horus who guarded the body and organs of the deceased in the tomb. Hapi especially guarded the lungs. In the neo-Enochian system, he is the servant of Horus the Elder.

    Fire/Water/Air: His pyramid has one side each of Fire, Water, and Air. (The fourth side does not matter in this case.) His image is that of a man with the head of a baboon mummified in white cloth. His headdress is yellow, and his pectoral collar is striped red, blue, and yellow. He stands upon a red, blue, and yellow base.

Figure 94: *Thoumathph/Duamutef*

14. **Thoumathph (Duamutef):** One of the sons of Horus who guarded the body and organs of the deceased in the tomb. Duamutef especially guarded the stomach. In the neo-Enochian system, he is the servant of Isis.

    Earth/Water/Air: His pyramid has one side each of Earth, Water, and Air. (The fourth side does not matter in this case.) His image is that of a man with the head of a jackal mummified in white cloth. He wears a blue headdress, and his pectoral collar is striped black, blue, and yellow. He stands upon a black, blue, and yellow base.

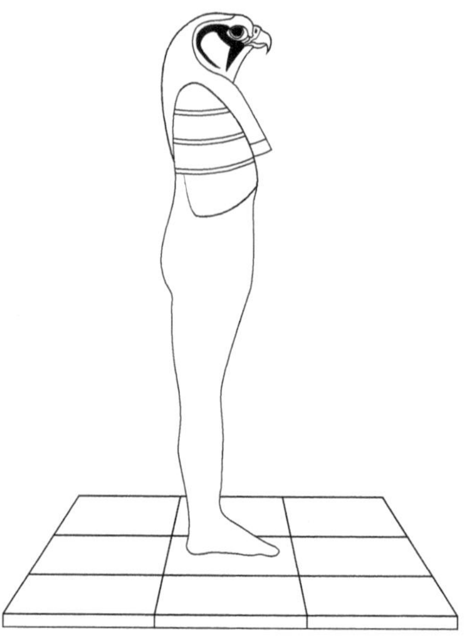

Figure 95: *Qebehsenuef*

15. **Qebehsenuef:** One of the sons of Horus who guarded the body and organs of the deceased in the tomb. Qebehsenuef especially guarded the intestines. In the neo-Enochian system, he is the servant of Horus.

    Earth/Air/Fire: His pyramid has one side each of Earth, Air, and Fire. (The fourth side does not matter in this case.) His image is that of a white-skinned man with the head of a falcon mummified in white cloth. His headdress is red, and his pectoral collar is striped black, yellow, and red. He stands upon a black, yellow, and red base.

Chapter Fourteen

A Neo-Enochian Angel Summoning

What You Will Need

To perform a neo-Enochian summoning ritual, you will need the following tools:[198]

- a double-cube altar (may be painted or covered with black or white, or you may use a covering of the proper elemental color)
- 2 pillar candles—white and black
- black or white robe
- lotus wand
- magickal sword
- elemental weapons: Fire Wand, Water Chalice, Air Dagger, and Earth Pentacle
- elemental substances: red candle for Fire, water in the chalice for Water, a rose symbolizing Air, and bread and salt for Earth

- 4 Watchtower tablets and the Table of Union drawn in full, vibrant colors
- the truncated pyramid of the angel you wish to evoke, its sphinx, and Coptic-Egyptian deity (these can be two-dimensional or you can fashion them in three dimensions; in either case, they must be drawn in vibrant color)
- a censer and elemental incense

For incense, you can use Martial incense for Fire, Lunar incense for Water, Mercury incense for Air, and Saturn incense for Earth (though I find Saturn incense too noxious for Earth, so I use patchouli instead).

Hang the four Watchtower tablets around your working space. The Oro Tablet will hang in the east, the Mph Tablet in the west, the Oip Tablet in the south, and the Mor Tablet in the north.

Set your altar in the center of your working space. Place the four elemental weapons on the top—Air Dagger toward the east, Water Chalice toward the west, Fire Wand toward the south, and Earth Pentacle toward the north. Arrange the four elemental substances upon the altar so they are in the same quarters as the elemental weapons. The censer should be placed between the eastern and southern sides. Place the Table of Union in the center, and place the two pillar candles on either side of it: the white candle on the right/southern side, and the black one on the left/northern side.

Upon the Table of Union place the truncated pyramid, sphinx, and Coptic deity. If you have drawn these in two dimensions, place the sphinx beneath the drawing of the pyramid. The Coptic deity should rest just to the east of the pyramid. If you have fashioned them in three dimensions, place the sphinx inside the pyramid and position the deity on the pyramid's top.

The Summoning Ceremony

Opening the Temple

Light all candles and the elemental incense. Take up the lotus wand, holding it by the lowest band of black, and move to the north-east corner of the temple. Face the altar and proclaim, "*Hekas, hekas, este bebeloi* (Far, far from this place be the profane)!"

Return to the altar and stand on its west side facing the east. Take the magickal sword and perform the Lesser Banishing Ritual of the Pentagram.[199]

Having returned to the altar, use the lotus wand (pointing the black end forward) to perform the Banishing Ritual of the Hexagram.

Return to the altar once more. Take up the chalice full of water and proceed clockwise around your temple one time, sprinkling the water in each of the four quarters while saying, "So therefore first, the Priest(ess) who governeth the works of Fire must sprinkle with the lustral waters of the loud, resounding sea."

Return the chalice to the altar and take up the censer. Proceed clockwise around the temple once more, censing the four quarters while saying, "And when, after all the phantoms have vanished, thou shalt see that holy and formless Fire, that Fire which darts and flashes through the hidden depths of the universe. Hear thou the voice of Fire!"

Return the censer to the altar and grasp the lotus wand by the uppermost band of white. Move to the east, then proceed clockwise around your temple space three times, making the Sign of the Enterer each time you pass the east.

Return again to the altar, raise your arms high, and perform the Adoration to the Lord of the Universe:

"Holy art Thou, Lord of the Universe!" (Sign of the Enterer)

"Holy art Thou, whom Nature hath not formed!" (Sign of the Enterer)

"Holy art Thou, the vast and the mighty one!" (Sign of the Enterer)

"Lord of the Light and of the Darkness." (Sign of Silence)

Invocations

Now grasp the lotus wand by the band that represents the element you wish to invoke. (The band of Leo for Fire, the band of Scorpio for Water, of Aquarius for Air, or that of Taurus for Earth.) Perform the Greater Invoking Ritual of the Pentagram for the proper element.

Standing at the altar once again, facing east, grasp the Lotus Wand by the upper white band. Perform the sign of the Rending of the Veil. Then raise your hands to heaven and recite the first and second Angelical Callings, invoking the Table of Union.

Remain at the altar, facing eastward. Raise your hands high and recite an invocation to the Coptic god who rules the pyramid upon the altar. It should ask him or her to be present during your work and to bring to you the angel or angels you wish to summon. The following is an example:

Invocation of the Coptic God

I invoke thee (name), *thou Great God(dess) who ruleth in the realm of* (element/sub-element). *Be thou present with me, and be thou the guardian of this mystic sphere. Keep far removed the evil and the unbalanced and look with favor upon this work. In the three great and secret names of God that ruleth the* (directional)[200] *quadrangle,* (three supreme divine names of Watchtower), *open the gates of the* (direction) *and bring to me the holy angel(s)* (names) *so that* (he / they) *will appear before me visibly and speak to me with an audible voice. Keep this sphere pure and holy so the angels of God will be moved to appear and reveal unto me the mysteries of their creation.*

Now put aside the lotus wand and take up the weapon of the element you are invoking. Move clockwise around the temple until you are facing the appropriate Watchtower. Make the sign of the Rending of the Veil, then recite the call assigned to the Watchtower (number three, four, five, or six).

Now recite an invocation of the Watchtower's king, such as the following:

Invocation of the Watchtower King

In the three secret and holy names of God born upon the banners of the (direction), (three supreme divine names of Watchtower), *and by the sacred letters of the mystical Table of Union* (tablet letters)[201], *I invoke the Great King of the* (directional) *quadrangle,* (name). (Vibrate the name of the king while tracing a spiral over the letters of his name before you.) *Thou who art the overseer and protector of the* (directional) *quarter of the universe, add the power and virtues of* (element) *to this work and send the angel(s)* (names) *that they may reveal unto me the mysteries of their creation.*

Then, if you are working with one of the three mixed sub-elements, recite the call associated with its subquadrant. (You do not need to do this if you are working with Fire of Fire, Water of Water, Air of Air, or Earth of Earth.)

Continue with an invocation of the angel(s) you are summoning by the name of their archangel(s) and the two divine names of the Calvary Cross (remember one name is for calling and the other is for commanding).

Invocation of the Archangel

> *O archangel* (name), *who rulest and governeth in the infinite realm of* (element / sub-element),[202] *who chargeth your angels to manifest the virtues of your power upon the physical world, hear my call in the exalted name* (calling name) *and send forth the holy angel* (name) *to this sacred place. In the mighty name* (commanding name), *empower him and charge him to appear visibly before me, to speak audibly to me and to reveal unto me whatsoever I desire.*

Invocation of the Servient Angel

> *I invoke, summon, and call ye forth, thou great angel* (name) *by the virtue and power of your archangel* (name) *and by the most holy name* (calling name) *written upon the foundations of the world. In and by these names, and by the highest names of God born upon the banners of the* (direction), (three supreme divine names of Watchtower), *and by the Great Elemental King* (name), *and by the sacred letters of the mystical Table of Union* (tablet letters), *I call ye from thy home and habitation in the astral realm of* (element / sub-element). *And I command you in the irresistible divine name* (commanding name) *to appear before me, speak with me, answer my questions, and accomplish my desires. By all of these names rehearsed, and by the power thereby vested in me and within this elemental weapon* (here hold the weapon aloft) *and within the sacred scepter of the lotus, so mote it be!*

Repeat the two invocations above, one for the archangel and one for the servient angel, for each angel you wish to call from the subquadrant. Then repeat the same two invocations in each of the remaining three quarters of the temple space, moving clockwise to each new quarter and ending again at the Watchtower you have opened.

Finally, return to the altar, standing so that you are facing the Watchtower with the altar between you and it. Replace the elemental weapon on the altar and take up the lotus wand. Hold it by the white band of Spirit and fix your attention upon the truncated pyramid before you. Recite a final prayer to the Coptic deity:

> O (name), *Lord/Lady of the pyramid of* (element/sub-element) *by whose names and images have I invoked the angels of the mighty Watchtowers of the universe, make unto me a strong seething. Open my eyes and my ears to the visions and voices of the Holy Ones. Before I was blind, but now I see! I once was deaf, but now I hear! Move, therefore, move and appear and open unto me the mysteries of creation. Strengthen and inspire me that I may enter in and become a partaker of the secrets of the Light Divine.*

At last, keeping your focus upon the truncated pyramid before you, welcome the summoned angel(s) and address them as you will. Receive their answers or any visions they give you. When you are done, the angel(s) will depart of their own accord.

Closing the Temple

When you are done with your working, say prayers of thanksgiving to the entities you have invoked in the working. Stand before the Watchtower to thank the angels summoned therefrom, and then perform the sign of the Closing of the Veil. Return to the altar, face east to thank the Coptic deity, and make the sign of the Closing of the Veil once more.

Lay aside the lotus wand. Take up the chalice, and then the censer, and purify the temple with water and fire exactly as was done in the opening.

Having finished the purification, take up the lotus wand by the white band and move to the east. Proceed counterclockwise around the temple three times, making the Sign of the Enterer each time you pass the east.

Return to the altar and perform again the Adoration to the Lord of the Universe.

Proclaim, "I now release any and all spirits who have been entrapped by this ceremony and are not needed in its operation. Go with the blessings of Yeheshua and Yehovasha. Return to your homes and habitations. May there be peace between me and thee, and may ye be always ready to come when ye are called!" (Make the sign of the Closing of the Veil.)

If you feel it is necessary, you may end by taking up the Sword and performing the Lesser Banishing Ritual of the Pentagram. However, I rarely suggest doing this, especially if you are fortunate enough to have an established space or room for ritual that others will not need to use after you are done.

Finally proclaim, "I now declare this temple duly closed. So mote it be!"

Appendix I

The Angelical Language

Table 55: *The Angelical Alphabet*

Graph	Un	Or	Gal	Ged	Veh	Pa
E	A	F	D	G/J	C/Ch/K	B

Drux	Ger	Mals	Ur	Na	Gon	Tal
N	Q/Qu	P/Ph	L	H	I/Y	M

Gisg	Fam	Van	Ceph	Don	Med	Pal
T	S	U/V	Z	R	O	X

Pronunciation Key (Fully Explained)

You may notice that this key is very different from the pronunciation guides we normally see for the Enochian language. Most often, such guides are alphabetical—meaning that they present the Angelical (or English-equivalent) letters and then suggest what sounds these letters might make individually. While it is good to know what sound each letter makes, it tells us little about what sounds are made when the letters are combined into actual syllables and words.

My pronunciation guide, on the other hand, is entirely phonetic. It begins with the sounds that make up the syllables. Then it presents the phonetic notations I have created to represent those sounds. These notations are intended to be simple and intuitive to the modern reader.

Vowels

Short vowels are mostly represented by single letters, while I have extended the long vowels to two letters:

Phonetic Sound	Notation
a –long (*cake, day*)	ay
a –short (*bat, cat*)	a
e –long (*beet, seat*)	ee
e –short (*bed, wed*)	e
i –long (*bite, kite*)	ii
i –short (*bit, sit*)	i
o –long (*boat, slope*)	oh
o –short (*bot, stop, father*)	o, ah
u –long (*boot, blue*)	oo
u –short (*but, cup*)	u

Note: There are some cases where an *A* falls at the end of a word. I feel this likely indicates something between a long and short *A*, or a schwa. In such cases, I have simply left a single *A* in my pronunciation. It can be treated as a short *A*, but it is more akin to a schwa sound. (I assume Dee, had he intended the long *A* sound, would have ended the words with *ay* or *eh*.) For example, the word *amma* ("cursed") likely ends with a sound somewhere in between the long and short *A* (schwa)—"am-a."

Consonants

If consonants are written together (as in br, cr, gr, st, th, and tr), simply pronounce the combined sound as you would in present-day English (break, crate, grab, start, and so forth). Otherwise, standard consonant sounds are indicated by the following:

Phonetic Sound	Notation
b (branch, blurb)	b
d (dog, during)	d
f (far, fork)	f
g (gap, gourd)	g
h (half, heavy)	h
j (jump, giant, bludgeon)	j
k (kind, can)	k
l (large, loud)	l
m (many, move)	m
n (north, never)	n
p (pace, pardon)	p
r (rain, banner)	r, er
s (serve, circle)	s
t (test, tax)	t
w (water, wind)	w
x (exit, except)	ks
y (yellow, your)	y
z (zoom, zebra)	z

"Long Consonants"

There are many cases where Dee indicated a consonant standing alone in a syllable. At these times, the letter does not make its usual consonant sound. Instead, the syllable is pronounced the same as the English name of the consonant. I have dubbed these "long consonants" and represent their sounds as follows:

Phonetic Sound	Notation
d	dee
f	ef
g	jee
j	jay
l	el
m	em
n	en
p	pee
q	kwah
r	ur
s	es
t	tee
y	wii
z	zohd, zed

Digraphs and Diphthongs

The digraphs and diphthongs are fairly standard in modern English:

Phonetic Sound	Notation
ch (*church, witch*)	ch
ch (*ache, chrome*)	kh
ou, ow (*out, town*)	ow
oi, oy (*oil, boy*)	oy
qu (*queen, quick*)	kw
sh (*shine, wish*)	sh
ph (*phone, philosophy*)	f
th (*that, whither, thorn*)	th

Also Note

There are a few instances when the letters *sg* occur in Angelical words, such as *Caosg* or *Vorsg*. In these cases, Dee does not indicate that the "g" sound should stand alone as its own syllable. Thus, I find it likely it is intended to combine with the *s* to make a kind of "zh" (or hard "sh") sound, as we hear in English words such as *measure*, *pleasure*, and *treasure*. I have indicated this sound in the Psalter with the digraph *zh*.

Accented Syllables

Dee included accent marks throughout the *48 Claves Angelicae* and *A True and Faithful Relation*. I have indicated these accents in my pronunciations by writing the related syllable in all caps. For instance, the word *Cacacom* ("to flourish") is recorded in the *48 Claves* as *ca-cá-com*. In the Psalter, I have given the pronunciation of "kay-SAY-som," showing an accent on the second syllable.

Appendix 2

An Angelical Psalter (Forty-Eight Callings)

Calls in English

Call One

"I reign over you," sayeth the God of Justice, "in power exalted above

the firmaments of wrath: in whose hands the Sun is as

a sword, and the Moon a through-thrusting fire: Which

measureth your garments in the midst of my vestures and

trussed you together as the palms of my hands. Whose seats

I garnished with the fire of gathering, and beautified your garments

with admiration. To whom I made a law to govern the Holy Ones,

and delivered you a rod (with) the ark of knowledge. Moreover,

you lifted up your voices and swore obedience and faith to Him

that liveth and triumpheth; whose beginning is not, nor end cannot be;

which shineth as a flame in the midst of your palace,

and reigneth amongst you as the balance of righteousness and

truth (truth)." Move, therefore, and

show yourselves. Open the mysteries of your creation. Be friendly unto me.

For I am a servant of the same your God; the true worshiper of the Highest.

Angelical Key

Key of the Second Table

"Ol sonf vorsg," goho Iad Balt, "lansh
"ohl sonv vorzh," goh-HOH yad balt, "lonsh

calz vonpho: Sobra z-ol ror i ta
kalz von-foh. SOB-ray zohd-OL ror ii tay

nazpsad, graa ta malprg; Ds
nayz-pee-sad, gray tay mal-purj: dee-es

holq qaa nothoa zimz, od
HOL-kwah kwah-AY-ay noth-OH-a zimz, ohd

commah ta nobloh zien. Soba thil
KOM-ah tay noh-bloh zeen. SOH-bay thil

gnonp prge aldi ds urbs oboleh
non-pee purj AL-dii dee-es yurbs OB-oh-lay

grsam. Casarm ohorela caba pir,
gur-sam. kay-SARM oh-hor-EL-a ka-BA per,

ds zonrensg cab erm iadnah. Pilah,
dee-es zon-renj kab erm yad-nah. pee-ii-lah,

farzm znrza adna gono iadpil
farz-em snur-za ad-nah gon-oh ii-AD-pil

ds hom toh; soba ipam, ul ipamis;
dee-es hom toh: SOH-bay ip-am, yewl ip-am-is;

ds loholo vep zomdux poamal,
dee-es LOH-hoh-loh vep zom-dooks poh-mal,

od bogpa aai ta piap baltle od
ohd bog-pa ay-AY-ii tay pii-ap bal-tayl ohd

vaoan (vooan)." Zacar, ca, od
vay-oh-AN (voo-AN)." ZAY-kayr, see-ay, ohd

zamran. Odo cicle qaa. Zorge.
zam-ran. od-oh sii-kayl kwah-AY-ay. zorj.

Lap zirdo noco mad; hoath Iaida.
lap zir-DOH NOH-kwoh mad; hohth jay-II-da.

Call Two

Can the wings of the winds understand your voices of wonder,

O you the Second of the First, whom the burning flames have framed within

the depths of my jaws; whom I have prepared as

cups for a wedding, or as the flowers

in their beauty for the chamber of righteousness. Stronger are your feet than the barren stone,

and mightier are your voices than the manifold winds. For

you are become a building such as is not but in the mind of

the All Powerful. "Arise," sayeth the First. Move

therefore unto His servants. Show yourselves in power

and make me a strong seething. For I am of Him that liveth forever.

Key of the Third Table

Adgt upaah zong om faaip sald,
ajt yew-pay-ah zong om fay-AY-ip sald,

viiv L, sobam ialpurg izazaz
vii-iv el, SOH-bam YAL-purj ii-zay-zaz

piadph; casarma abramg ta
pii-AD-ef; kay-SAR-ma ay-BRAY-mig tay

talho paracleda, qta lorslq
tal-ho par-AK-lee-da, kwah-tay lors-el-kwah

turbs ooge baltoh. Givi chis lusd orri,
turbs oh-oj bal-toh. jiv-ii kiis lus-dee or-ii,

od micalp chis bia ozongon. Lap
ohd mii-KALP kiis bii-a OH-zohn-gon. lap

noan trof cors tage oq manin
noh-AN trof kors tayj oh-kwah man-in

Iaidon. "Torzu," gohel. Zacar
jay-II-don. "tor-ZOO," GOH-hel, ZAY-kayr

ca cnoqod. Zamran micalzo,
see-ay see-NOH-kwod. zam-ran mii-KAYL-zoh,

od ozazm urelp. Lap zir Ioiad.
ohd oz-az-em yer-elp. lap zer joh-JAD.

Call Three

"Behold," sayeth your God. "I am a Circle

on whose hands stand twelve Kingdoms. Six are the seats of

living breath; the rest are as sharp sickles

or the horns of death; wherein the creatures of the earth

are and are not except by mine own hand; which

sleep and shall rise. In the first I made you stewards

and placed you in twelve seats of government, giving unto

every one of you power successively over 456, the true ages

of time, to the intent that from the highest vessels and the corners

of your governments you might work my power; pouring down

the fires of life and increase upon the earth continually. Thus, you are become the skirts of

justice and truth (truth)."

In the Name of the same your God, lift up, I say,

yourselves. Behold, His mercies flourish and

Key of the Fourth Table

"Micma," goho piad, "Zir comselh
"mik-ma," goh-HOH pii-AD, "zer KOM-sel

azien biab oslondoh. Norz chis othil
az-EEN bii-ab os-LON-doh. norz kiis oh-THIL

gigipah; undl chis tapuin
jij-ii-pah; und-el kiis TAY-pew-in

qmospleh teloch; quiin toltorg
kwah-mos-play tee-LOCH; kwii-in tol-TORJ

chis ichisge m ozien; dst
kiis jay-KIIS-jee em oh-ZEEN; dee-es-tee

brgda od torzul. Ili eol balzarg
burj-da ohd tor-ZOOL. II-lii ee-OHL bal-zarj

od aala thilnos netaab, dluga
ohd AY-ay-la thil-nos nee-TAY-ab. dee-LOO-ga

vomzarg lonsa capmiali vors cla, homil
vom-sarj lon-sha kap-mii-AY-lii vorz kla, hom-il

cocasb, fafen izizop od miinoag
KOH-kasb, fay-fen iz-is-op ohd mii-ii-noh-ayg

de gnetaab vaun nanaeel; panpir
dee nee-TAY-ab von nay-NAY-ee-el; pan-per

malpirgi caosg pild. Noan unalah
mal-per-jii kay-OZH pild. noh-AN un-al-ah

balt odvaoan (odvooan).
"balt ohd-vay-oh-AN (ohd-voo-AN)."

Dooiap mad, goholor, gohus,
doh-OH-ii-ap mad, goh-HOH-lor, goh-US,

amiran. Micma, iehusoz cacacom od
am-ir-an. mik-ma, jay-US-os kay-SAY-som ohd

Call Three continued

Name is become mighty amongst us.

In whom we say, move,

descend and apply yourselves unto us as partakers of

the secret wisdom of your creation.

Key of the Fourth Table continued

dooain	noar	micaolz	aaiom.
doh-OH-ay-in	*noh-ar*	*mii-KAY-ohlz*	*ay-AY-om.*

Casarmg	gohia,	z-acar,
kay-SAR-mij	*goh-HII-a,*	*ZOHD-ay-kayr,*

uniglag	od	imvamar	pugo	plapli
yew-nii-glag	*ohd*	*im-vay-mar*	*pug-oh*	*play-plii*

ananael	qaan.
an-AN-ee-el	*kwah-AY-an.*

Call Four

"I have set my feet in the south and have looked about me

saying, Are not the Thunders of Increase numbered

33 which reign in the Second Angle; under whom

I have placed 9639 whom none hath yet numbered

but One. In whom the second beginning of things are

and wax strong; which also successively are

the number of time; and their powers are as the first 456.

Arise you sons of pleasure and visit the earth,

for I am the Lord your God which is and liveth."

In the Name of the Creator, move

and show yourselves as pleasant deliverers; that you may praise Him amongst

the sons of men.

Key of the Fifth Table

"Othil lasdi babage od dorpha
"oh-THIL las-dii bay-BAY-jee ohd dorf-fa

gohol, gchisge avavago cormp
goh-HOHL, jee-KIIS-jee av-AY-vay-go kormf

pd dsonf vivdiv; casarmi
pee-dee dee-sonv viv-DII-vee; kay-SAR-mij

oali mapm, sobam ag cormpo
OH-ay-lii map-em, SOH-bam ag korm-FOH

crpl. Casarmg croodzi chis
krip-el. key-SAR-mij kroh-OD-zii kiis

odugeg; dst capimali chis
ohd-yew-JEJ; dee-es-tee kay-pii-MAY-lii kiis

capimaon; odlonshin chis talo cla.
kap-ii-MAY-on; ohd-lon-shin kiis tay-el-loh kla.

Torgu norquasahi od fcaosga,
tor-GOO nor-kway-SAY-hii ohd ef-kay-OS-ga,

bagle zirenaiad dsi odapila."
BAY-gayl zii-er-NAY-ad dee-sii ohd-ap-ii-la."

Dooaip qaal, z-acar
doh-OH-ay-ip kwah-AY-el, ZOHD-ay-kayr

odzamran obelisong; restil aaf
ohd-zam-ran oh-bel-is-ong; rest-el ay-AF

normolap.
nor-moh-lap.

Call Five

"The Mighty Sounds have entered into the third Angle and are become

as olives in the olive mount looking with gladness upon the earth and

dwelling within the brightness of the heavens as continual comforters, unto whom

I have fastened pillars of gladness 19, and gave them

vessels to water the earth with Her creatures; and

they are the brothers of the First and Second; and the beginning of

their own seats which are garnished with continually burning lamps 69636; whose

numbers are as the first, the ends, and

the contents of time." Therefore, come you and obey

your creation. Visit us in peace and comfort.

Conclude us as receivers of your mysteries. For why? Our Lord and Master

is all one.

Key of the Sixth Table

"Sapah zimii duiv od noas
"SAY-fah ZII-mii DOO-iv ohd noh-as

taqanis adroch dorphal caosg, od
tay-kway-nis ad-roch dor-fal kay-OZH, ohd

faonts piripsol tablior, casarm
fay-onts per-IP-sol TAY-blii-or, kay-SARM

amipzi nazarth af, od dlugar
ay-mip-zii nay-zarth af, ohd dee-LOO-gar

zizop z-lida caosgi toltorgi; od
ziz-op zohd-lid-a kay-OZH-ii tol-TOR-jii; ohd

z-chis esiasch L taviv; od iaod
zohd-kiis ee-sii-ash el tay-viv; ohd YAY-ohd

thild ds hubar peral; soba
thild dee-es hoo-BAR pee-AR-al; SOH-bay

cormfa chista la, uls, od
korm-FA kiis-tay lah, yewls, ohd

qcocasb." Ca, niis od darbs
kwah-KOH-kasb." see-ay, nii-IS ohd darbs

qaas. Fetharzi od bliora.
kwah-AY-as. feth-AR-zii ohd blii-OH-ra.

Iaial ednas cicles. Bagle? Geiad
jay-yal ed-nas sii-kayls. BAY-gayl? jej-AYD

il.
ii-el.

Call Six

The spirits of the fourth Angle are nine, mighty in the Firmaments of Water;

whom the First hath planted a torment to the wicked and a garland to

the Righteous; giving unto them fiery darts to van the earth

and 7699 continual workmen whose courses visit with comfort

the earth; and are in government and continuance

as the second and the third. Wherefore, hearken unto my voice. I have talked of you

and I move you in power and presence, whose works

shall be a song of honor and praise of your God

in your creation.

Key of the Seventh Table

Gah sdiv chis em, micalzo pilzin;
jah es-DII-vee kiis em, mii-KAYL-zoh pil-zin;

sobam el harg mir babalon od obloc
SOH-bam el harg mir bay-BAY-lon ohd ob-lok

samvelg; dlugar malpurg arcaosgi,
sam-velj; dee-LOO-gar mal-purj ar-kay-OZH-ii,

od acam canal sobolzar fbliard
ohd ay-KAM san-al soh-BOL-zar ef-blii-ard

caosgi; odchis anetab od miam
kay-OZH-ii; ohd-kiis ay-NEE-tayb ohd mii-AM

taviv od d. Darsar, solpeth bien. Brita,
tay-viv ohd dee. dar-sar, sol-peth bii-en. brit-a,

od zacam gmicalzo, sobhaath
ohd ZAY-kam jee-mii-KAYL-zoh, sob-HAY-ath

trian luiahe odecrin mad
TRII-an loo-JAY-hee oh-dee-KRIN mad

qaaon.
kwah-AY-ay-on.

Call Seven

The east is a house of virgins

singing praises amongst the flames of the First Glory; wherein

the Lord hath opened His Mouth, and they become 28

living dwellings in whom the strength of men rejoiceth

and they are appareled with ornaments of brightness such as work wonders

on all creatures. Whose kingdoms and continuance

are as the Third and Fourth; strong towers and

places of comfort, the seats of mercy and continuance.

O you servants of mercy, move, appear,

sing praises unto the Creator, and

be mighty amongst us. For

to this remembrance is given power and our strength

waxeth strong in our Comforter.

Key of the Eighth Table

Raas isalman paradiz
ray-as ii-SAYL-man pay-ray-DII-zohd

oecrimi aao ialpirgah; quiin
oh-EE-kriim-ii ay-ay-OH YAL-pur-jah; kwii-in

Enay butmon, od inoas ni
en-ay but-mon, ohd in-OH-as nii

paradial casarmg ugear chirlan;
pay-ray-DII-al kay-SAR-mij yew-JEE-ar kir-lan;

od zonac luciftian corsta vaulzirn
ohd zoh-nak loo-sif-TII-an kors-tay VOL-zern

tolhami. Soba londoh odmiam
tol-HAY-mii. SOH-bay lon-DOH ohd-MII-am

chistad odes; umadea od
kiis-tad oh-DES; yew-MAY-dee-a ohd

pibliar; othilrit odmiam.
pib-lii-AR; oh-THIL-rit ohd-MII-am.

Cnoquol rit, z-acar, zamran,
see-NOH-kwol rit, ZOHD-ay-kayr, zam-ran,

oecrimi qadah, od
oh-EE-kriim-ii kwah-AY-dah, ohd

omicaolz aaiom. Bagle
oh-mii-KAY-ohl-zohd. ay-AY-om. BAY-gayl

papnor idlugam lonshi, od umplif
pap-nor id-LOO-gam lon-shii, ohd um-plif

ugegi bigliad.
yew-JEE-jii big-lii-ad.

Call Eight

"The midday the first is as the third heaven made of hyacinth pillars

26; in whom the Elders are become strong;

which I have prepared for my own righteousness," sayeth the Lord,

"Whose long continuance shall be bucklers to

the stooping dragons and like unto the harvest of a widow.

How many are there, which remain in the glory of the earth,

which are and shall not see death until

this house fall and the dragon

sink." Come away, for the Thunders

have spoken. Come away, for the crowns of

the Temple, and the coat of Him that is, was, and shall be Crowned,

are divided. Come, appear to the terror of the earth;

and to our comfort; and of such as are prepared.

Key of the Ninth Table

"Bazemlo ita piripson oln nazavabh
"bas-em-loh ii-tay per-IP-son ohln nay-zay-VAB

ox; casarmg uran chis ugeg;
oks; kay-SAR-mij yew-RAN kiis yew-JEJ;

dsabramg baltoha," gohoiad,
dee-say-bray-mig bal-toh-ha," goh-HOH-ii-ad,

"Solamian trian talolcis
"soh-LAY-mii-an TRII-an tay-LOL-sis

abaivonin od aziagiar rior.
ay-bay-II-voh-nin ohd ay-zii-AY-jii-er rii-or.

Irgilchisda, dspaaox busd caosgo,
ir-jil-KIIS-da, dee-SAY-ay-oks buzd kay-OS-go,

dschis odipuran teloah cacrg
dee-es-kiis ohd-II-pew-ran TEE-loh-ah KAY-kurg

oisalman loncho od vovina
oh-ii-SAYL-man lon-koh ohd voh-VII-na

carbaf." Niiso, bagle avavago
kar-baf." nii-II-soh, BAY-gayl av-AY-vay-go

gohon. Niiso, bagle momao
goh-HON. nii-II-soh, BAY-gayl MOH-may-oh

siaion, od mabza iadoiasmomar,
sii-AY-ii-on, ohd MAB-za jad-oh-JAS-moh-mar,

poilp. Niis, zamran ciaofi caosgo;
poylp. nii-IS, zam-ran sii-ay-oh-fii kay-OS-go;

od bliors; od corsi ta abramig.
ohd blii-ORS; ohd kor-sii tay ay-BRAY-mig.

Call Nine

A mighty guard of fire with two-edged swords flaming

(which have vials 8 of wrath

for two times and a half; whose wings

are of wormwood and of the marrow of salt), have settled

their feet in the west and are measured

with their ministers 9996. These gather up

the moss of the earth as the rich man doth his treasure.

Cursed are they whose iniquities they are.

In their eyes are millstones greater than

the earth, and from their mouths run seas of

blood. Their heads are covered with

diamond and upon their hands are

marble sleeves. Happy is he on whom

they frown not. For why? The God of Righteousness rejoiceth in them.

Come away, and not your vials. For

the time is such as requireth comfort.

Key of the Tenth Table

Micaoli bransg prgel napta ialpor
mii-KAY-oh-lii branzh pur-jel nap-ta YAL-por

(dsbrin efafafe p vonpho
(dee-es-brin ee-FAY-fay-fee pee von-foh

olani od obza; sobca upaah
oh-el-AY-nii ohd ob-za; SOB-kay yew-pay-ah

chis tatan od tranan balye), alar
kiis tay-tan ohd tray-nan bay-lii-ee), AY-lar

lusda soboln od chisholq
lus-da soh-bohln ohd KIIS-hohl-kwa

cnoqvodi cial. Unal aldon
see-noh-KWOH-dii sii-al. yew-NAL AL-don

mom caosgo ta lasollor gnay limlal.
mom kay-OS-go tay las-OHL-or nay lim-lal.

Amma chiis sobca madrid z-chis.
am-a kiis SOB-kay MAY-drid zohd-kiis.

Ooanoan chis aviny drilpi
oh-oh-AY-noh-an kiis ay-VII-nee dril-pii

caosgin, od butmoni parm zumvi
kay-OS-jin, ohd but-moh-nii parm zum-vii

cnila. Dazis ethamz
see-NII-la. daz-IS ee-THAM-zohd

achildao, od mirc ozol chis
ay-KIL-day-oh, ohd mirk oh-ZOHL kiis

pidiai collal. Ulcinin asobam
pii-dii-ay-ii kol-lal. yewl-SII-nin ay-SOH-bam

ucim. Bagle? Iadbaltoh chirlan par.
yew-sim. BAY-gayl? ii-ad-BAL-toh kir-lan par.

Niiso, od ip ofafafe. Bagle
nii-II-soh, ohd ip oh-FAY-fay-fee. BAY-gayl

acocasb icorsca unig blior.
ay-KOH-kasb ii-KORS-kay yew-nig blii-OR.

Call Ten

The Thunders of Judgment and Wrath are numbered and harbored in the north

in the likeness of an oak whose branches

are 22 nests of lamentation and weeping

laid up for the earth; which

burn night and day and vomit out

the heads of scorpions and live sulfur mingled with

poison. These be the thunders that 5678

times in the twenty-fourth part of a moment roar with a hundred mighty

earthquakes, and a thousand times as many

surges, which rest not neither know any

(long) time here. One rock

bringeth forth 1000 even as the heart of man

doth his thoughts. Woe, woe, woe

woe, woe, woe, yea, woe

be to the earth. For her iniquity is, was,

and shall be great. Come away, but not your noises.

Key of the Eleventh Table

Coraxo chis cormp od blans lucal
koh-RAYKS-oh kiis kormf ohd blanz loo-kal

aziazor paeb soba lilonon
ay-ZII-ay-zor pay-eb SOH-bay lii-loh-non

chis op virq eophan od raclir
kiis oh-pee vir-kwah ee-oh-fan ohd ray-kler

maasi bagle caosgi; ds
may-ay-sii BAY-gayl kay-OZH-ii; dee-es

ialpon dosig od basgim od oxex
YAL-pon doh-sig ohd bas-jim ohd oks-eks

dazis siatris od salbrox cinxir
daz-IS sii-ay-TRIS ohd sal-broks sinks-ir

faboan. Unalchis const ds daox
fay-boh-an. yew-nal-kiis konst dee-es day-oks

cocasg ol oanio yor torb vohim
KOH-kazh oh-el oh-AY-nii-oh yor torb VOH-im

gizyax, od matb cocasg plosi
jiz-wii-aks, ohd may-teb KOH-kazh ploh-sii

molui, ds pageip larag om droln
mol-vii, dee-es pay-jee-ip lay-rag om drohln

(matorb) cocasb emna. Lpatralx
(may-torb) KOH-kasb em-na. el-PAY-tralks

yolci matb nomig monons olora
yol-sii may-teb noh-mig moh-nons oh-loh-ra

gnay angelard. Ohio ohio ohio
nay an-jee-lard. oh-hii-oh oh-hii-oh oh-hii-oh

ohio ohio ohio, noib, ohio
oh-hii-oh oh-hii-oh oh-hii-oh, noh-ib, oh-hii-oh

caosgon, bagle madrid i, zirop,
kay-OS-gon, BAY-gayl MAY-drid ii, zii-ROP

chiso drilpa. Niiso, crip ip nidali.
kiis-oh dril-pa. nii-II-soh, krip ip nii-day-lii.

Call Eleven

The Mighty Seat groaned and they were five

Thunders which flew into the east, and

the Eagle spake and cried with a loud voice, "Come away!"

And they gathered themselves together and became the house of death,

of whom it is measured, and it is as they are

whose number is 31. Come away, for

I have prepared for you. Move, therefore, and

show yourselves. Open the mysteries of your creation. Be friendly unto me.

For I am a servant of the same your God; the true worshiper of the Highest.

Key of the Twelfth Table

Oxiayal holdo od zirom o
oks-AY-al hol-doh ohd zer-OM oh

coraxo ds zildar raasy, od
koh-RAYKS-oh dee-es zil-dar ray-ay-see, ohd

vabzir camliax od bahal, "Niiso!"
vab-zer kam-lii-aks ohd BAY-hal, "nii-II-soh!"

Od aldon od noas salman teloch,
ohd AL-don ohd noh-as SAYL-man tee-LOCH,

casarman holq, od ti ta z-chis
kay-SAR-man HOL-kwah, ohd tii tay zohd-kiis

soba cormf iga. Niisa, bagle
SOH-bay kormf ii-ga. nii-II-sa, BAY-gayl

abramg noncp. Zacar, ca, od
ay-BRAY-mig non-sef. ZAY-kayr, see-ay, ohd

zamran. Odo cicle qaa. Zorge.
zam-ran. od-oh sii-kayl kwah-AY-ay. zorj.

Lap zirdo noco mad; hoath Iaida.
lap zir-DOH NOH-kwoh mad; hohth jay-II-da.

Call Twelve

O you that reign in the south and are 28

the lanterns of sorrow, bind up your girdles and

visit us. Bring down your train 3663 that the Lord may be magnified

whose name amongst you is wrath.

Move, I say, and show yourselves. Open

the mysteries of your creation. Be friendly unto me. For I am

a servant of the same your God; the true worshiper of the Highest.

Call Thirteen

O you swords of the south, which have forty-two

eyes to stir up wrath of sin,

making men drunken which are empty.

Behold the promise of God and His power which

is called amongst you a bitter sting. Move and show yourselves.

Open the mysteries of your creation. Be friendly unto me. For I am

a servant of the same your God; the true worshiper of the Highest.

Key of the Thirteenth Table

Nonci dsonf babage od chis ob
non-sii dee-sonv bay-BAY-jee ohd kiis ob

hubaio tibibp, allar atraah od
hoo-BAY-ii-oh tib-ib-ip, AL-lar ay-tray-ah ohd

ef. Drix fafen mian ar enay ovof
ef. driks fay-fen mii-AN ar en-ay oh-vof

soba dooain aai ivonph.
SOH-bay doh-OH-ay-in ay-AY-ii ii-VONV.

Zacar, gohus, od zamran. Odo
ZAY-kayr, goh-US, ohd zam-ran. od-oh

cicle qaa. Zorge. Lap zirdo
sii-kayl kwah-AY-ay. zorj. lap zir-DOH

noco mad; hoath Iaida.
NOH-kwoh mad; hohth jay-II-da.

Key of the Fourteenth Table

Napeai babagen, dsbrin ux
nay-pee-ay bay-BAY-jen, dee-es-brin yewks

ooaona lring vonph doalim,
oh-oh-AY-oh-na el-ring vonv doh-ay-lim,

eolis ollog orsba dschis affa,
ee-OH-lis ohl-log ors-ba dee-es-kiis af-fa,

micma isro mad od lonshitox ds
mik-ma iz-roh mad ohd lon-shii-toks dee-es

iumd aai grosb. Zacar od zamran.
jay-umd ay-AY-ii grozb. ZAY-kayr ohd zam-ran.

Odo cicle qaa. Zorge. Lap zirdo
od-oh sii-kayl kwah-AY-ay. zorj. lap zir-DOH

noco mad; hoath Iaida.
NOH-kwoh mad; hohth jay-II-da.

Call Fourteen

O you sons of fury, the daughters of the just, which

sit upon twenty-four seats, vexing all creatures of the earth

with age, which have under you 1636; Behold

the voice of God, promise of Him which is called

amongst you fury (or extreme justice). Move and show yourselves. Open

the mysteries of your creation. Be friendly unto me. For I am

a servant of the same your God; the true worshiper of the Highest.

Call Fifteen

O thou the Governor of the First Flame, under whose

wings are 6739 which weave

the earth with dryness, which knowest

the great name Righteousness and the seal of

honor. Move and show yourselves. Open

the mysteries of your creation. Be friendly unto me. For I am

a servant of the same your God; the true worshiper of the Highest.

Key of the Fifteenth Table

Noromi bagie, pasbs oiad, ds
noh-ROM-ii bag-EE, pas-bes oh-ii-AD, dee-es

trint mirc ol thil, dods tolham caosgo
trint mirk oh-el thil, dods tol-HAYM kay-OS-go

homin, dsbrin oroch quar; micma
hom-in, dee-es-brin oh-ROK kwar; mik-ma

bial oiad, aisro tox dsium
bii-al oh-ii-AD, ay-ii-sroh toks dee-sii-um

aai baltim. Zacar od zamran. Odo
ay-AY-ii bal-tim. ZAY-kayr ohd zam-ran. od-oh

cicle qaa. Zorge. Lap zirdo
sii-kayl kwah-AY-ay. zorj. lap zir-DOH

noco mad; hoath Iaida.
NOH-kwoh mad; hohth jay-II-da.

Key of the Sixteenth Table

Yls tabaan lialprt, casarman
yils tay-BAY-an el-YAL-purt, kay-SAR-man

upaahi chis darg dsoado
yew-pay-hii kiis darj dee-soh-ay-doh

caosgi orscor, ds omax
kay-OZH-ii ors-kor, dee-es oh-MAKS

monasci baeovib od emetgis
mon-ay-sii bee-oh-vib ohd em-et-jis

iaiadix. Zacar od zamran. Odo
yay-II-ad-iks. ZAY-kayr ohd zam-ran. od-oh

cicle qaa. Zorge. Lap zirdo
sii-kayl kwah-AY-ay. zorj. lap zir-DOH

noco mad; hoath Iaida.
NOH-kwoh mad; hohth jay-II-da.

Call Sixteen

O thou of the Second Flame, the house of justice which

has thy beginning in glory and shalt comfort the just;

which walkest upon the earth with feet 8763 that understand

and separate creatures; Great art thou in the God of Stretch Forth and Conquer.

Move and show yourselves. Open the mysteries of

your creation. Be friendly unto me. For I am a servant of

the same your God; the true worshiper of the Highest.

Call Seventeen

O thou whose wings are

thorns to stir up vexation, and hast 7336

lamps living going before thee; whose God

is Wrath in Anger. Gird up thy loins and hearken.

Move and show yourselves. Open the mysteries of

your creation. Be friendly unto me. For I am a servant of

the same your God; the true worshiper of the Highest.

Key of the Seventeenth Table

Yls vivialprt, salman balt ds
yils viv-ii-AL-purt, SAYL-man balt dee-ess

acroodzi busd od bliorax balit;
ak-roh-OD-zii buzd ohd blii-OH-raks bal-it;

dsinsi caosg lusdan emod dsom
dee-sin-sii kay-OZH lus-dan ee-mod dee-som

od tliob; Drilpa geh yls madzilodarp.
ohd tlii-ob; dril-pa jey yils mad-ZII-loh-darp.

Zacar od zamran. Odo cicle
ZAY-kayr ohd zam-ran. od-oh sii-kayl

qaa. Zorge. Lap zirdo noco
kwah-AY-ay. zorj. lap zir-DOH NOH-kwoh

mad; hoath Iaida.
mad; hohth jay-II-da.

Key of the Eighteenth Table

Yls dialprt, soba upaah chis
yils dii-AL-purt, SOH-bay yew-pay-ah kiis

nanba zixlay dodsih, odbrint taxs
nan-ba ziks-lay dod-sih, ohd-brint taks-is

hubaro tastax ylsi; sobaiad
hoo-BAY-roh tas-taks yil-sii; soh-BAY-ad

ivonpovnph. Aldon daxil od toatar.
ii-VON-foh-unv. AL-don daks-il ohd toh-AY-tar.

Zacar od zamran. Odo cicle
ZAY-kayr ohd zam-ran. od-oh sii-kayl

qaa. Zorge. Lap zirdo noco
kwah-AY-ay. zorj. lap zir-DOH NOH-kwoh

mad; hoath Iaida.
mad; hohth jay-II-da.

Call Eighteen

O thou mighty Light and Burning Flame of comfort,

which openest the glory of God to the center

of the earth. In whom the secrets of truth 6332

have their abiding, which is called

in thy kingdom Joy, and

not to be measured. Be thou a window of comfort unto me.

Move and show yourselves. Open the mysteries of

your creation. Be friendly unto me. For I am a servant of

the same your God; the true worshiper of the Highest.

Key of the Nineteenth Table

Yls micalzo ialpirt ialprg bliors,
yils mii-KAYL-zoh YAL-pert YAL-purj blii-ORS,

ds odo busdir oiad ovoars
dee-es od-oh buz-der oh-ii-AD oh-voh-ars

caosgo. Casarmg laiad eran
kay-OS-go. kay-SAR-mij lay-II-ad ee-RAN

brints casasam, ds iumd
brints kay-SAY-sam, dee-es jay-umd

aqlo adohi moz, od
AY-kwah-loh ay-DOH-hii moz, ohd

maoffas. Bolp comobliort pambt.
may-AHF-fas. bulp koh-moh-blii-ort pamt.

Zacar od zamran. Odo cicle
ZAY-kayr ohd zam-ran. od-oh sii-kayl

qaa. Zorge. Lap zirdo noco
kwah-AY-ay. zorj. lap zir-DOH NOH-kwoh

mad; hoath Iaida.
mad; hohth jay-II-da.

The Call of the Aethyrs

O you heavens which dwell [in the ___ *Aethyr*]

are mighty in the Parts of the Earth, and

execute the judgment of the Highest. To you

it is said, Behold the face of your God,

the beginning of comfort; whose eyes

are the brightness of the heavens; which provided

you for the government of the earth and her

unspeakable variety; furnishing you

with a power (of) understanding to dispose all things according to

the providence of Him that sitteth upon the Holy Throne; and rose up

in the beginning saying, "The earth,

let her be governed by her parts, and let there be

division in her, that the glory of her may be

always drunken and vexed in itself.

Her course, let it run with the heavens, and as

a handmaid let her serve them. One season, let it confound

Key of Tables Twenty to Forty-Nine

Madriiax dspraf [___]
MAY-drii-yaks dee-es-praf [___]

chismicaolz saanir caosgo, od
kiis-mii-KAY-ohlz say-AY-ner kay-OS-go, ohd

fisis balzizras Iaida. Nonca
FIS-iis bal-zii-sras jay-II-da. non-sa

gohulim, micma adoian mad,
goh-HOO-lim, mik-ma ay-doh-II-an mad,

iaod bliorb; sabaooaona
YAY-ohd blii-ORB; say-bay-oh-oh-AY-oh-na

chis luciftias piripsol; ds abraassa
kiis loo-SIF-tii-as per-IP-sol; dee-es ab-RAY-sa

noncf netaaib caosgi od tilb
non-sef nee-TAY-ay-ib kay-OZH-ii ohd tilb

adphaht damploz; tooat noncf
ad-fot DAM-ploz; toh-OH-at non-sef

gmicalzoma lrasd tofglo marb
jee-mii-KAYL-zoh-ma el-RAZD TOF-gloh marb

yarry Idoigo; od torzulp
YAR-ee ii-dee-oy-go; ohd tor-ZOOLP

iaodaf gohol, "Caosga,
YAY-oh-daf goh-HOHL, "kay-OS-ga,

tabaord saanir, od christeos
tay-BAY-ord say-AY-ner, ohd kris-TEE-os

yrpoil tiobl, busdirtilb noaln
yur-POY-il tii-AHB-el, buz-der-tilb noh-aln

paid orsba od dodrmni zilna.
pay-id ors-ba ohd dod-rum-nii zil-na.

Elzaptilb, parmgi piripsax, od ta
el-ZAP-tilb, parm-jii per-IP-saks, ohd tay

qurlst booapis. Lnibm, oucho
kurlst boh-OH-ay-pis. el-nib-em, oh-yew-choh

The Call of the Aethyrs continued

another, and let there be no creature upon

or within her the same. All her members, let them differ in

their qualities, and let there be no one creature

equal with another. The reasonable creatures of the earth (or men), let them vex and

weed out one another; and the dwelling places, let them forget

their names. The work of man and his pomp,

let them be defaced. His buildings, let them become caves for

the beasts of the field. Confound her understanding with darkness. For why?

It repenteth me I made man. One while

let her be known, and another while a stranger;

Because she is the bed of an harlot,

and the dwelling place of him that is fallen.

O you heavens, arise! The lower heavens

beneath you, let them serve you. Govern

those that govern; cast down such as

fall. Bring forth with those that increase,

Key of Tables Twenty to Forty-Nine continued

symp, od christeos agtoltorn mirc
simp, ohd kris-TEE-os ay-jee-tol-torn mirk

q tiobl lel. Ton paombd, dilzmo
kwah tii-AHB-el el-el. ton pay-omd, dilz-moh

aspian, od christeos agltoltorn
as-pii-an, ohd kris-TEE-os ag-el-tol-torn

parach asymp. Cordziz, dodpal od
pay-RAK ay-simp. KORD-ziz, dod-pal ohd

fifalz lsmnad; od fargt, bams
fii-falz els-mad; ohd farj-et, bams

omaoas. Conisbra od avavox,
oh-may-OH-as. koh-NIS-bra ohd av-VAY-voks,

tonug. Orscatbl, noasmi tabges
too-nuj. ors-kat-bel, noh-ays-mii tab-jes

levithmong. Unchi omptilb ors. Bagle?
lev-ith-mong. un-kii omp-tilb ors. BAY-gayl?

Moooah olcordziz. Lcapimao
moh-oh-WAH ohl-KORD-ziz. el-kay-PII-may-oh

ixomaxip, odcacocasb gosaa;
iks-oh-MAKS-ip, ohd-kay-KOH-kazb goh-say-ay;

baglen pii tianta ababalond,
BAY-gayl-en pii-ii tii-AN-ta ay-BAY-bay-lond,

odfaorgt telocvovim.
ohd-fay-ORJT tee-LOCH-voh-vee-im.

Madriiax, torzu! Oadriax
MAY-drii-yaks, tor-ZOO! oh-AY-drii-aks

orocha, aboapri. Tabaori
oh-ROH-ka, ay-BOH-ay-prii. tay-BAY-oh-rii

priaz artabas; adrpan corsta
prii-AYZ ar-tay-bas; ay-dir-pan kors-tay

dobix. Yolcam priazi arcoazior,
dob-iks. yol-kam prii-AY-zii ar-koh-ay-zhor,

The Call of the Aethyrs continued

and destroy the rotten. No place let it remain

in one number. Add and diminish until

the stars be numbered." Arise, move,

and appear before the covenant of his mouth, which

he hath sworn unto us in his justice. Open the mysteries of your creation,

and make us partakers of undefiled knowledge.

Key of Tables Twenty to Forty-Nine continued

odquasb	qting.	Ripir	paaoxt
ohd-kwazb	*kwah-tinj.*	*rii-PER*	*PAY-ay-okst*

sagacor.	Uml	od	prdzar	cacrg
say-GAY-kor.	*um-el*	*ohd*	*purd-zar*	*KAY-kurg*

aoiveae	cormpt."	Torzu,	zacar,
ay-oy-VEE-ay	*kormft."*	*tor-ZOO,*	*ZAY-kayr,*

odzamran	aspt	sibsi	butmona,	ds
ohd-zam-ran	*aspt*	*sib-sii*	*but-moh-na,*	*dee-es*

surzas	tia	baltan.	Odo	cicle	qaa,
sur-zas	*tii-a*	*bal-tan.*	*od-oh*	*sii-kayl*	*kwah-AY-ay,*

od	ozazma	plapli	iadnamad.
ohd	*oz-az-ma*	*play-plii*	*yad-nay-mad.*

Bibliography

Agrippa, Henry Cornelius. *Three Books of Occult Philosophy*. Llewellyn, 1992.

Almadel of Solomon (found in the *Lemegeton*), http://www.esotericarchives.com/solomon/lemegeton.htm.

Arbatel of Magic, http://www.esotericarchives.com/solomon/arbatel.htm.

Cicero, Chic, and Sandra Tabatha Cicero. *Book of the Concourse of the Watchtowers*. H.O.G.D Books, 2012.

———. *Creating Magical Tools: The Magician's Craft*. Llewellyn, 1999.

———. *Ritual Use of Magical Tools: Resources for the Ceremonial Magician*. Llewellyn, 2000.

Crowley, Aleister. *Liber LXXXIV Vel Chanokh: A Brief Abstract of the Symbolic Representation of the Universe by Doctor John Dee Through the Skrying of Sir Edward Kelley*, http://pturing.firehead.org/occult/renaissance/Liber_Chanokh.pdf.

———. *The Vision & the Voice with Commentary and Other Papers: The Collected Diaries of Aleister Crowley, 1909–1914 E.V.* Weiser Books, 1999.

Dee, John. *Digital Scans of the Enochian Manuscripts* (i.e., all of Dee's original journals), http://www.themagickalreview.org/enochian/mss/.

———. *The Heptarchia Mystica*, http://www.esotericarchives.com/dee/hm.htm.

———. *John Dee's Five Books of Mystery*, ed. Joseph Peterson. RedWheel/Weiser, 2008.

———. *A True and Faithful Relation of What Passed for Many Years Between Dr. John Dee…and Some Spirits,* ed. Méric Casaubon, http://www.themagickalreview.org/enochian/tfr.php.

DuQuette, Lon Milo. *Enochian Vision Magick: An Introduction and Practical Guide to the Magick of Dr. John Dee and Edward Kelley.* Weiser Books, 2008.

——— with Christopher Hyatt. *Enochian World of Aleister Crowley*. New Falcon Publications; twentieth anniversary edition, 2011.

The Heptameron, http://www.esotericarchives.com/solomon/heptamer.htm.

James, Geoffrey. *The Enochian Magick of Dr. John Dee*. Llewellyn, 2002.

Kaplan, Aryeh. *Jewish Meditation.* Schocken Books, 1985. (Especially see pp. 40–41.)

Kelley, Edward. *The Theatre of Terrestrial Astronomy,* http://www.levity.com/alchemy/terrastr.html.

King James Bible, http://www.biblegateway.com.

Laycock, Donald. *The Complete Enochian Dictionary: A Dictionary of the Angelic Language as Revealed to Dr. John Dee and Edward Kelley.* Weiser Books, 2001.

Leitch, Aaron. *The Angelical Language, Volume I: The Complete History and Mythos of the Tongue of Angels*. Llewellyn, 2010.

———. *The Angelical Language, Volume II: An Encyclopedic Lexicon of the Tongue of Angels*. Llewellyn, 2010.

———. *A Discourse on the Enochian Watchtowers*, http://kheph777.tripod.com/art_discourse.html.

———. *The Quest for the Divine Language*, http://www.llewellyn.com/journal/article/2108.

———. *Secrets of the Magickal Grimoires, The Classical Texts of Magick Deciphered*. Llewellyn, 2005.

———. *Shem haMephoresh, the Divine Name of Extension*, http://www.hermeticgoldendawn.org/leitch-shemhamephoresh.html.

Lemegeton, http://www.esotericarchives.com/solomon/lemegeton.htm.

Liber Juratus, http://www.esotericarchives.com/juratus/juratus.htm.

Lumpkin, Joseph B. *The Books of Enoch: A Complete Volume Containing 1 Enoch (The Ethiopic Book of Enoch), 2 Enoch (The Slavonic Secrets of Enoch), 3 Enoch (The Hebrew Book of Enoch)*. Fifth Estate, 2011.

Mclean, Adam, ed. *A Treatise on Angel Magic*. Weiser, 2006.

The Pauline Arts (in the *Lemegeton*), http://www.esotericarchives.com/solomon/lemegeton.htm.

Peterson, Joseph. *Esoteric Archives CD*, http://www.esotericarchives.com/cd.htm.

———, ed. *John Dee's Five Books of Mystery by John Dee.* RedWheel/Weiser, 2008.

———. *Twilit Grotto: Archives of Western Esoterica,* http://www.esotericarchives.com.

Regardie, Israel. *The Complete Golden Dawn System of Magic.* Original Falcon Press, 2010.

———. *The Golden Dawn: The Original Account of the Teachings, Rites and Ceremonies of the Hermetic Order.* Llewellyn, 2002.

Scholem, Gershom. *Major Trends in Jewish Mysticism.* Schocken, 1995.

———. *Origins of the Kabbalah.* Princeton University Press, 1991.

Skinner, Stephen, and David Rankine. *The Practical Angel Magic of Dr. John Dee's Enochian Tables: Tabularum Bonorum Angelorum Invocationes.* Llewellyn, 2010. (This is *Book H.*)

Trithemius, Johannes. *De Septum Secundeis,* http://www.renaissanceastrology.com/heavenlyintelligences.html.

———. *Steganographia,* http://www.esotericarchives.com/tritheim/stegano.htm.

Tyson, Donald. *Enochian Magick for Beginners: The Original System of Angel Magick.* Llewellyn, 2002.

Wilson, Dean F. *Enochian Magic in Theory.* Kerubim Press, 2012.

Endnotes

1 In this way, Enochian magick has something in common with the infamous *Book of Abramelin*, which is also a magickal system popularly known as very advanced and dangerous, yet is, in fact, intended to progress one from beginner to adept over a period of months and years.

2 Before this rediscovery, two attempts were made to create new versions of the book. We call these the *Slavonic Book of Enoch* (or *2 Enoch*) and the *Hebrew Book of Enoch* (or *3 Enoch*). These texts would have their own influence upon the Enochian legends, but their history does not directly concern us here.

3 Personally, I suspect it was never meant to be translated, and only the angels associated with the book can reveal the mysteries concealed in its pages.

4 A leaf is one piece of paper in a book, with a front and a back side, thus containing two pages.

5 Dee's journals actually mention several different mystical books. One of these was a small Book of Silvered Leaves that—so the angels promised—would contain ineffable celestial mysteries. Enochian students have often confused the Book of Silvered Leaves with the *Book of Loagaeth*; however, they are two distinct books. Dee never fashioned the Book of Silvered Leaves, nor did he record what might have been written in it.

6 A similar system was outlined by Agrippa in his *Three Books of Occult Philosophy*, which is likely Dee's source.

7 I will explain this hidden Part of the Earth in chapter 10.

8 See http://dictionary.reference.com/browse/ether—especially definitions 3, 4, and 5.

9 See my *Discourse on the Enochian Watchtowers.*

10 After my own analysis of the Great Table, I suspect each Watchtower can be associated with a zodiacal triplicity—and, thus, an element. However, none of this is mentioned in Dee's journals, so I will not outline it here. See my *Discourse on the Enochian Watchtowers.*

11 These nations are not listed in Dee's journals. I have given them merely as examples of nations that typically fall into these four categories.

12 See *A True and Faithful Relation,* p. 184 (Wednesday, June 27, 1584).

13 The angels transmitted each Watchtower one after the other. Dee wrote them into the Great Table in a "Z pattern," or zig-zag—putting the first Watchtower in the upper-left position, the second in the upper-right position, the third in the lower-left position, and the final in the lower-right position. The angels corrected this by telling him to switch the two lower Watchtowers so that the four actually ran clockwise around the Great Table.

14 See *A True and Faithful Relation,* pp. 172–181 (June 25, 1584).

15 See *A True and Faithful Relation* beginning on April 4, 1587.

16 To be fair to poor Mary, her father's actions (both officially and toward her personally) were heartless and self-centered. He destroyed Mary's family and home life, and refused to allow her to see her mother. She had real reason to hate the Church of England, or at least those who had established it.

17 There is some indication that Kelley may have been a spy himself—perhaps even for the Catholics. However, an exploration of this aspect of Kelley's shadowy past is beyond the scope of this primer.

18 Annael did not state how long his term in office would last. However, the *Arbatel of Magic*—which had a profound influence on Dee's Heptarchic system—suggests a 490-year cycle. According to that text, the angel of Mercury took over in the year 1900, which in Dee's system would make Raphael the supreme archangel now.

19 The name "Fortitudo Dei"—which can be translated as "Strength of God"—made Dee initially mistake this angel for Gabriel. Gabriel is Hebrew for "Strength of God." However, the angel soon affirmed that he was, indeed, Michael.

20 The angel Me is one of the "Family of Light" angels, whom I will describe in chapter 6.

21 I will not cover the Corpus Omnium table in this primer; however, it is discussed in exhaustive detail in my *Angelical Language, Volume I.*

22 Illemese actually revealed a single call that was to be repeated thirty times (one of each aethyric heaven), changing only the name of the Aethyr in each instance.

23 The Seal of the True God is an important piece of Enochian magickal equipment that I will describe in detail in chapter 7.

24 I will not be covering this group of angels in this book. I will discuss them in a forthcoming advanced Enochian work.

25 I include a full discussion of Counting the Omer and the Fifty Gates of Binah in my *Angelical Language, Volume I.*

26 See Agrippa's *Three Books of Occult Philosophy*, book I, chapter 31, "How Provinces and Kingdoms Are Distributed to Planets."

27 There is no mention of the throne of God in relation to the Great Table in Dee's journals; however, there is reason to believe the relationship was intended. See my *Discourse on the Enochian Watchtowers* for a full explanation.

28 I have published a fuller discussion of this topic in my *Quest for the Divine Language.* Plus, of course, I focus entirely upon Dee's contribution to the quest in *The Angelical Language, Volumes I* and *II.*

29 I cover the Gnostic influences within the forty-eight callings in depth in *The Angelical Language, Volume I.*

30 Dee left us a copy of his own *Book of Supplication* in his personal grimoire. However, the author of *Book H* does not appear to have had access to that document. Therefore, we have two versions of the *Book of Supplication* used in the Great Table initiation rite: one written by Dee and one written by the author of *Book H.* As we shall see later, the angels instructed that each aspirant should write his own version of the *Book of Supplication.*

31 Dee's personal grimoire would not help matters once it was found, because he had included a copy of the Reformed Table next to the original Great Table in the book. This perhaps indicates that even Dee was unsure whether or not the Reformed Table had a part to play in the magickal system.

32 Second only to the Vault of Christian Rosencrutz, of which the four Watchtowers were just one part.

33 The Table of Union will be explained in the neo-Enochian section of the grimoire (chapter 12).

34 You can see these colorful Watchtowers for yourself in the two-volume set *Creating and Using Magical Tools* by Chic and Sandra Tabatha Cicero.

35 See Joseph Peterson's *John Dee's Five Books of Mystery.*

36 Crowley's *Liber Vel Chanokh* can be found online at http://hermetic.com/crowley/libers/liber084.pdf.

37 At some point in history, this diagram was inscribed upon a round golden talisman that still exists today in the British Museum. Many have assumed the talisman was created by Dee himself for use in the Enochian system of magick. However, because it is a copy of an illustration from Casaubon's *True and Faithful Relation*, it was apparently made after the publication of that book and therefore long after Dee's passing.

38 You can see its original form in *The Enochian Magick of Dr. John Dee*, p. 119.

39 See the *Sepher Bahir*.

40 There are actually ten Sephirotic realms in total. Seven of them relate to the planets. The other three Sephiroth embody the physical realm, the sphere of the zodiac, and the "first swirlings" of creation.

41 See Agrippa's *Three Books of Occult Philosophy*, book 2, chapter 10, "Of the Number Seven, and the Scale Thereof."

42 Cumael appears in Dee's journals. However, his name is traditionally spelled Camael, which is likely a corruption of the name Samael.

43 You may notice that this list is very similar to the previous list given for the archangels of the Sephiroth. In fact, they are historically the same list that eventually took on two different forms. The list of Sephirothic archangels appears in Agrippa's work, while the list of planetary archangels appears in grimoires like *The Heptameron*. By Dee's time, both lists were being treated as separate groups of angels—one on a higher plane and the other on a lower plane.

44 You may note the switch between Michael and Raphael in this list when compared to the archangels of the Sephiroth (see previous note). Both of these archangels have traditional associations with both Mercury and Sol, and it appears different occultists have chosen to associate them more with one planet or the other. Again, by Dee's time the two lists had become separate traditions in their own right, and Dee adopted them both.

45 This name appears this way in Dee's journals. In other sources it is usually spelled Anael.

46 See the *Arbatel of Magic*. In Dee's journals, Annael revealed that the seven archangels govern the world in succession (and that he was in charge at the time), but he did not reveal how long each period of rule lasted. This information is included in Arbatel, which had a massive impact on Dee's Heptarchic system. There the period of rule is given as 490 (or 10 × 49) years.

47 See *John Dee's Five Books of Mystery*, pp. 152–165 (book 3, April 28, 1582). Also note pp. 381–382 (appendix, April 29, 1583): "And so are the other 7 characters...proper to every king and prince according to their order."

Finally, see pp. 399–400 (appendix, May 5, 1583) for the construction of the seven talismans.

48 *Three Books of Occult Philosophy*, book 2, chapter 22, "Of the tables of the Planets, their virtues, forms, and what Divine names, Intelligences and Spirits are set over them."

49 Also spelled Sabathiel.

50 This name appears this way in Dee's journals. It is more properly spelled Shemeshiel in Hebrew.

51 This name appears this way in Dee's journals. It is more properly spelled Kokabiel in Hebrew.

52 There is another Hagonel found in the Heptarchic system—his name will appear in the list of the Family of Light. It is unclear whether or not the two are directly related, but it is unlikely they are the same angel.

53 See *John Dee's Five Books of Mystery*, p. 211 (book 4, November 17, 1582). Dee notes that only six of the forty-two Ministers are "in subjection." I assume this means only those six are subject to our call.

54 Ibid., p. 236, note 273 (book 4, November 20, 1582).

55 In astrology, Venus rules Libra, the cardinal sign of Air.

56 For Baligon's functions, see *John Dee's Five Books of Mystery*, pp. 242–243 (book 4, November 20, 1582).

For Bagenol's functions, see pp. 199–200 (book 4, November 18, 1582). *Note*: These powers are originally listed with Prince Bralges; however, Dee later notes an intruding spirit corrupted this session and several of the powers of the princes were switched or missing. Bagenol's powers were not mentioned, but as Baligon's prince he should rule the spirits of Air.

57 Ibid., p. 243 (book 4, November 20, 1582).

58 The seals of the kings and six of the princes are all found in *John Dee's Five Books of Mystery*, pp. 184–187 (book 4, November 15, 1582).

59 The princes were described as a group in *John Dee's Five Books of Mystery*, pp. 184–187 and p. 188, note 11 (book 4, November 15, 1582). Further details about the princes' appearances were recorded on other pages, which I will note with each prince.

60 Later, we shall see there is another angel—a son of the Sons of Light—named Hagonel. These two angels are *not* one and the same.

61 See *John Dee's Five Books of Mystery*, p. 188 (book 4, November 15, 1582).

62 Ibid. and p. 201, note 78 (Friday, November 18).

63 Ibid., p. 243 (November 20, 1582).

64 For Bobogel's functions, see *John Dee's Five Books of Mystery,* p. 223 (book 4, November 19, 1582). For Bornogo's functions, see p. 195 (book 4, November 16, 1582).

65 Ibid., pp. 184–185 (book 4, November 15, 1582) and pp. 216–217 (book 4, November 17,1582).

66 Ibid., p. 221 (book 4, November 19, 1582).

67 Ibid., p. 229 (note 233) and p. 230 (November 19, 1582).

68 Ibid., pp. 217–219 (November 17, 1582).

69 Ibid., pp. 216–217 (November 17, 1582).

70 In astrology, Mars rules Scorpio, the fixed sign of Water.

71 For Babalel's functions, see *John Dee's Five Books of Mystery,* p. 231 (note 247, November 19, 1582), and p. 233 (note 256, November 20, 1582). For Befafes's functions, see pp. 195–196 (November 16, 1582).

72 For Babalel's appearance, see *John Dee's Five Books of Mystery,* pp. 231–233 (November 19, 1582). For the servient angel named Multin, see p. 233 (November 20, 1582).

73 For Befafes's appearance, see *John Dee's Five Books of Mystery,* p. 234 (November 20, 1582). For Befafes's alternate name of Obelison, see pp. 234–235.

74 Ibid., pp. 235–236 (November 20, 1582).

75 See Prince Befafes, who gives life to creatures of the sea, and Baligon/Bagenol, who govern creatures of the air.

76 For Bynepor's functions, see *John Dee's Five Books of Mystery,* pp. 236–237 (note 273) and pp. 238–239 (November 20, 1582). For Butmono's functions, see p. 198 (November 18, 1582). *Note*: Butmono's functions were originally listed with Prince Blisdon. However, Dee later notes an intruding spirit corrupted this session and several of the powers of the princes were switched or missing. As Bynepor's prince, Butmono should govern the life of all things.

77 Ibid., pp. 236–239 (November 20, 1582).

78 In astrology, Mercury rules Virgo, the mutable sign of Earth.

79 For Bnaspol's functions, see *John Dee's Five Books of Mystery*, p. 240 (November 20, 1582). For Blisdon's functions, see pp. 196–198 (November 18, 1582). *Note*: Blisdon's powers were originally listed with Prince Butmono. However, Dee later notes an intruding spirit corrupted this session and several of the powers of the princes were switched or missing. As Bnaspol's prince, Blisdon should govern the bowels of the earth.

80 This same concept is mentioned in the *Book of Abramelin* (book 1, chapter 8), where the aspirant can lay claim to a certain portion of the buried treasures saved up for the Antichrist.

81 For Bnaspol's appearance, see *John Dee's Five Books of Mystery*, p. 240 (November 20, 1582).

82 This is a traditional color for Mercury and can be seen in alchemical texts as well as the *Key of Solomon the King*. Note that it is also the color of the silk that covers the Enochian Holy Table.

83 For Blisdon's appearance, see *John Dee's Five Books of Mystery*, p. 240 (November 20, 1582).

84 Ibid.

85 For Bnapsen's functions, see *John Dee's Five Books of Mystery*, p. 241 (November 20, 1582). For Brorges's functions, see p. 199 (November 18, 1582).

86 For Bnapsen's appearance, see *John Dee's Five Books of Mystery*, p. 241 (November 20, 1582).

87 Ibid.

88 There is much confusion in the journals over the functions of King Blumaza and Prince Bralges. At first glance, their functions appear to be missing from the record, but they can be found. First, the ruling prince of the Heptarchia (Bagenol, going by the name Hagonel) outlines all the powers of the princes *except* for his own (see *John Dee's Five Books of Mystery*, pp. 194–201, November 16, 1582). However, Dee later suspects this information was corrupted and several of the powers of the princes were switched or missing (see p. 236, note 273, November 20, 1582).

Later, Hagonel reveals a table of forty-two ministers that he *appears* to govern (see pp. 203–207, November 17, 1582). However, that table of ministers would eventually prove to belong to Monday / Luna, and thus to Prince Bralges. These ministering angels of Monday, along with their king and prince, are in charge of all the kings of the earth; thus, these functions belong to Prince Bralges and—by extension—to King Blumaza (see p. 201, note 78, Friday, November 18, 1582).

89 For some reason, Bralges does not appear at this point in the journals. Instead, it is Prince Hagonel who introduces Bralges's ministers. (See *John Dee's Five Books of Mystery*, pp. 203–207, November 17, 1582.)

90 Ibid., p. 206 (November 17, 1582). *Note*: All references to the ministers on pp. 205–206 mention groups of *six* angels rather than seven. However, Carmara quickly corrected this, and Dee made a marginal notation about his confusion; see p. 207, note 107. From that point on, all references are to groups of seven.

91 See *John Dee's Five Books of Mystery*, pages 204, 205–207, and 210–212 (November 17, 1582).

92 Ibid., pp. 204–206 (November 17, 1582).

93 See *A True and Faithful Relation*, pp. 10–27 (May–June, 1583).

94 See *John Dee's Five Books of Mystery*, p. 187, note 8, Thursday, November 15, 1582.

95 Ibid., p. 188, Thursday, November 15, 1582.

96 Ibid., p. 247, note 324, Wednesday, November 21, 1582.

97 This Hagonel is not the same Hagonel who is prince of the Heptarchia.

98 See *John Dee's Five Books of Mystery*, pp. 70–71 (book 1, Saturday, March 10, 1582), pp. 79–80 (book 1, Wednesday, March 14, 1582), and pp. 87–148 (book 2, March 1582).

99 On Dee's own Seal of the True God, Zedekiel is spelled "Zedekieil." It is very likely the second "i" was an error on Dee's part as he carved the seal.

100 Such lengthy divine "names" are common in the Qabalah, where we find examples as long as forty-two or even seventy-two letters.

101 The eighth secret name is never mentioned in Dee's journals, and there are several mysteries associated with the name and how to find it within the seal's circumference. This will be covered in a later advanced text.

102 See *John Dee's Five Books of Mystery*, pp. 70–72 (book 1, March 10, 1582), p. 245 (book 4, November 21, 1582), pp. 374–379 (appendix, April 28, 1583), pp. 381–382 (appendix, April 29, 1583), pp. 395–398 and 399–400 (appendix, May 5, 1583).

103 See the *Key of Solomon the King*, book 1, chapter 2, "Of the Days and Hours and of the Virtue of the Planets" and book 1, chapter 8, "Concerning Pentacles and the Manner of Constructing Them." Also note the wand made of hazel wood in this grimoire—hazel being a wood sacred to Mercury.

104 See *John Dee's Five Books of Mystery*, p. 72 (book 1, March 10, 1582) and p. 374 (appendix, April 28, 1583).

105 The description can also be found in Francis Barrett's *The Magus*, book 2, part 3, "Of the making of the CRYSTAL and the Form of Preparation for a VISION."An illustration of the table can be found in my own *Secrets of the Magickal Grimoires.*

106 See *John Dee's Five Books of Mystery*, pp. 374–379 (appendix, April 28, 1583).

107 Agrippa mentions talismans of Mercury engraved upon plates of tin; see the *Three Books of Occult Philosophy*, book 2, chapter 22, "Of the Tables of the Planets...": "The sixth table is of Mercury...and if it be with Mercury being fortunate engraven upon Silver, *or Tin* or yellow Brass, or be writ upon Virgin Parchment, it renders the bearer thereof grateful, and fortunate to do what he pleaseth: it bringeth gain, and

prevents poverty, conduceth to memory, understanding, and divination, and to the understanding of occult things by dreams..." (emphasis mine). I assume the seven Enochian ensigns are essentially Mercurial—like the talismans of the *Key of Solomon*—to further aid communication between the human operator and the angels.

108 It is possible that the Ensign of Mercury should now take the topmost position, meaning the ensigns would have to run clockwise from Mercury to Saturn, Luna, Venus, Sol, Mars, and finally Jupiter.

109 Dee recorded three visions of the Holy Table. In the first, the upper tablecloth was simply red. In the second, the cloth had changed to "changeable (mixed) red and green." Finally, in the third vision, the cloth had evolved once more to its pied, or peacock, coloring: "the most changeable that can be gotten."

110 Meet = fitting, proper, acceptable.

111 See *John Dee's Five Books of Mystery*, pages 63, 64, 66–67, and 68 (note 61). Also see pp. 19–20 (note 55), where it is described and compared with Trithemius's *Art of Drawing Spirits into Crystals* and Barrett's *Magus*.

112 See below in this section for information on the actual crystal given to Dee by an angel.

113 Compare this to Trithemius's *Art of Drawing Spirits into Crystals*, where the crystal ball is set in a frame displaying the names Michael, Gabriel, Raphael, and Uriel.

114 See *The Holy Almandal: Angels and the Intellectual Aims of Magic* by Jan R. Veenstra, p. 214: "A twelfth-century student of catoptromancy [divination using a mirror] explained the intricacies of Artesius's art by regarding the sun as a mirror that reflects the images of all things, so that capturing the sun's rays in shining objects may produce a reflection of present realities and perhaps reveal the secrets of nature...It is mainly through this theory that optics, i.e., the mathematical study of rays, came to play such an important role in magic and astrology, for Dee believed that optics could teach one to 'imprint the rays of any star more strongly upon any matter subjected to it,' and mirrors or lenses were naturally the most adequate means of reaching that effect."

115 Likewise, the *Almadel of Solomon* mentions a crystal ball but does not list it as an indispensable part of the *Almadel* itself.

116 See *John Dee's Five Books of Mystery*, p. 253 and p. 395 (note 105). Also see p. 19 (note 54).

117 Zedekiel, Madimiel, Semeliel, Nogahel, and Corabiel are the five angels who appear in the angles of the pentagram upon the Seal of the True God. They represent Jupiter, Mars, Sol, Venus, and Mercury. Why Saturn and Luna are excluded is not clear.

118 See *John Dee's Five Books of Mystery*, p. 69 (book 1, March 10, 1582), p. 151 (book 2, April 28, 1582), pp. 380–388 (appendix, April 29, 1583), and pp. 395 and 398 (appendix, May 5, 1583).

119 See the instructions for the Parts of the Earth magickal system in chapter 10 of this book.

120 See *John Dee's Five Books of Mystery*, pp. 78–79 (book 1, March 14, 1582) and pp. 151–152 (book 3, April 28, 1582).

121 *Three Books of Occult Philosophy*, book 3, chapter 11, "Of the Divine Names, and Their Power and Virtue." Compare this with Judges 13:18: "Why do you ask my name, it is a name that works wonders (*pele*)." Also see Exodus 15:11: "Who is like thee, glorious in holiness, fearful in praises, working wonders (*pele*)?" Also see Psalms 77:14: "Thou art the God that doest wonders (*pele*)."

122 See *John Dee's Five Books of Mystery*, pages 212–214, 236, and 399–402. Also see *Heptarchia Mystica*, chapters 5 and 6.

123 Ibid., p. 213 (book 4, November 17, 1582). Also p. 230 (note 239, November 19, 1582). Also pp. 399, 401–402 (appendix, May 5, 1583).

124 Similar backward letters would later be included in the Great Table of the Earth.

125 Dee was instructed to purify himself for nine days before attempting Gebofal, the practice of the *Book of Loagaeth*. I feel that same instruction applies equally well to Heptarchic invocations. In *The Key of Solomon the King*, you can find a nine-day purification that is likely similar to what Dee would have done.

126 See *The Enochian Magick of Dr. John Dee*, p. 53 (*The Mystical Heptarchy*, chapter 5): "The Oration to God to be Spoken *Every Day*, Three Times Successively" (I have added the emphasis).

127 Dee does not indicate one should face east; however, this is standard practice for Solomonic work.

128 See *John Dee's Five Books of Mystery*, p. 213 (book 4, November 17, 1582): "First cast thine eye unto the general prince, governor or angel that is principal in this world." In the margin, Dee notes: "Is it not Annael with whom I began?"

129 Dee does not specify exactly where on the Holy Table to set the talisman of the prince. However, based upon the similarities between the Holy Table and the Table of Practice described in the *Pauline Arts*, I suspect it was intended to set the prince's talisman directly atop the ensign.

130 See *The Enochian Magick of Dr. John Dee*, pp. 153–155 (Or *The Mystical Heptarchy*, chapter 5.) Note that I have modernized the punctuation, spelling, and some of the more archaic wording. I have also changed

aspects of the prayers that were specific to Dee personally, rewording them to apply to anyone reciting the prayer.

131 *The Mystical Heptarchy* reads: "...to deliver unto me, long since (through the eye and ear of Edward Kelley)..."

132 *The Mystical Heptarchy* reads: "...by thy Divine Beck..."

133 Isagoge = a scholarly introduction to a subject.

134 See *The Enochian Magick of Dr. John Dee*, p. 57 (Or *The Mystical Heptarchy*, chapter 6).

135 Here state the office and function of the king as it relates to your goal. Dee provided his own versions of the angels' offices (see *The Enochian Magick of Dr. John Dee*, pp. 59–64). However, most of them are personalized for Dee himself, mentioning things the angels revealed or promised to him. The rest are simply quotes from the journals—where an angel would mention his abilities or past deeds—and stitched together rather haphazardly. In your own invocations, I would suggest stating the offices of the angels as they specifically relate to your intended goal.

136 *The Mystical Heptarchy* reads: "...I may be holpen..."

137 See *The Enochian Magick of Dr. John Dee*, p. 58 (Or *The Mystical Heptarchy*, chapter 6).

138 Here state the office and function of the prince as it relates to your goal.

139 Dee's records do not mention repeating the invocations seven times. However, as seven is a sacred number to the Heptarchia, it is a good number of times to repeat their invocations if necessary.

140 This is a problem I have been working to solve. I will share my findings in future publications.

141 See previous endnote.

142 You can get the Forty-Nine Tables of *Loagaeth* on Joseph Peterson's *Esoteric Archives CD*: http://www.esotericarchives.com/cd.htm. You can see the original journals on *The Magickal Review*: http://www.themagickalreview.org/enochian/.

143 I have formed an online forum for discussion of the Angelical language and the *Book of Loagaeth*. The archives there already contain much useful information on creating your own copy: http://groups.yahoo.com/group/angelical_linguistics.

144 It is unclear in the journals, but these words might translate as "Let those that fear God, and are worthy, read."

145 See *John Dee's Five Books of Mystery*, p. 394 (appendix, May 5, 1583): "Humble yourselves nine days before. Yea, unrip (I say) the cankers of

your infected souls, that you may be apt and meet to understand the Secrets that shall be delivered."

146 See *The Key of Solomon the King* for a nine-day purification process that is likely similar to what Dee would have done.

147 See *A True and Faithful Relation*, pp. 196–197 (July 7, 1584). Again, I have modernized the punctuation and spelling and some of the more archaic wording.

148 The original prayer of Enoch says "fifty times" in these last two lines. However, Enoch was supposed to be practicing the Jewish ritual of "Counting the Omer," which takes fifty days. Meanwhile Dee's Christianized version (Gebofal) takes place over forty-nine days instead.

149 This system first appears in Agrippa's *Three Books of Occult Philosophy*, book 1, chapter 31, "How Provinces and Kingdoms Are Distributed to Planets."

150 The associations between the signs of the zodiac and the twelve tribes of Israel are also found in Agrippa's *Three Books of Occult Philosophy*, book 2, chapter 14, "Of the Number Eleven, and the Number Twelve..."

151 The names of these nations are taken from Ptolemey's *Geographia*, which was written in the second century CE and is thus outdated today. I have undertaken a project to update the names and locations of these nations, but space does not permit me to share the work here. I will provide it in a future publication.

152 Note that Lil is the first and highest Aethyr, closest to God's throne, and contains the three Parts of the Earth that cover the Fertile Crescent—the cradle of civilization.

153 See the next section for more about Paraoan.

154 See *A True and Faithful Relation*, pages 183 and 188 (Paraoan is first mentioned on p. 179), Tuesday, June 26; Wednesday, June 27; and Monday, July 2,1584.

155 See *The Enochian Magick of Dr. John Dee*, p. 112.

156 This is supported by other aspects of Dee's system that include hidden (or "blinded") references to the End Times—most of which I have decided to leave hidden for the purposes of this book. I will cover them in more depth in a later publication.

157 Dee discovered the spelling changes himself and asked the angels if he should correct the Great Table to better match the names of the parts. However, he was told to leave the spelling differences as they were. See *A True and Faithful Relation*, p. 188.

158 See chapter 11 for more on the Great Table of the Earth.

159 There are, of course, only seven letters in Paraoan. If there are four pairs of two letters, that leaves us one letter short—and this is the reversed letter L that appears in the lower-right corner of the Great Table (see the diagram in the next section). It is the first letter of Lexarph, the rest of which appear on the large central cross.

160 Remember the final thirty Angelical Calls are all the same, except that the name of the Aethyr is changed for each one.

161 See *John Dee's Five Books of Mystery*, p. 395 (appendix, May 5, 1583).

162 See chapter 2 for more details on the Watchtowers and the four world civilizations.

163 See *A True and Faithful Relation,* pp. 168–171 (Wednesday, June 20, 1584).

164 See Revelation 9. The colors of the horses are given as white, red, black, and "pale." Some scholars suppose the pale color was actually a pale greenish tint.

165 Generally, the four stages of alchemy are given the colors red, white, black, and yellow. However, some texts expand these four stages to seven, and one of the seven stages is an iridescent green, or "peacock." Edward Kelley would later write an alchemical treatise listing thirteen stages, with four of them given the colors black, peacock, white, and red, respectively: *The Theatre of Terrestrial Astronomy* by Edward Kelley. See http://www.levity.com/alchemy/terrastr.html.

166 See *A True and Faithful Relation,* p. 173 (Monday June 25, 1584).

167 The letters stand for the Latin phrase *Iesus Nazarenus, Rex Iudaeorum,* "Jesus of Nazareth, King of the Jews."

168 See figure 15, ensign of Mercury, p. 90.

169 See *A True and Faithful Relation,* p. 15. This page 15 is not in the front of the book, but nearly all the way at the end, after p. 448. It is the same entry where Dee records the infamous Reformed Great Table of Raphael.

170 See Agrippa's *Three Books of Occult Philosophy*, book 2, chapter 14: "Now the number twelve is divine, and that whereby the Celestials are measured; it is also the number of the signs in the zodiac over which there are twelve angels as chief, supported by the irrigation of the great name of God."

171 Also see Agrippa's *Three Books of Occult Philosophy*, book 2, chapter 14: the "Scale of the Number 12" includes "The Great Name (YHVH) returned back into twelve banners."

172 The relationship between the twelve names of God and the zodiac will be explored in a later publication concerning the advanced Enochian mysteries.

173 Note that Dee's original Great Table shows the name as aLndOod. The capital *O* is the initial letter of the forty-second Part of the Earth named Ooanamb. However, when writing the name of the elder, he replaces the *O* with a *V* to make the name as I have shown in the list here. As a point of interest, he replaces this *O* with a *V* in the Reformed Great Table of Raphael, though he never indicates that the name of the forty-second Part of the Earth should change accordingly.

174 Some sources list this name as "Arinnaq" (with a final *Q*). However, this letter on the Great Table is actually a capital *P* written backward (the first letter of Paraoan), which makes it look like an oversized lowercase *Q*.

175 See *A True and Faithful Relation*, p. 178 (Monday, June 25, 1584): "If you will make them of seven letters...that is, when the wrath of God is to be increased."

176 Ibid.: "You must take but one (of the two letters). (One is) comiter, and (the other is) in extremes judiciis" (*comiter* = "in a friendly manner," *judiciis* = "like a tyrant").

177 See my *Shem haMephoresh: The Divine Name of Extension.*

178 Again, see Dee's diagram of the Holy City for the triplicities in each cardinal direction. This is another relationship I will explore in a later publication concerning the advanced Enochian mysteries.

179 Calvary is the town where Christ was crucified. The exact spot was called *Golgatha*, the "Place of the Skull."

180 Dee wrote this demon's name as Cfa. This is likely intended to indicate that the letter *P* in this name takes the same sound as "ph" (or "f").

181 Dee wrote these names as Xpen and Xpaen. However, the letter *C* appears on the Great Table instead of *E*, so Dee may have made a transcription error here.

182 Dee wrote this name as Dabtt. However, the letter *L* appears on the Great Table instead of *B*, so Dee may have made a transcription error here.

183 See *A True and Faithful Relation*, p. 184. Further instructions are contained in descriptions of the Book of Supplication (see next footnote).

184 See *A True and Faithful Relation*, pp. 182, 184, and 188–189.

185 See James's *Enochian Magick of Dr. John Dee*, book 5, pp. 117–177.

186 Geoffrey James makes a very similar assumption in his *Enochian Magick of Dr. John Dee*, appendix A.

187 See *A True and Faithful Relation*, p. 179.

188 Ibid.

189 Note that there are several differences in lettering between the Great Table found in *Book H* and the Reformed Great Table of Raphael in Dee's journals. I have favored Dee's journals in this Great Table.

Also, there is a rather large point of confusion in the Reformed Great Table. In Dee's journal, he recorded line 8 of the "Mor" Table differently than he had done on the original Great Table. On the original, it is: R O c a n c h i a s o m. However, on the Reformed Table it is changed to: o c a n c h i a s o m t (that is, the initial *R* is removed and a *T* is added onto the end). Adding further confusion, *Book H* changes it yet again, to: A o c a n c h i a s o m (simply replacing the initial *R* of the original Great Table with an *A*—likely a typographical error). Again, I have favored the Reformed Table as it appears in Dee's journal (beginning the line with *O* and ending with *T*—as do most modern Golden Dawn groups).

190 Flashing colors are found directly opposite to the ground color on an artist's color wheel. The Golden Dawn used these "opposing" colors to draw figures and details on talismans on top of the background color. Thus, for example, a talisman of Fire would be painted red, while the lettering on the talisman would be painted in green. Try this, and you will quickly see how green "flashes" when viewed on a red background.

191 The Hebrew letter Heh with a dot inside it (הּ) indicates the second Heh in the Tetragrammaton, often called Heh-final or Heh-sophith.

192 As we will see later, the Golden Dawn assigned the symbol of Saturn to Earth in the Enochian Watchtowers. Otherwise, the sigil of Earth would appear as 🜃.

193 Remember that there was no indication in Dee's work that these were words in their own right. Instead, they are the names of three Parts of the Earth: Lexarph, Comanan, and Tabitom, excluding the initial *L*.

194 See my *Clarification of Geomancy for Golden Dawn Students*, http://kheph777.tripod.com/gd_geomancy.html.

195 For the Sun/Leo and the Moon/Cancer you'll have a choice of two geomantic figures, or you can include both on the pyramid.

196 This is why Saturn stands in as the symbol of Earth in the Golden Dawn Enochian system.

197 Images of these gods are shown in Regardie's *Golden Dawn*, pp. 664–665, and described further on pp. 686–688. Note that I have made modifications to the colors so they better reflect the elemental natures of the deities.

198 Note that the Enochian Holy Table is not used in neo-Enochian workings; neither is the Ring of Solomon nor the Holy Lamen. However, the ring and lamen *can* be worn if you have them and wish to include them.

199 If you do not have a magickal sword, you may use the lotus wand, holding it by the lowest band of black.

200 That is, Eastern, Western, Southern, or Northern.

201 That is, EXARP, HCOMA, NANTA, or BITOM.

202 That is, the element of the Watchtower and (if it applies) the sub-element of the subquadrant.

To Write to the Author

If you wish to contact the author or would like more information about this book, please write to the author in care of Llewellyn Worldwide and we will forward your request. Both the author and the publisher appreciate hearing from you and learning of your enjoyment of this book and how it has helped you. Llewellyn Worldwide cannot guarantee that every letter written to the author can be answered, but all will be forwarded. Please write to:

Aaron Leitch

℅ Llewellyn Worldwide

2143 Wooddale Drive

Woodbury, MN 55125-2989

Please enclose a self-addressed stamped envelope for reply or $1.00 to cover costs. If outside the USA, enclose an international postal reply coupon.

Many of Llewellyn's authors have websites with additional information and resources. For more information, please visit our website:

www.llewellyn.com